Premodern Monsters

A Varied Compilation of Pre-modern Judeo-Christian
and Japanese Buddhist Monstrous Discourses

Edited by
Allan E.C. Wright
University of Alberta

Series in Anthropology

VERNON PRESS

www.vernonpress.com

In the Americas:
Vernon Press
1000 N West Street, Suite 1200
Wilmington, Delaware, 19801
United States

In the rest of the world:
Vernon Press
C/Sancti Espiritu 17,
Malaga, 29006
Spain

Series in Anthropology

Library of Congress Control Number: 2024932857

ISBN: 979-8-8819-0141-7

Also available: 978-1-64889-903-4 [Hardback]; 979-8-8819-0049-6 [PDF, E-Book]

Cover design by Vernon Press with elements by Maroyendesign on Freepik.

Table of Contents

Introduction

Allan E.C. Wright

University of Alberta

The history of all hitherto-existing societies is the history of monsters.
Homo sapiens is a bringer-forth of monsters as reason's dream. They are
not pathologies but symptoms, diagnoses, glories, games, and terrors...
All our moments are monstrous moments.

China Mieville, *Theses on Monsters.*

While it has been suggested that the genesis of "Monster" studies was J.R.R. Tolkien's essay "Beowulf: The Monster and the Critics",[1] academia did not immediately follow suit and engage with the material, concept, and data. Tolkien questioned the idea that *Beowulf* was simply an important historical and linguistic document. As a literary work, he argued that the poem itself outshines its historical content. Tolkien states, "Beowulf is in fact so interesting as poetry, in places poetry so powerful, that this quite overshadows the historical content, and is largely independent even of the most important facts (such as the date and identity of Hygelac)".[2] Tolkien identifies the monsters of the tale as the essential framework to highlight the poem's ideas. His examination of Beowulf countered the prevailing historical linguistic scholarship at the time and is a significant turning point for the advancement of monster studies.

Monster studies slowly began to gain academic acceptance after Jeffrey Jerome Cohen's famous theses in 1996.[3] Cohen outlined various methodologies that one can use as a theoretical base to examine monsters and monstrosities.

---

[1] For example, see Asa Simon Mittman and Marcus Hensel "Introduction: 'A Marvel of Monsters.'" in *Classical Readings on Monster Theory: demonstrare. Volume 1*, edited by Asa Simon Mittman and Marcus Hensel (Yorkshire: Arc Humanities Press, 2018), xi. Mittman and Hensel present and establish the sparse and scarce examinations of Monster Studies before Jeffrey Jerome Cohen.

[2] J.R.R. Tolkien "Beowulf: The Monsters and the Critics". In *Classical Readings on Monster Theory: demonstrare. Volume 1*, eds. Asa Simon Mittman and Marcus Hensel (Yorkshire: Arc Humanities Press, 2018).

[3] See Jeffrey Jerome Cohen, ed., *Monster Theory: Reading Culture* (Minneapolis: University of Minnesota Press, 1996).

He states, "the monster is best understood as an embodiment of difference, a breaker of category, and a resistant Other known only through process and movement, never through dissection-table analysis".[4] Cohen argues that monsters are a part of a Cultural Body. The thesis suggests that when a monster is created, it embodies a culture's time and place that incorporates strong sentiments such as fear and anxiety. His second thesis proclaims that monsters will always escape. In general, monsters will continually reinvent themselves for specific cultural matrixes. A monster might vanish or perish in a particular narrative; however, the same monster, which represents the same fears and possibly adds to them, can reappear in other narratives. Cohen employs vampires as an example, "the undead returns in slightly different clothing, each time to be read against contemporary social movements or a specific, determining event... each reappearance and its analysis is still bound in a double act of construction and reconstitution"[5]. Next, Cohen argues that monsters are harbingers of categories that create a categorical crisis. This thesis suggests that monsters can rebuke, protect, and challenge social boundaries as they reject easy classifications. Cohen elaborates,

> This refusal to participate in the classificatory 'order of things' is generally true of monsters: they are disturbing hybrids whose externally incoherent bodies resist attempts to include them in any systematic structuration. And so the monster is dangerous, a form suspended between forms that threaten to smash distinctions... by refusing easy compartmentalization of their monstrous contents, they demand a radical rethinking of boundary and normality.[6]

Incorporating a monster within a narrative can force one to question and re-examine one's preconceived notions and biases surrounding social discourses. Cohen's next thesis states that monsters live and thrive at differences. Cohen argues that differences, whether race, gender, economic, or political, are made into a being, sometimes physically, who makes a home and dwells among the larger population. In other words, Monsters are "outsiders" who have integrated into sociocultural settings. Monsters can be "too much like us" and hidden within plain sight. However, they are still somehow different and seditious. This dichotomy provides populations with a dialectical "other". The "monsters" threaten to destroy the population and the whole social order itself. Cohen explains, "By revealing that difference is arbitrary and potentially free-floating, mutable rather than essential, the monster threatens to destroy not just individual members of a society, but the very cultural apparatus through which

---

[4] Cohen, preface, x.
[5] Cohen, 5-6.
[6] Cohen, 6.

individuality is constituted and allowed".[7] Thesis five argues that monsters police physical and socially constructed borders. Monsters provide a warning against various realms and domains. They provide a symbolic representation of punishing curiosity, whatever that inquisitiveness might be. The monster, then, polices different boundaries, intellectually, physically, and socially. It can police dangerous and sacred physical locations as well as eliminate potential subversive and perceived immoral thoughts and actions. In other words, Monsters limit, or unequivocally prevent, the fluid motion of already established classification systems. The prohibition demarcates and even prohibits various classification systems to indicate that these borders cannot, and must not, be crossed. Monsters are employed as warnings where "curiosity is more often punished than rewarded...The monster prevents mobility".[8] Cohen's sixth thesis claims that the fear of monsters is a form of desire. The monster can move between the various realms and practices. This fluidity can induce escapist imaginations. Monsters can be linked to "forbidden" and taboo actions and thoughts, producing sentiments of escapism. This means that monsters can be appealing because they act as figureheads for rebellion against typical societal constraints. Therefore, some audiences might envy its freedom from classification systems. Cohen states, "We distrust and loathe the monster; at the same time, we envy its freedom".[9] Finally, Cohen's conclusion argues that monsters stand at the threshold of becoming. Monsters are human creations, our intellectual "children". They can provide an in-depth knowledge of history and specific discourses within history. They can ask how humanity perceives their society and the world around them. They can ask us to examine our cultural and individual thoughts and practices to challenge or reinforce them. Monsters "bring not just a fuller knowledge of our place in history and the history of knowing our place, but they bear self-knowledge, human knowledge... These monsters ask us how we perceive the world... They ask us to reevaluate our cultural assumptions about race, gender, sexuality, our perception of difference, our tolerance toward its expression".[10] In other words, Monsters ask why we produced them. Overall, Cohen brought monster scholarship from the fringes of academia into a suitable and important subject for research and analysis. Derived from Cohen's theses, scholars continue utilizing theoretical approaches to monster studies. Demarcations of physical boundaries[11] or moral inclinations, representations of cultural bodies, and the

---

[7] Cohen, 12.

[8] Cohen, 12.

[9] Cohen, 17.

[10] Cohen, 20.

[11] For example, forests can be sites of mystery, fear, and disorientation. Numerous forests have been associated with the "fear of the unknown". Within the mythology of

harbingers of category crisis are a few examples of scholarly theories approaching the subject derived from Cohen.

The subject of monsters is now being tackled without apology. Books, articles, and essays concerning monsters have risen significantly in the past 30 years. Specifically, scholars have examined how monsters in various mediums, narratives, and discourses reflect social/moral proclivities and demarcations, insider/outsider anxieties, and general fears within a population at any given time and location. Stephen T. Asma refers to these tensions as "moral imaginations". Asma states, "We use imagination in order to establish our agency in chaotic and uncontrollable situations... People frequently underestimate the role of art [and narrative] and imagery in their moral convictions".[12] Responses can demonize creatures and people that threaten this order, the order of our body, home, community, society, and the cosmos. Monsters reveal what classifications of the "sacred" are deemed "good" and "natural". This produces strong sentiments within a population, reinforcing specific social structures and moral proclivities. Richard Kearney provides a similar observation in this book, *Strangers, Gods and Monsters*.[13] Kearney argues that a critical component of identity is moulded by the monstrous. The monstrous are not simply characters or archetypes in mythologies but a vital component of public imagination and discourse.

The term "monster" can be challenging to define. However, this is not necessarily a negative as it opens various possibilities and interpretations of a "monster". This ambiguity exhibits the vast potential for monster studies. Latin's *monstrum*, or *monstrare*, is defined as "to show" or "reveal", which leads to definitions of the "monstrous" from various perspectives and data sets. A monster can be a hybrid creature comprised of different animals and humans; it can be an utterly unfamiliar creature, and it can also be other people. Stemming

---

Robin Hood, the Sheriff of Nottingham's deputies were anxious about venturing into Sherwood Forest for the fear of what would transpire. Additionally, many folktales, such as Hansel and Gretel and Little Red Riding Hood, also include a predatory beast living in confines of a forest. Many fictional and supposedly non-fictional narratives have utilized the labels "haunted forest", and "enchanted forest", as descriptives for specific locations. The inhabitants who reside in these forests are usually represented by some form of anti-social hermit, witches, trolls, and other mischievous beings. Generally, it is difficult to graph an entire forest and its dwellers. Therefore, if one cannot predict what creatures populate a dense and mystifying landscape, fear follows.

[12] See Stephen T. Asma "Monsters and the Moral Imagination" in *The Monster Theory Reader,* edited by Jeffrey Andrew Weinstock (Minneapolis: University of Minnesota Press, 2020), 289-294, 291.

[13] Richard Kearney, *Strangers, Gods, and Monsters: Interpreting Otherness* (London: Routledge, 2003).

from Sigmund Freud,[14] the Monster can also be perceived as an embodiment or representation of the *unheimlich*, or "uncanny". It's the awareness of a so-called threatening "presence" towards our *Heimlich*, our sentiments of security. The threat should be "outside", but somehow, it has manifested itself within the home comforts. This notion of "home" is vast. It can be related to the physical body, a physical dwelling, a small community, or larger cultural systems and even extend to the cosmos. The "uncanny" invades this supposed safe space, creates sentiments of fear, and reveals individual and social insecurities and anxieties. The uncanny, and monsters by extension, "is that which invades one's sense of personal, social, or cosmic order and security".[15] In other words, monsters are something unwelcome that invades our individual and social sense of the "sacred". Timothy K Beal's general definition states, "Monsters are conglomerations of many different forms of otherness—cosmological, political, psychological, and religious otherness".[16] I would also add physical differences to this list. Overall, the definition of "monster(s)" is wide-ranging and refers to something specific. Asma argues that the term "monsters" and the socio-cultural constructions surrounding it are vital for lexicons. As Asma states, "…the concept of monster cannot be erased from our language and thinking. Other, more polite terms and concepts cannot replace them because they still refer to something that has no satisfactory semantic substitute or refinement. The term's imprecision, within parameters, is part of its usefulness".[17]

This collection exclusively focuses on the monstrous pre-modernity within Judeo-Christian and Japanese Buddist discourses. While meaningful, engaging, and fascinating, many monster studies have generally revolved around monsters post-eighteenth century. Marina Levina & Diem-my T. Bui's *Monster Culture in the 21st Century: A Reader*[18] is a primary example. The reader is a collection of essays focused on the topics of modern monstrous identities and monstrous technologies. There are, of course, exceptions, such as Brandon R. Grafius's "Text and Terror: Monster Theory and the Hebrew Bible".

---

[14] See Sigmund Freud "The Uncanny" In *The Standard Editions of the Complete Psychological Works of Sigmund Freud*. XVII, Translated by James Strachey, Anna Freud, et al (London: Hogarth Press, 1955).

[15] Timothy K. Beal. *Religion and its Monsters*. (New York: Routledge, 2002), 5.

[16] Beal, 103.

[17] Asma, 293.

[18] Marina Levina, & Diem-my T. Bui, eds. *Monster Culture in the 21st Century: A Reader* (London: Bloomsbury, 2013). For another example, see Douglas E. Cowan, *Sacred Terror: Religion and Horror on the Silver Screen* (Waco: Baylor University Press, 2008). There is, of course, notable exceptions. For example, see

Additionally, Heather Macumber's *Recovering the Monstrous in Revelation (Horror and Scripture)* provides an analysis of the Book of Revelation through the context of its monsters.[19] This collection aims to follow the pre-modern monstrous examinations, including discourses from various periods and cultures, to provide a slight glimpse of its socio-historical diversity. It is an eclectic compilation that attempts to provide a variety of time, location, culture, etc., and demonstrates the diversity in the approaches to monster studies from two distinct traditions.

In chapter one, Heather McCumber examines the ancient combat motif and the Hebrew Bible. McCumber argues that within the Hebrew Bible, there is a lack of a distinct combat motif. In other words, there is *no* definitive clash between a deity and a chaos monster. The lack of a combat myth is intentional. By downplaying or omitting the monstrous, the outcome of such a battle is already predetermined and assured. Therefore, the "dragon" of empire (Babylonian or Greek) in the Hebrew Bible threatens the social body, but it is ultimately deemed feeble due to God's power. In her essay, McCumber states, "The monstrous body in these prophetic and apocalyptic texts is not a symbol of chaos; instead, the dragon's destruction represents Israel's hope for communal renewal from attempted efforts at colonization outlines the vital function of traversing social identities and systematic boundary markers."

In chapter two, Greg Lamb looks at the "monstrous" language, primarily employed in the New Testament text Philippians. He argues that the author, Paul, uses monstrous and dehumanizing language, such as his warnings to "Beware!" to demarcate perceived "outsiders" to the new *Ekklesia*. In other words, Lamb suggests that Paul utilizes monstrous and dehumanizing terminology to identify potential outsiders who, according to Paul, might attempt to disrupt and unsettle the newly found communities. Therefore, Paul employs monstrous language to mark the social boundaries of those he deems subversive.

Chapter 3 examines an insider/outsider dichotomy concerning the important classification of the "monstrous". In general, the separation between the designations of Orthodoxy and Heresy are socially constructed classifications. This examination looks at the Nestorius controversy and the resulting built classification lines of what is deemed Orthodoxy and Heresy, with the latter becoming deemed monstrous. In other words, the classification lines that labelled Nestorius a heretic are an example of socially constructed classification lines created by employing discourse and ingenuity.

---

[19] Heather Macumber, *Recovering the Monstrous in Revelation (Horror and Scripture)* (Lanham, Boulder, New York, London: Lexington Press/Fortress Academic, 2021).

In chapter 4, Helena Martin examines "monstrous birth" narratives from the early English Reformation. Coinciding with these narratives is a newer form of communication, pamphlets. Pamphlets provide an insight into the complicated social imagination. In other words, pamphlets and other sources regarding these "monstrous births" were utilized for the population as a possible interpretation of their social incongruities. Martin argues that early scholarly (theological) work has only partially examined the narrative. Previously, the primary concern was for a select group of readers who did not provide information to the common population. Martin then examines various sources and argues that they are exposed while reinforcing social boundaries.

Within chapter 5, Dunja Jelesijevic examines a fifteenth-century play, Dōjōji. Jelesijevic analyzes the Noh Dōjōji in relation to folk legends and illustrated Buddhist scrolls of the Kiyohime narrative. Specific emphasis is placed on how the play muddles gender and gender dynamics. Meaning the play redirects the focus to the female character. Through ritual and performance, the play subverts the anticipated resolution present within the other legends. Jelesijevic then argues that the importance of the woman's serpent costume indicates how the protagonist is continually constructed through carefully constructed identities. These identities scrutinize and dispute the various ways these identities conglomerate in the narrative. Ritual contexts navigate these discourses surrounding Buddhist concepts and folk legends. The Dōjōji provides a performative element to highlight the narrative of the Kiyohime legend. Therefore, the performance transforms the tale into a nuanced discourse revolving around various concepts about suffering and navigating social boundaries.

In chapter 6, Laura Nuffer examines narratives surrounding the Japanese monsters *Yamauba*, or "mountain hags." Nuffer argues that modern scholars have attempted to retrieve the "mountain hags" by redescribing them to be rebellious entities who challenge the traditional patriarchal society. Nuffer, however, argues that earlier sources contradict this interpretation. Instead, Nuffer suggests that the *yamauba* narratives reinforce the existing cultural, and thus, patriarchal standards. Nuffer examines two narratives that present female ageing as monstrous. Ultimately, these narratives are utilized to demonstrate to women that a fulfilling life, one of "safety and happiness," are not found with a liberator archetype, but by remaining steadfast within the realm of the household.

Finally, in chapter 7, Kevin Bond examines a genre of Japanese literature known as *engi* (Buddhist temple foundation legends). Specifically, this literature describes high-ranking Buddhist monks employing spells in order to tame and conquer malevolent spirits. Bond focuses on the supernatural antagonists, the *oni* and *yōkai*. Bond examines the Buddhist tactics to establish and reinforce "sacred geography" to exhibit spiritual power.

Cultural Monster studies are continuing to grow and hold academic interest. This collection is an addition to these engaged voices. It comprises essays that share an interest in the "monstrous" and the category of monsters. The point of such a collection is to enlarge the corpus of the growing academic subject of monsters and to provide a snippet of its diversity and possibilities. Monster studies should not be limited to a narrow socio-historical and cultural period. Scholars can dive into any historical period within any culture and examine what the populations consider monstrous. As Cohen suggests:

> Monsters are our children. They can be pushed to the farthest margins of geography and discourse, hidden away at the edges of the world and in the forbidden recesses of our minds, but they always return. And when they come back, they bring not just a fuller knowledge of our place in history and the history of knowing our place, but they bear self-knowledge, *human* knowledge… These monsters ask us how we perceive the world.[20]

Cohen states that if one can understand, or at least attempt to understand, a society's constructed monsters, one can better understand the specific cultural fears, desires, fascinations, and anxieties. Kearney highlights the importance of monster studies: "They, [monsters], subvert our established categories and challenge us to think again. And because they threaten the known with the unknown, they are often set apart in fear and trembling".[21] Cultural monster studies will continue to grow as long as social fear, anxieties, and uncertainties exist.

Bibliography

Asma, Stephen T. "Monsters and the Moral Imagination". In *The Monster Theory Reader*, Edited by Jeffrey Andrew Weinstock. Minneapolis: University of Minnesota Press, 2020.

Beal, Timothy K. *Religion and its Monsters*. New York: Routledge, 2002.

Cohen, Jeffrey Jerome Cohen, ed. *Monster Theory: Reading Culture*. Minneapolis: University of Minnesota Press, 1996.

Freud, Sigmund. "The Uncanny". In *The Standard Editions of the Complete Psychological Works of Sigmund Freud*. XVII, Translated by James Strachey, Anna Freud, et al. London: Hogarth Press, 1955.

Grafius, Brandon R. "Text and Terror: Monster Theory and the Hebrew Bible". In *Currents in Biblical Research* 16.1 (Nov, 2017).

---

[20] Cohen, 20. *Original emphasis.*
[21] Kearney, 3.

Kearney, Richard. *Strangers, Gods, and Monsters: Interpreting Otherness.* London: Routledge, 2003.

Levina, Marina and Diem-my T. Bui, eds. *Monster Culture in the 21st Century: A Reader.* London: Bloomsbury, 2013.

Macumber, Heather. *Recovering the Monstrous in Revelation (Horror and Scripture).* Lanham, Boulder, New York, London: Lexington Press/Fortress Academic, 2021.

Mieville, China. "Theses on Monsters". Conjunctions. No. 59. Colloquy (2012).

Mittman, Asa Simon and Marcus Hensel. "Introduction: 'A Marvel of Monsters.'" In *Classical Readings on Monster Theory: demonstrare.* Volume 1, edited by Asa Simon Mittman and Marcus Hensel. Yorkshire: Arc Humanities Press, 2018.

Tolkien, J.R.R. "Beowulf: The Monsters and the Critics". In *Classical Readings on Monster Theory: demonstrare.* Volume 1, edited by Asa Simon Mittman and Marcus Hensel. Yorkshire: Arc Humanities Press, 2018.

Chapter 1

Disappointing Dragons: The Powerless Monster of the Hebrew Bible

Heather Macumber

University of Providence

Abstract

The story of the chaos monster has dominated biblical scholarship, a tale of a dragon that resurfaces throughout Israel's history in the guise of successive political empires. The combat between the god of order and the monster of chaos is remembered as an epic battle that gains popularity in later biblical reception. However, an examination of Jer 51, Ezek 29 and 32, and Dan 7 demonstrates a surprising lack of conflict or battle in the Hebrew Bible. Unlike the *Enuma Elish* or *Baal Cycle*, a focus on an extended fight between the god/goddess and the chaos monster is absent. This paper argues that the downplaying and/or elimination of such a key element of the combat myth is an intentional mechanism of resisting empire. The victory of the battle is all but assured in the biblical texts and the focus moves to the punishment and execution of the monstrous body. The resurfacing of the dragon under new empires speaks to the recurring impulse to demarcate boundaries and navigate identities under colonial rule whether Babylonian or Greek. The threat of the monster expressed primarily through its hybrid and threatening body is emphasized by the biblical writers. However, despite the potential danger of the monster, they are quickly rendered powerless in their contact with the God of Israel. This omission serves as a reassurance to the readers that the power of the empire was limited as the monsters' threat to the divine world is quickly neutralized. Moreover, the punishment and execution of the monstrous body serves as a spectacle or a warning of lines that should not be crossed.

Keywords: Hebrew Bible, *Chaoskampf,* Mesopotamian, Ugaritic, and Greek Combat Myths, Dragons

* * *

Introduction

The combat myth (aka *Chaoskampf*) has a long history in biblical scholarship. It is traditionally understood as a battle between a warrior deity and a chaos monster for supremacy among the gods. Hermann Gunkel's articulation of the *Chaoskampf*, highly influenced by the Babylonian *Enuma Elish*, argued for strong links between the combat myth and creation.[1] The later discovery of the Ras Shamra tablets containing the *Baal Epic* challenged this reliance on the Babylonian material by featuring a combat myth centred on kingship rather than creation.[2] Fundamental to Gunkel's articulation of the *Chaoskampf* was the understanding that this battle between two opposing divine forces also represented a larger struggle of order versus chaos. In this paradigm, the preferred deity is cast as the hero pitted against an enemy typically described as a monstrous and chaotic dragon. Examples of combat myths are found throughout the ancient world, exhibiting various areas of resemblance and overlap while preserving their distinctions and adaptations.[3] This article focuses on the following three prominent articulations of the combat myth: (1) Marduk versus Tiamat (*Enuma Elish*); (2) Baal versus Yamm/Mot (*Baal Cycle*); and (3) Zeus versus Typhon (Hesiod *Theog*, Apollodorus *Biblio.*) before proceeding to the biblical material.

---

[1] Hermann Gunkel, *Creation and Chaos in the Primeval Era and the Eschaton: A Religio-Historical Study of Genesis 1 and Revelation 12*, trans. K. William Whitney Jr., The Biblical Resource Series (Grand Rapids: Eerdmans, 2006). For a recent volume that engages and challenges the work of Hermann Gunkel, see Richard Henry Beal and Jo Ann Scurlock, eds., *Creation and Chaos: A Reconsideration of Hermann Gunkel's Chaoskampf Hypothesis* (Winona Lake: Eisenbrauns, 2013).

[2] John Day, *God's Conflict with the Dragon and the Sea: Echoes of a Canaanite Myth in the Old Testament*, University of Cambridge Oriental Publications 35 (Cambridge: Cambridge University Press, 1985), 1–7; Carola Kloos, *Yhwh's Combat with the Sea: A Canaanite Tradition in the Religion of Ancient Israel* (Amsterdam: G.A. van Oorschot, 1986).

[3] The following books trace a variety of different combat myth and dragon traditions across numerous cultures: Joseph Fontenrose, *Python: A Study of Delphic Myth and Its Origins* (Berkeley and Los Angeles: University of California Press, 2022); Neil Forsyth, *The Old Enemy: Satan and the Combat Myth* (Princeton: Princeton University Press, 1989); Daniel Ogden, *Drakōn: Dragon Myth and Serpent Cult in the Greek and Roman Worlds* (Oxford: Oxford University Press, 2013); Debra Scoggins Ballentine, *The Conflict Myth and the Biblical Tradition* (New York: Oxford University Press, 2015); Robert D. Miller II, *The Dragon, the Mountain, and the Nations: An Old Testament Myth, Its Origins, and Its Afterlives*, Explorations in Ancient Near Eastern Civilizations 6 (University Park: Eisenbrauns, 2018); Daniel Ogden, *The Dragon in the West: From Ancient Myth to Modern Legend* (Oxford: Oxford University Press, 2021).

Scholars have proposed a variety of different patterns of the combat myth as it appears throughout ancient Near Eastern, Greek, and biblical sources.[4] Gunkel's model influenced generations of scholars and is presented as follows: (1) primordial water personified as a dragon; (2) dragon has helpers; (3) monsters of the deep and the deities of heaven are juxtaposed; (4) arrogance and rebellion of the monsters; (5) failure of other gods to fight the monsters; (6) victory of the divine warrior with a focus on his weaponry; (7) the world is formed from the corpse of the monster; (8) praise for the hero.[5] His main source material was the *Enuma Elish*, but he also amalgamates several biblical texts in an attempt to retrieve or recreate an original *Chaoskampf*.[6] Instead of finding one schema, an alternate pattern proposed by Joseph Fontenrose is more descriptive of the varieties of dragon fights present in ancient Near Eastern and Greek texts. Unlike Gunkel, there is little effort to draw links or parallels to the biblical material:

1. The Enemy was of divine origin.

2. The Enemy had a distinctive habitation.

3. The Enemy had an extraordinary appearance and properties.

4. The Enemy was vicious and greedy.

5. The Enemy conspired against heaven.

6. A divine Champion appeared to face him.

7. The Champion fought the enemy.

8. The Champion nearly lost the battle.

9. The Enemy was finally destroyed after being outwitted, deceived, or bewitched.

10. The Champion disposed of the Enemy and celebrated his victory.[7]

This outline is especially helpful as it focuses on the threat and activity of both the enemy and the champion as equally threatening opponents.

---

[4] A related pattern is that of the divine warrior as outlined by Paul D. Hanson: combat-victory, theophany of Divine Warrior, salvation of the Israelites, building of the temple and procession, and manifestation of Yahweh's universal reign (Paul D. Hanson, *The Dawn of Apocalyptic* [Philadelphia: Fortress Press, 1975], 299–310).

[5] Gunkel, *Creation and Chaos in the Primeval Era and the Eschaton*, 75–77.

[6] Gunkel, 75–77.

[7] This is a simplified reproduction of Fontenrose's more detailed chart (Fontenrose, *Python*, 9–11).

Finding a standard pattern that encompasses such different cultures and historical periods is challenging.[8] Debra Ballentine approaches the conflict themes in diverse sources as a constellation rather than a checklist, especially where extant narratives are missing.[9] Like others, she notes a similar configuration across various cultures but argues that one cannot treat the *Enuma Elish* as the original standard.[10] Instead, each tradition should be approached with an awareness of changes and adaptations, especially where the combat myth is employed to communicate or reinforce a particular viewpoint or ideology.[11] To illustrate this point, Ballentine issues the following caution in evaluating how a text's hierarchy of divine characters is presented:

> If we characterize Tiamat, Yammu, Môtu, Leviathan, or the sea as "chaos", we overlook the alternative divine hierarchy each story works so hard to reject; we adopt the interested stance of the text, reproducing its negative portrayal of these characters; and we apply anachronistic notions when interpreting these ancient West Asian stories, whether Greek *cháos* or modern "chaos" as "cosmic evil" or "utter disorder".[12]

The legacy of the chaos monster as evil and aggressive is strongly embedded in current understandings of how the combat myth operates in biblical texts.[13] This tradition is likely influenced by later developments of the dragon and devil in the New Testament and later Christian sources. However, when the focus shifts from the actions of the divine warrior to the body and activity of the dragon, a new constellation emerges featuring a rather powerless monster. Each of the examples from Mesopotamia, Ugarit, and Greece presents both the "hero" and the "challenger" as powerful warriors preparing for battle against each other. They are mirror images as they are simultaneously threatening in appearance, dangerously armed for battle, before finally meeting in a single

---

[8] Neil Forsyth critiques Fontenrose's structure and develops his own schema (Forsyth, *The Old Enemy*, 441–55).

[9] Ballentine, *The Conflict Myth and the Biblical Tradition*, 74–75.

[10] Ballentine, 23.

[11] Ballentine, 2–8. See also the following on comparison: Bruce Lincoln, *Apples and Oranges: Explorations In, On, and With Comparison* (Chicago: University of Chicago Press, 2018), 25–33.

[12] Ballentine, *The Conflict Myth and the Biblical Tradition*, 189.

[13] For scholars that challenge these binaries regarding divine creatures, see Timothy K. Beal, *Religion and Its Monsters* (New York: Routledge, 2002); Ballentine, *The Conflict Myth and the Biblical Tradition*, esp. 186-98; Safwat Marzouk, *Egypt as a Monster in the Book of Ezekiel*, Forschungen zum Alten Testament. 2. Reihe 76 (Tübingen: Mohr Siebeck, 2015), 45–69; Heather Macumber, *Recovering the Monstrous in Revelation*, Horror and Scripture (Lexington Books/Fortress Academic, 2021).

conflict. These clashes remain within the cosmic realm and are predominantly concerned with establishing kingdoms and rulers.

In contrast, the biblical iterations of the combat myth featuring a dragon are missing key elements found in their ancient counterparts, particularly a battle between two well-matched forces.[14] Within this larger paradigm, there are three main features that I will explore consistently found in the Mesopotamian, Ugaritic, and Greek materials: (1) symmetry between opponents; (2) help is required from other gods; (3) a moment of defeat or genuine peril. Unlike Marduk, Baal, and Zeus, whose struggles and limitations are key parts of the narrative, the biblical texts significantly adapt these features to reassert the independence and power of Israel's God.[15] This movement away from depicting any weakness on the part of their deity likely reflects the community's experience under colonial powers symbolized as dragons or beasts in Jer 51, Ezek 29, 32, and Dan 7.[16] The monstrous body in these prophetic and apocalyptic texts is not a symbol of chaos. Instead, the destruction of the dragon represents Israel's hope for restoration from colonial oppression.

Symmetry between Opponents

Each of these mythic texts displays a mirror-like quality in which both opponents are presented as equally dangerous and threatening. This is helpfully outlined in Fontenrose's list of narrative themes that juxtapose the actions of the enemy (#1-5) with those of the champion and subsequent battle (#6-10).[17] However, one might be predisposed to see Marduk, Baal, or Zeus as the "hero", instead, reading all cosmic deities as monstrous removes these biases to appreciate

---

[14] Rebecca Watson argues that the sea is never a serious opponent for God and that a true combat between equally threatening forces is entirely missing from the biblical texts (Rebecca S. Watson, *Chaos Uncreated: A Reassessment of the Theme of "Chaos" in the Hebrew Bible* [Berlin: Walter de Gruyter, 2012], 25, 369). In this article, I apply similar criteria to the prophetic and apocalyptic texts that feature a fight between God and an opponent (usually portrayed as a dragon).

[15] Terminology for the nation of Israel varies across different historical time periods (ex. Israel for pre-exilic, Judah for exilic, Yehud for post-exilic, etc.). I have chosen to employ the more generic term Israel but use Judah in discussing specific historical and political realities for the audiences of Jeremiah and Ezekiel.

[16] Other biblical texts that reference the combat against the dragon include: Isa 27:1; 30:7; 51:9-11; Pss 74:13-14; 87:4; Job 7:12; 26, etc.

[17] Fontenrose, *Python*, 9–11. This is not a fixed pattern for Fontenrose as he notes replacements, reductions, substitutions, and different combinations that are found throughout these myths featuring a combat between two divine opponents (Fontenrose, 6–8).

their inherent similarity.[18] Monsters are not necessarily evil but something that is out of order and challenges boundaries in their bodies and liminal capabilities.[19] It is customary to view the gods Tiamat, Yamm/Mot, and Typhon as the monstrous villains; however, as Ballentine argues, they are not "agents of chaos but rather agents of an alternative divine power structure".[20] This symmetry between opponents is highlighted in the epic battles between Marduk and Tiamat, Baal and Yamm/Mot, and Zeus and Typhon as they seek supremacy over the cosmos. In *Theogony*, Hesiod describes Typhon's hybrid and threatening appearance in great detail: "Out of his shoulders came a hundred fearsome snake-heads with black tongues flickering, and the eyes in his strange heads flashed fire under the brows; and there were voices in all his fearsome heads, giving out every kind of indescribable sound".[21] Similarly, Apollodorus focuses on Typhon's composite body but also emphasizes his superhuman size, whose height and width are cosmic in scope, reaching the stars and stretching to the east and west. Typhon's presentation conforms to typical descriptions of monsters as hybrid, supersized, and terrifying, especially his association with snakes and vipers.[22]

Conversely, Zeus's form is not described using typical markers of horror, but as the privileged deity, it is easy to overlook his otherness and breaking of boundaries. Instead of finding clues to Zeus' monstrosity in his appearance, it is more helpful to consider the effect of his presence that disturbs the very foundations of the world.[23] Hesiod notes his immense power as the "loud-thundering Zeus", who is acknowledged as the most powerful of the gods. In the battle against the Titans, Zeus' terrifying power is further revealed: "Now Zeus is held in his power no longer. Straightaway, his lungs were filled with fury, and he began to display his full might. From heaven and Olympus together he came, with continuous lightning flashes, and the bolts flew thick and

---

[18] The term monster, contrary to popular thought should not be equated with something evil, instead its Latin roots points to its use as a sign or warning (Beal, *Religion and Its Monsters*, 6–10).

[19] For an introduction to monster theory as a lens to read a culture, see Jeffrey Jerome Cohen, "Monster Culture (Seven Theses)", in *Monster Theory: Reading Culture*, ed. Jeffrey Jerome Cohen (Minneapolis: University of Minnesota Press, 1996), 3–25.

[20] Ballentine, *The Conflict Myth and the Biblical Tradition*, 186.

[21] Hesiod, *Theogony and Works and Days*, trans. M. L. West, Oxford World's Classics (Oxford: Oxford University Press, 1988), 825-830.

[22] The presence of phobic creatures like snakes is also expected among creatures classified as horrific or undesirable (Noel Carroll, *The Philosophy of Horror: Or, Paradoxes of the Heart* [New York: Routledge, 2003], 48–52).

[23] Jeffrey J. Cohen speaks of "signifiers of monstrous passing" left in the wake of the monster who eludes capture (Cohen, "Monster Culture [Seven Theses]", 6).

fast from his stalwart hand amid thunder and lightning, trailing supernatural flames".[24] Though Typhon's description makes him the more obvious "monster", both Zeus and Typhon are set up as equally terrifying powers.

In Greek traditions, the actual conflict between the dragon and its opponent is also symmetrical.[25] Typhon and Zeus's battle begins with both adversaries issuing terrifying sounds that indicate their power and strength.[26] Typhon's body, composed of snakes and a myriad of fearsome animal heads, utters indescribable sounds, including a bellowing bull, a lion, a pack of hounds, and the sound of hissing. Similarly, Zeus's arrival comes with the sound of his thunder, causing the earth, heaven, seas, and the underworld to react with fear. As Fiona Mitchell observes, in this sonic contest, Typhon's sounds only echo the mountains, while Zeus' thunder and footsteps cause the mountains to quake in fear.[27] Indeed, Zeus and Typhon engage in what Daniel Ogden calls a "mirror battle" as both use fire as a weapon against each other.[28] In Hesiod's retelling, Zeus fights with lightning from heaven while Typhon shoots fire upward toward Zeus. The battle between the two figures is extended to the cosmos as the whole earth and sea react to these deadly twin forces unleashed upon it. Fear is a common response to the monstrous that is well illustrated by the trembling of Hades and the Titans to the battle between the two deities that rages above them.[29] Thus, each side is likewise threatening, and the outcome remains unclear until Zeus contains Typhon in Tartarus, signalling his ascendency as chief deity.[30]

This equilibrium between opponents is not confined to the Greek myths but is also evident in the *Enuma Elish* and the *Baal Cycle*. There is a long history of describing the goddess Tiamat as a chaos monster despite little textual evidence.[31]

---

[24] This is not the only instance where Zeus' power is overwhelming and monstrous. His ability to shapeshift is well attested but it is the unveiling of his true power in his encounter with Semele that proves deadly to her (Apollodorus, *Bibl.* 3.4.3; Nonnus, *Dion.* 8.286-406). See Richard Buxton, *Forms of Astonishment: Greek Myths of Metamorphosis* (Oxford: Oxford University Press, 2009), 158–59.

[25] Ogden, *Drakōn*, 215.

[26] Fiona Mitchell, *Monsters in Greek Literature: Aberrant Bodies in Ancient Greek Cosmogony, Ethnography, and Biology*, Routledge Monographs in Classical Studies (London and New York: Routledge, 2021), 32–33.

[27] Mitchell, 33.

[28] Ogden, *Drakōn*, 218.

[29] Carroll, *The Philosophy of Horror*, 17.

[30] Mitchell, *Monsters in Greek Literature*, 31.

[31] Gunkel, *Creation and Chaos in the Primeval Era and the Eschaton*, 22–23; Brevard Childs, *Myth and Reality in the Old Testament*, Studies in Biblical Theology 37 (Eugene: Wipf and Stock, 2009), 37; Bernhard W. Anderson, *Creation Versus Chaos: The Reinterpretation of Mythical Symbolism in the Bible* (Minneapolis: Fortress Press, 1987), 39; Gregory Mobley,

Recent scholars have challenged the alignment of Tiamat with chaotic evil by arguing that interpreters are conditioned to read Marduk as the hero and the champion, resulting in the demonizing of the mother goddess.[32] Despite her frequent identification as a dragon, she is overwhelmingly associated with the primordial waters from which the gods are created.[33] The narrative itself does not portray her unambiguously as a villain but reveals how the death of her mate provokes her. Anšar's challenge to his son Anu reveals the threat now posed by Tiamat, "…You set out and killed Apsû, and as for Tiāmat, whom you made furious, where is her equal?"[34] In response to the actions of Ea and Marduk, Tiamat gives birth to a myriad of hybrid and horrific creatures that strike their opponents with horror and distress upon confronting them.[35] As Beal demonstrates, her equal is indeed Marduk, who is depicted in similarly monstrous and terrifying terms.[36] His form defies description as it is "incapable of being grasped with the mind", perhaps due to his startling possession of four eyes and ears.[37] Beyond this symmetry of fearsome physical attributes, both Marduk and Tiamat are accompanied by a ghastly retinue of creatures. This balance between the two opponents continues as Tiamat threatens Marduk with venom while he counters with his plant antidote. Thus, it is not a battle of chaos versus order but two equally powerful factions vying for control of the divine world. A similar duality is presented in the *Baal Cycle*, where both Yamm and Mot vie for control against Baal. Again, it is customary to read Baal as the hero and Mot and Yamm as the villainous monsters associated with death and chaos.[38] However, they are all part of the same

---

The Return of the Chaos Monsters: And Other Backstories of the Bible (Grand Rapids: Eerdmans, 2012), 17–19. For a helpful overview of the scholarship on linking chaos with Tiamat, see David Toshio Tsumura, *Creation and Destruction: A Reappraisal of the Chaoskampf Theory in the Old Testament* (Winona Lake: Eisenbrauns, 2005), 36–41.

[32] Karen Sonik, "From Hesiod's Abyss to Ovid's *rudis indigestaque moles*: Chaos and Cosmos in the Babylonian 'Epic of Creation,'" in *Creation and Chaos: A Reconsideration of Hermann Gunkel's Chaoskampf Hypothesis*, ed. JoAnn Scurlock and Richard Beal (Winona Lake: Eisenbrauns, 2013), 14, 16, 22–33; Ballentine, *The Conflict Myth and the Biblical Tradition*, 186–89.

[33] Sonik, "From Hesiod's Abyss to Ovid's", 16.

[34] All translations of the *Enuma Elish* are taken from: W. G. Lambert, *Babylonian Creation Myths*, Mesopotamian Civilizations 16 (Winona Lake: Eisenbrauns, 2013).

[35] These creatures include monster serpents, dragon, hairy hero-men, lion monsters, lion men, scorpion men, mighty demons, fish men and bull men (*EE* II 1-34).

[36] Beal, *Religion and Its Monsters*, 18.

[37] Marduk's description upon departing for battle with Tiamat is equally horrific, "He was clad in a tunic, a fearful coat of mail, and on his head he wore an aura of terror. Bēl proceeded and set out on his way, he set his face toward the raging Tiāmat" (*EE* IV 57-60).

[38] For a rebuttal of this position see Brendon C. Benz, "Yamm as the Personification of Chaos?: A Linguistic and Literary Argument for a Case of Mistaken Identity", in *Creation and Chaos: A Reconsideration of Hermann Gunkel's Chaoskampf Hypothesis*, 2013, 1–2.

divine family, and both Yamm and Mot are called the beloved of El. Thus, these defeated deities are not identified with primordial chaos but are instead considered part of the same cosmic world, though positioned on opposite sides of a power struggle.[39] This equivalence between opponents challenges the boundaries arbitrarily drawn between gods and monsters.

Help Is Needed from Other Gods

A second feature of ancient combat is the limited power of the preferred deity in their confrontation with an opponent. In each of the mythological traditions, the effort required to defeat the monster is made evident by numerous moments where the "hero" requires help. This is accomplished either through the giving of weapons or the military assistance of other divine beings. The absolute power of the gods is not common, as many myths depict the limited nature of these divine characters.[40] The *Baal Cycle* ends with the celebration of the supremacy of the god Baal over his opponent, Mot; however, this position of authority is only achieved with the aid of other deities. First, the worker deity Kothar wa-Hasis intervenes to help Baal multiple times by creating magical weapons for his battle against Yamm. The assistance provided by Kothar may go beyond the manufacture of weapons to include the use of magical incantations that imbue them with power.[41] Moreover, the struggle to defeat Yamm is made evident by the failure of Baal's first weapon and the necessity for a second.[42] In fact, as noted by Shawn W. Flynn, the victory belongs as much to Kothar as to Baal in his successful defeat of Yamm with the second weapon.[43]

Baal's limitations are further highlighted in his battle with Mot, where he is defeated and descends to the underworld. Rescue comes from his sister Anat, who has already stepped in previously to help secure a palace for Baal, restrained

---

[39] Beal, *Religion and Its Monsters*, 22; Ballentine, *The Conflict Myth and the Biblical Tradition*, 187–88.

[40] Mark S. Smith and Wayne Pitard, *The Ugaritic Baal Cycle: Volume II. Introduction with Text, Translation and Commentary of KTU/CAT 1.3-1.4* (Leiden: Brill, 2009), 18–19. The weakness of Baal is recognized by scholars: Simon B. Parker, ed., *Ugaritic Narrative Poetry*, trans. Mark S. Smith and Simon B. Parker, Writings from the Ancient World 9 (Atlanta: Scholars Press, 1997), 84; Corrine Carvalho, "Fight like a Girl: The Performance of Gender and Violence in the Baal Cycle", in *Mighty Baal: Essays in Honor of Mark S. Smith*, ed. Stephen C. Russell and Esther J. Hamori, Harvard Semitic Studies 66 (Leiden ; Brill, 2020), 34–35.

[41] Mark S. Smith, *The Ugaritic Baal Cycle. Volume 1, Introduction with Text, Translation and Commentary of KTU 1.1-1.2*, Supplements to Vetus Testamentum 55 (Leiden: Brill, 1994), 341.

[42] Miller II, *The Dragon, the Mountain, and the Nations*, 99.

[43] Shawn W. Flynn, *YHWH Is King: The Development of Divine Kingship in Ancient Israel*, Supplements to Vetus Testamentum 159 (Leiden: Brill, 2014), 24.

Baal from killing Yamm's messengers, and slayed numerous monsters.[44] Finding her brother's corpse abandoned in a field, she calls on Shapsh to help her carry Baal over her shoulder and bring him to Mount Sapan for burial. Anat does not concede victory to Baal's enemies but rather confronts Mot and demands the return of her brother. She then slays Mot by splitting him and grinding him like grain to be scattered in the field before birds devour his flesh. Anat closely follows the pattern of the divine warrior; however, without the final rewards of kingship or power awarded to others.[45] She is portrayed as an independent deity who owns her own house, shows little respect for the high god El, and is free from male control.[46] In contrast, Baal is consistently shown as a deity who relies on the help and support of others to defeat his opponents.[47]

The need for outside help to kill the dragon or monster is common in other mythological stories. Though the Babylonian god Marduk is the one ultimately responsible for destroying Tiamat, his victories remain partially indebted to other gods. Thorkild Jacobsen compares the independence of Ea's destruction of Apsu as "anarchy" without the approval or help of the rest of the divine community.[48] In contrast, Marduk's rise to power and investiture as lord is achieved with the approval of other deities. This begins at his creation; Anu gives Marduk the four winds to stir up Tiamat. Finally, once Marduk's kingship is recognized, he is first blessed by the assembled gods before being outfitted with a mace, a throne, and a rod.

Moreover, the next line states, "They gave him an irresistible weapon that overwhelms the foe", specifically for the purpose of cutting the throat of Tiamat. The single combat between Marduk and Tiamat overshadows the support of other gods; however, Marduk does not act independently like his father, Ea, but is indebted to other deities for his success. Similarly, the limitations on the champion's power are echoed in the battle between Zeus and Typhon. Like other divine beings previously considered, Zeus also receives his greatest

---

[44] Wayne Pitard discusses the difficulty in determining the amount and identity of monsters that Anat slays (Wayne T. Pitard, "Just How Many Monsters Did Anat Fight? (KTU 1.3 III 38-47)?", in *Ugarit at Seventy-Five*, ed. K. Lawson Younger [Winona Lake, Ind: Eisenbrauns, 2007], 76).

[45] Anat is not presented as subservient to Baal when she aids him in battle, instead it is Baal who is depicted as the weaker partner (Kelly J. Murphy, "Myth, Reality, and the Goddess Anat: Anat's Violence and Independence in the Ba'al Cycle", *Ugarit-Forschungen* 41 [2009]: 537).

[46] Murphy, 533–39.

[47] Smith and Pitard, *The Ugaritic Baal Cycle*, 17.

[48] Thorkild Jacobsen, *The Treasures of Darkness: History of Mesopotamian Religion* (New Haven: Yale University Press, 1976), 172.

weapon, the thunderbolt, from outside helpers.[49] Nevertheless, his weapons ultimately fail, and Zeus needs to be rescued by the gods Hermes and Aegipan after being captured and wounded by Typhon. Finally, Typhon's eventual defeat by Zeus was greatly aided by the trickery of the Fates, whose offer of berries weakened the dragon.[50] Thus, whether it is equipping the preferred deity or rescuing them from peril, the champion does not act alone.

Temporary Defeat of the Champion

Central to many of these stories is the initial defeat of the "hero" at the hands of the monster or adversary.[51] As Rebecca Watson notes, the struggle is real, and there is a moment of doubt that the opponent can actually be defeated.[52] Although Marduk's slaying of Tiamat is the climax of the narrative, he is not the first deity to confront the angry goddess. The god Ea, responsible for the killing of Apsu, the mate of Tiamat, finds himself unable to face the terrifying goddess:

85 [My father], Tiāmat's deeds are too much for me.

86 I perceived her planning, but [my] incantation was not equal (to it).

87 Her strength is might; she is full of dread,

88 She is altogether very strong; none can go against her.

89 Her very loud noise does not diminish,

90 I became afraid of her cry and turned back[53]

An increased sense of impending defeat is found in the *Enuma Elish* as the first two gods are found wanting in the face of Tiamat's terrifying power. The despair of the gods is palpable as there is no one willing to confront Tiamat, so they sit in silence. It is not until the elevation of Marduk as avenger that someone is willing to challenge the goddess.[54] Unlike other "heroes", Marduk

---

[49] Later in *Theogony*, Hesiod reveals that Zeus' uncles gift him with numerous weapons including the thunder, the glowing thunderbolt, and lightning after he frees them (Hesiod *Theog.* 503-6).

[50] A later 3rd cent. CE tradition also includes the help of Pan in luring and destroying Typhon (Oppian *Halieutica* 3.16-25). See Spyros Syropoulos, *A Bestiary of Monsters in Greek Mythology* (Oxford: Archaeopress, 2018), 48.

[51] Fontenrose, *Python*, 11; Forsyth, *The Old Enemy*, 46–47.

[52] Watson, *Chaos Uncreated*, 25–26.

[53] Enuma Elish II, 85-90.

[54] Ballentine notes the similarities between Ninurta and Marduk whose bravery in facing their opponent is juxtaposed against other deities that refuse to fight (Ballentine, *The Conflict Myth and the Biblical Tradition*, 32). See also Lambert, *Babylonian Creation Myths*, 450.

himself does not suffer a defeat. However, his rival Qingu's reaction upon meeting Marduk in battle mimics the earlier gods' reactions to Tiamat: "As he looked, he lost his nerve, His determination went, and he faltered".[55] The temporary defeat of the champion is a repeated motif in the *Enuma Elish*, cementing Marduk's lack of hesitation to confront the threat of Tiamat as evidence of his exceptional nature over other deities.[56]

As noted previously, Baal is neither all-powerful nor independent from other Ugaritic divine beings. The *Baal Cycle* features two different opponents, Yamm and Mot, that Baal must overcome to attain his kingship. In the first battle against Yamm, Baal makes two attempts to kill him, and he is only successful with the help of Kothar's weapons. After Yamm collapses, Baal dismembers his body, thereby gaining his kingship. Mot, the god of death, issues a similar fight for supremacy after Baal receives his palace and kingship.[57] However, in this instance, Baal is unsuccessful, and Mot boasts that he ate and crushed him like a lamb. The finality of Baal's loss is further reinforced by the mourning of the gods and the burial of his body by Anat. It takes the actions of his sister Anat to rescue him and restore him to his position as king.

Similarly, in the Greek traditions, Zeus' victory over Typhon is nearly lost at the climax of the battle when Typhon uses Zeus' weapon, "an adamantine harpe", against him. Despite his wounds, Typhon ensnares Zeus in his coils and proceeds to constrict him before stripping the sinews of his hands and feet. Ogden notes, "In deploying the *harpē* against Zeus, Typhon brings him into a physical state curiously parallel to his own: he uses it to strip the sinews out of Zeus' arms and legs, presumably rendering his limbs as twisting as his anguiform members".[58] Thus, Zeus is temporarily debilitated as Typhon carries him away to the Corycian Cave, which is guarded by the dragon Delphyne. As noted above, Zeus is both healed and rescued by Hermes and Aegipan before returning to finally triumph over Typhon and assume his place as chief deity. In each of these traditions, the preferred god's defeat of the dragon or opponent comes at great risk, demonstrating not only the limited power of the hero but the very real danger of their adversary.

---

[55] Enuma Elish IV, 67-68
[56] Ballentine, *The Conflict Myth and the Biblical Tradition*, 32.
[57] Unlike Yamm, Mot is not conceived as a dragon but is the god of death and the underworld characterized by his enormous mouth that consumes his enemies (*KTU* 1.4 VIII 14-20; 1.5 I 4-8; 1.5 II 2-6; 1.6 II 17-23).
[58] Ogden, *Drakōn*, 236.

Dragon Fights in the Hebrew Bible

The combat myths in Mesopotamian, Ugaritic, and Greek traditions are foundational texts employed by scholars to understand biblical combat traditions. Thus, it is surprising that dragons in the Hebrew Bible differ so radically from their ancient Near Eastern and Greek counterparts.[59] As discussed, these mythic traditions focus on the aggression and threatening appearance and powers of the dragon, leaving little doubt that the "hero" is at a disadvantage. This feature is less apparent in biblical dragon fights, where the figure of the dragon remains shadowy and nebulous. Some sources attest to the multiple heads of the dragon (Ps 74:13) or its fleeing and twisting nature (Isa 27:1) or large size (Ezek 29:3).[60] However, especially in Jer 51 and Ezek 29 and 32, there is little extended description of the dragon's appearance or threatening abilities. In each instance, it is understood as a *tannin*, a term used for sea monsters, serpents, and potentially crocodiles.[61] This ambiguity is well illustrated in Ezekiel's description of a *tannin* thrashing in the Nile whose identity as a dragon/sea serpent or a crocodile is contested by scholars (Ezek 32:2).[62] A hint of the dragon's power is implied in Ezek 32 which accentuates the massive size of the monster's dismembered and mutilated corpse whose blood and body fill valleys and mountains (Ezek 32:4-6). The situation in Dan 7 finds a closer parallel to the extended descriptions of the dragon in surrounding cultures with the detailed elaboration on the four beasts emerging from the sea (Dan 7:1-8).[63] However, as noted by John Day, "Whilst the four beasts, and especially the last, appear to play the role ascribed to the dragon Leviathan in Canaanite mythology, the fact remains that the precise form of the beasts does not correspond to that of Leviathan and other dragons attested in Ugaritic".[64] Indeed, even the last beast, which is arguably the most threatening,

---

[59] The clear exception to this trend is God's extended description and praise of Leviathan in Job 41. However, this is not in the context of a battle as the other texts under consideration.

[60] The use of a sword is also likely in Isa 51:9 which states, "Was it not you who cut Rahab in pieces, who pierced the dragon?"

[61] Both Ezek 29 and 32 use *tannim* rather than *tannin* in the MT; however, most scholars continue to read it is as *tannin* as per other ancient versions (LXX, Syriac, Targums).

[62] In his commentary Daniel I. Block reads it as primarily a crocodile but acknowledges that "it carries mythological overtones" (Daniel I. Block, *The Book of Ezekiel. Chapters 25-48*, New International Commentary on the Old Testament [Grand Rapids: Eerdmans, 1998], 137). In contrast, Day sees in Ezek 29 and 32 a mythic allusion to Leviathan and argues against its identification as a crocodile (Day, *God's Conflict with the Dragon and the Sea*, 94–95).

[63] For a discussion of the monstrous bodies of the beasts, see my article: Heather Macumber, "A Monster without a Name: Creating the Beast Known as Antiochus IV in Daniel 7", *The Journal of Hebrew Scriptures* 15 (2015): 1–26.

[64] Day, *God's Conflict with the Dragon and the Sea*, 152–53.

is never clearly described, and its body remains ambiguous and unformed for the reader.[65] When compared to the vivid imagery in the *Enuma Elish*, the *Baal Cycle*, and Hesiod's *Theogony*, the lack of descriptors for the dragon or beast in the biblical material is noticeable. The result is that the symmetry between the champion and the enemy so prevalent in ancient Near Eastern and Greek texts is not replicated in biblical dragon fights, whose focus remains on the actions of Israel's God as a divine warrior.

A second prominent feature of the ancient Near Eastern and Greek texts is the joint effort required to defeat the dragon. This help comes especially in the form of weapons that are crafted or given to the "hero" by other divine beings. Although one finds a similar reference to the use of weapons by God in the fight against the dragon, there is no corresponding narrative explaining the origins of such weapons.[66] Israel's God employs a variety of implements, including a sword described as "cruel, great and strong" (Isa 27:1), a net (Ezek 32:3), and fishhooks to grasp the dragon's jaw (Ezek 29:4).[67] In these prophetic and apocalyptic texts, there is no origin story detailing the creation or acquirement of such divine weapons. Additionally, the dragon fights focus on the independent actions of the God of Israel, who has no additional divine helpers. This autonomy of the divine warrior against the dragon stands out from other biblical texts where divine beings march to war with God (Judg 3:27; 1 Sam 13:13; Joel 2:1-11; Hab 3). Moreover, a central symbol of the Hebrew Bible is the divine court, where God and numerous divine beings congregate to make decisions and enact judgments over the world and its inhabitants.[68] Instead, these dragon fights only feature an independent deity who alone is responsible for defeating the powerless monster (Jer 51:44; Ezek 29:4-5; 32:3-6).

An exception to this pattern is discernible in Dan 7, which features the aforementioned divine court convening (featuring the Ancient One and the Son of Man) and the subsequent judgment upon the beasts (Dan 7:11-12; 26). Initially, there is no expected battle between God and the dragon, and in fact, it is unclear who is responsible for killing the final beast. Moreover, Robert D. Miller points out that this text does not fit the normal dragon slaying pattern, as one might expect the Son of Man to be given charge of the defeat of the

---

[65] Macumber, "A Monster without a Name", 21–22.

[66] There are also traditions of God using the storm as a weapon especially in the psalms (e.g. Ps 29; 83:13-15).

[67] The fishhook is also repeated in Job 40:26 where God asks, "Can you draw out Leviathan with a fishhook, or press down its tongue with a cord?" For more details on God's use of a fishhook against both mythical creatures and human opponents, see Marzouk, *Egypt as a Monster in the Book of Ezekiel*, 182–83.

[68] Patrick D. Miller, "Cosmology and World Order in the Old Testament: The Divine Council as Cosmic-Political Symbol", *Horizons in Biblical Theology* 9, no. 2 (1987): 53–78.

beast.[69] However, there is a final echo of the combat myth in Daniel's vision of the horn, "As I looked, this horn made war with the holy ones and was prevailing over them, until the Ancient One came; then judgement was given for the holy ones of the Most High, and the time arrived when the holy ones gained possession of the kingdom (Dan 7:21)".[70] Indeed, one might argue that the expected pattern established in ancient Near Eastern and Greek texts where the preferred deity receives help is reversed in this instance. Here, it is the holy ones who are under attack until the arrival of the Ancient One, another name for Israel's God.[71] Thus, in Jer 51, Ezek 29, 32 and Dan 7, the combat myth is not adapted identically, but similar themes of the independent nature of God's fight against the dragon are apparent.

A final defining characteristic of the ancient dragon fights under consideration is the temporary defeat of the "hero" that underscores the threat of the opponent. Nonetheless, the dragons of the Hebrew Bible are never shown as dangerous to God, nor do they ever gain the upper hand in any of the battles. Baal, Zeus, and the gods of the *Enuma Elish* are evenly matched against their adversaries, and some are even temporarily defeated. In contrast, the danger posed by dragons in the Hebrew Bible is primarily directed against the human community rather than Israel's God. The prophetic texts of Ezek 29, 32 and Jer 51 were written during Judah's occupation and Jerusalem's eventual destruction by the Babylonian empire in the 6th century. BCE.[72] In these prophetic texts, Jeremiah and Ezekiel use the traditional metaphor of the dragon to symbolize Judah's present historic enemies: Nebuchadnezzar, the king of Babylon and the Pharaoh of Egypt. Both prophets adapt the conventional features of the combat myth to a situation where their audience is powerless and in the grip of a colonial authority that threatens to consume them. Thus, the defeat of the hero is completely omitted from their versions, and instead, the focus is on the destruction and dismemberment of the dragon.

For Jeremiah's audience, Babylon is the target who, earlier in chapter 50, was described as having "gnawed" the bones of Judah (Jer 50:17). In chapter 51, the prophet describes the Babylonian king Nebuchadnezzar's actions in the following way:

---

[69] Miller II, *The Dragon, the Mountain, and the Nations*, 243.

[70] All biblical translations are from the New Revised Standard Version.

[71] There is debate regarding the identity of the "holy ones" and whether they should be viewed as divine beings or as the human community. I take the position of John J. Collins who sees the "holy ones" as divine beings (John J. Collins, "Son of Man and the Saints of the Most High in the Book of Daniel", *Journal of Biblical Literature* 93, no. 1 [March 1974]: 50–66).

[72] During the exilic period, the former nation of Israel consisted of the southern part known as Judah.

> King Nebuchadnezzar of Babylon has devoured me; he has crushed me;
> he has made me an empty vessel; he has swallowed me like a monster;
> he has filled his belly with my delicacies; he has spewed me out.[73]

In classic monster imagery, Babylon is depicted as a beast that devours its prey, a vivid metaphor for colonial occupation. Judah is the defeated party, and Jeremiah reassures his audience that God will rescue them from the belly of the monster (Jer 51:44). There is no explicit slaying of the dragon. Still, Babylon's fate is set, as God pronounces that the city will become a ruin and an object of horror (Jer 51:37). Conversely, the dragon of Ezekiel is not Nebuchadnezzar of Babylon, but the Pharaoh of Egypt who fails to aid Judah against the Babylonians prompting such a harsh judgement.[74] Judah is caught between two colonial powers, Babylon and Egypt, and Ezekiel contains strong rhetoric against trusting in the aid provided by their southern neighbour.[75] The case against Pharaoh, especially in vv. 6b-7 reveals a glimpse into the way that the combat myth is adapted to a context where the dragon is rendered powerless. Pharoah is accused of being "a staff of reed" to Judah that will shatter when they lean upon it, providing a false sense of security against the Babylonians (Ezek 29:6). Thus, in this context, omitting any mention of the power of the dragon is designed to convince the people not to seek aid from Egypt in their rebellion against the Babylonians. There is no imminent danger to God as judgement is quickly rendered against Pharaoh's claim to the Nile as his possession and creation (Ezek 29:9). In these texts, it is less of a battle and more analogous to an execution, as God raises a sword against Egypt to render it desolate (Ezek 29:8-12).

The dragon imagery resurfaces in Ezek 32, again directed against Pharoah and likely written after Jerusalem had fallen to the Babylonians.[76] Ezekiel mocks the power of Pharaoh by denying his claim as a "lion among the nations" but instead labels him "a dragon in the seas" (Ezek 32:2). The prophet goes further in drawing his unflattering portrait by belittling the power of the dragon, "…you thrash about in your streams, trouble the water with your feet, and foul your streams" (Ezek 32:2). The denial of the image of a lion, a royal symbol with connotations of power and the ability to protect,[77] further builds upon Ezekiel's earlier rhetoric to erode his audience's trust in Egypt. Similar to other biblical examples, Ezekiel omits any hint of a battle yet retains the destruction and dismemberment of the dragon's body found in other ancient

---

[73] Jer. 51:34
[74] Ballentine, *The Conflict Myth and the Biblical Tradition*, 102–3.
[75] Marzouk, *Egypt as a Monster in the Book of Ezekiel*, 29–42.
[76] Block, *The Book of Ezekiel. Chapters 25-48*, 200.
[77] Block, 200–201.

combats. The dragon's corpse now becomes the focus for the audience as it is hauled out of the waters and thrown into the open fields to be eaten by the wild birds and animals (Ezek 32:4). As Marzouk argues, this extended description of the dragon's dismemberment reinforces Egypt as an object of horror for Ezekiel's audience.[78] Although scholars retain the language of combat, there is no explicit fight between God and the dragon. This is simply a tale of defeat and humiliation. This pattern is repeated in Dan 7, where the historical context shifts from the 6th to the second century BCE, in which the Greek empire led by Antiochus IV has colonized Israel. Unlike Jeremiah and Ezekiel, the physical appearance and danger posed by the beasts are highlighted, especially the fourth beast who "...shall devour the whole earth, and trample it down, and break it into pieces" (Dan 7:23). Despite the increased level of threat, the combat is again muted and the beast's death is reported without embellishment (Dan 7:11). The exclusion of an authentic battle between two formidable opponents is a consistent feature of these biblical texts whose rhetorical purpose is to promote the dominance of their deity by showcasing the limited abilities of the dragon.

Conclusion

It is common to observe the correspondence between ancient combat myths and biblical material. Ballentine notes several similarities, including the arrogance of the enemy, the image of a dragon for the adversary, the use of nets to capture the dragon, the humiliation of the opponent's corpse, and the resulting reinforcement of the deity's power.[79] These similarities are all accurate, but this article has also shown that attention to features missing from ancient combat myths is also an important consideration. The downplaying and elimination of common narrative themes, especially those relating to the limitation of the power of Israel's deity, provide an opportunity to analyze the rhetorical use of the combat myth In the texts of Jer 51, Ezek 29, 32 and Dan 7, any potential menace from the monster primarily targets the human community, and the dragons or beasts are quickly rendered powerless in their contact with the God of Israel. Thus, the victory of the battle is all but assured in the biblical texts, and the focus moves to the punishment and execution of the monstrous body. In each of these prophetic and apocalyptic examples, the audiences all faced the threat of colonial powers and the use of the combat myth is adapted to their particular historical situation. Omissions or adaptations to the myth serve to reassure the audience that the power of the empire was limited and

---

[78] Marzouk, *Egypt as a Monster in the Book of Ezekiel*, 179–80.
[79] Ballentine, *The Conflict Myth and the Biblical Tradition*, 102. These relate specifically to Ezek 29 and 32 and their comparison to the ancient combat myths.

any danger of the monster to the divine world was quickly neutralized. The monstrous body in a culture alerts one to the borders of what is considered acceptable, and in the Hebrew Bible, a strong boundary is drawn around the dominance of their God. Unlike ancient mythic texts, the symmetry between equally powerful opponents is not acceptable. Rather than retain any limits on their deity, the writers of Jeremiah, Ezekiel, and Daniel strip their dragons of any authentic threat.

Bibliography

Anderson, Bernhard W. *Creation Versus Chaos: The Reinterpretation of Mythical Symbolism in the Bible*. Minneapolis: Fortress Press, 1987.

Ballentine, Debra Scoggins. *The Conflict Myth and the Biblical Tradition*. New York: Oxford University Press, 2015.

Beal, Richard Henry, and Jo Ann Scurlock, eds. *Creation and Chaos: A Reconsideration of Hermann Gunkel's Chaoskampf Hypothesis*. Winona Lake: Eisenbrauns, 2013.

Beal, Timothy K. *Religion and Its Monsters*. New York: Routledge, 2002.

Benz, Brendon C. "Yamm as the Personification of Chaos?: A Linguistic and Literary Argument for a Case of Mistaken Identity". In *Creation and Chaos: A Reconsideration of Hermann Gunkel's Chaoskampf Hypothesis*, 127–45, 2013.

Block, Daniel I. *The Book of Ezekiel. Chapters 25-48*. New International Commentary on the Old Testament. Grand Rapids: Eerdmans, 1998.

Buxton, Richard. *Forms of Astonishment: Greek Myths of Metamorphosis*. Oxford: Oxford University Press, 2009.

Carroll, Noel. *The Philosophy of Horror: Or, Paradoxes of the Heart*. New York: Routledge, 2003.

Carvalho, Corrine. "Fight like a Girl: The Performance of Gender and Violence in the Baal Cycle". In *Mighty Baal: Essays in Honor of Mark S. Smith*, edited by Stephen C. Russell and Esther J. Hamori, 32–46. Harvard Semitic Studies 66. Leiden ; Brill, 2020.

Childs, Brevard. *Myth and Reality in the Old Testament*. Studies in Biblical Theology 37. Eugene: Wipf and Stock, 2009.

Cohen, Jeffrey Jerome. "Monster Culture (Seven Theses)". In *Monster Theory: Reading Culture*, edited by Jeffrey Jerome Cohen, 3–25. Minneapolis: University of Minnesota Press, 1996.

Collins, John J. "Son of Man and the Saints of the Most High in the Book of Daniel". *Journal of Biblical Literature* 93, no. 1 (March 1974): 50–66.

Day, John. *God's Conflict with the Dragon and the Sea: Echoes of a Canaanite Myth in the Old Testament*. University of Cambridge Oriental Publications 35. Cambridge: Cambridge University Press, 1985.

Flynn, Shawn W. *YHWH Is King: The Development of Divine Kingship in Ancient Israel*. Supplements to Vetus Testamentum 159. Leiden: Brill, 2014.

Fontenrose, Joseph. *Python: A Study of Delphic Myth and Its Origins*. Berkeley and Los Angeles: University of California Press, 2022.

Forsyth, Neil. *The Old Enemy: Satan and the Combat Myth*. Princeton: Princeton University Press, 1989.

Gunkel, Hermann. *Creation and Chaos in the Primeval Era and the Eschaton: A Religio-Historical Study of Genesis 1 and Revelation 12*. Translated by K. William Whitney Jr. The Biblical Resource Series. Grand Rapids: Eerdmans, 2006.

Hanson, Paul D. *The Dawn of Apocalyptic*. Philadelphia: Fortress Press, 1975.

Hesiod. *Theogony and Works and Days*. Translated by M. L. West. Oxford World's Classics. Oxford: Oxford University Press, 1988.

Jacobsen, Thorkild. *The Treasures of Darkness: History of Mesopotamian Religion*. New Haven: Yale University Press, 1976.

Katz, Diane. "Reconstructing Babylon: Recycling Mythological Traditions Towards a New Theology". In *Babylon: Wissenskultur in Orient Und Okzident*, edited by Eva Cancik-Kirschbaum, Margarete Ess, and Joachim Marzahn, 123–34. Berlin: de Gruyter, 2011.

Kloos, Carola. *Yhwh's Combat with the Sea: A Canaanite Tradition in the Religion of Ancient Israel*. Amsterdam: G.A. van Oorschot, 1986.

Lambert, W. G. *Babylonian Creation Myths*. Mesopotamian Civilizations 16. Winona Lake: Eisenbrauns, 2013.

Lincoln, Bruce. *Apples and Oranges: Explorations In, On, and With Comparison*. Chicago: University of Chicago Press, 2018.

Macumber, Heather. "A Monster without a Name: Creating the Beast Known as Antiochus IV in Daniel 7". *The Journal of Hebrew Scriptures* 15 (2015): 1–26.

———. *Recovering the Monstrous in Revelation*. Horror and Scripture. Lexington Books/Fortress Academic, 2021.

Marzouk, Safwat. *Egypt as a Monster in the Book of Ezekiel*. Forschungen zum Alten Testament. 2. Reihe 76. Tübingen: Mohr Siebeck, 2015.

Miller II, Robert D. *The Dragon, the Mountain, and the Nations: An Old Testament Myth, Its Origins, and Its Afterlives*. Explorations in Ancient Near Eastern Civilizations 6. University Park: Eisenbrauns, 2018.

Miller, Patrick D. "Cosmology and World Order in the Old Testament: The Divine Council as Cosmic-Political Symbol". *Horizons in Biblical Theology* 9, no. 2 (1987): 53–78.

Mitchell, Fiona. *Monsters in Greek Literature: Aberrant Bodies in Ancient Greek Cosmogony, Ethnography, and Biology*. Routledge Monographs in Classical Studies. London and New York: Routledge, 2021.

Mobley, Gregory. *The Return of the Chaos Monsters: And Other Backstories of the Bible*. Grand Rapids: Eerdmans, 2012.

Murphy, Kelly J. "Myth, Reality, and the Goddess Anat: Anat's Violence and Independence in the Ba'al Cycle". *Ugarit-Forschungen* 41 (2009): 525–41.

Ogden, Daniel. *Drakōn: Dragon Myth and Serpent Cult in the Greek and Roman Worlds*. Oxford: Oxford University Press, 2013.

———. *The Dragon in the West: From Ancient Myth to Modern Legend*. Oxford: Oxford University Press, 2021.

Parker, Simon B., ed. *Ugaritic Narrative Poetry*. Translated by Mark S. Smith and Simon B. Parker. Writings from the Ancient World 9. Atlanta: Scholars Press, 1997.

Pitard, Wayne T. "Just How Many Monsters Did Anat Fight? (KTU 1.3 III 38-47)?" In *Ugarit at Seventy-Five*, edited by K. Lawson Younger, 75–88. Winona Lake, Ind: Eisenbrauns, 2007.

Smith, Mark S. *The Ugaritic Baal Cycle. Volume 1, Introduction with Text, Translation and Commentary of KTU 1.1-1.2.* Supplements to Vetus Testamentum 55. Leiden: Brill, 1994.

Smith, Mark S., and Wayne Pitard. *The Ugaritic Baal Cycle: Volume II. Introduction with Text, Translation and Commentary of KTU/CAT 1.3-1.4.* Leiden: Brill, 2009.

Sonik, Karen. "From Hesiod's Abyss to Ovid's *rudis indigestaque moles*: Chaos and Cosmos in the Babylonian 'Epic of Creation.'" In *Creation and Chaos: A Reconsideration of Hermann Gunkel's Chaoskampf Hypothesis*, edited by JoAnn Scurlock and Richard Beal, 21–45. Winona Lake: Eisenbrauns, 2013.

Syropoulos, Spyros. *A Bestiary of Monsters in Greek Mythology.* Oxford: Archaeopress, 2018.

Tsumura, David Toshio. *Creation and Destruction: A Reappraisal of the Chaoskampf Theory in the Old Testament.* Winona Lake: Eisenbrauns, 2005.

Watson, Rebecca S. *Chaos Uncreated: A Reassessment of the Theme of "Chaos" in the Hebrew Bible.* Berlin: Walter de Gruyter, 2012.

Chapter 2

Becoming "Monsters"? Paul's use of Dehumanizing Terms as Boundary Markers in Philippians

Gregory E. Lamb

Southeastern Baptist Theological Seminary

Abstract

Philippians is seen by many as a light-hearted, joy-filled letter, despite its often-dark themes of suffering, violence, death, martyrdom, and the dehumanizing terminology "dogs" (τοὺς κύνας), "evil workers" (τοὺς κακοὺς ἐργάτας), and "mutilation" (τὴν κατατομήν) in Phil 3:2. While much ink has been spilt by scholars in attempts to identify exactly whom Paul is referring to in 3:2 and that Paul's abrupt shift in tone in 3:1–2—from irenic to polemic—betrays the editing effects of a later redactor, there is no scholarly consensus.

Scholarship remains divided regarding the literary integrity of Philippians. J. Reumann et al. see Philippians as a composite document, whereas J. Hellerman et al. argue for the literary integrity of the epistle. Regarding the identities of Paul's referents, some argue that Paul refers to "Judaizers" (so M. J. Keown), others suggest "Cynics" (so M. D. Nanos), while still others posit temple cults such as those of Diana as Paul's intended target (so K. Ehrensperger). However, relatively little scholarly discussion has ensued regarding the demarcating aspects of the monstrous, dehumanizing terms Paul uses in 3:2 as boundary markers denoting outsiders to the nascent Christ community/communities in Philippi.

Paul has previously used terminology often associated with "deformed monsters" (ἔκτρωμα) in 1 Cor 15:8 in reference to his own "abnormal, untimely birth" and unlikely inclusion as an apostle of Christ. In Phil 3:2, it appears that Paul uses dehumanizing terminology to identify enemy outsiders of the Jesus movement who, like Saul of Tarsus, seek to derail and destroy the Christ communities in Philippi and throughout the first-century Mediterranean world.

Thus, Paul refers to these outsiders as subhuman "monsters," deformed, mutilated beings, who live unworthily of Christ's gospel (1:27), whose allegiances are to their own selfish desires and to this world (3:18–19), and whose eschatological end is destruction (3:19).

Thus, I argue that a more fruitful approach to Phil 3:2 is found in understanding Paul's repeated threefold warning to "Beware!" (βλέπετε) as a rhetorical boundary marker vividly highlighting outsiders, who hold worldly rather than heavenly citizenship (3:20) and are to be avoided at all costs by the Philippian saints. Such an approach fills at least two lacunae in biblical studies: (1) it moves discussions of 3:2 away from the seeming scholarly stalemates of identification and literary integrity; and (2) it moves discussions forward in terms of Paul's conception of insider and outsider groups amongst the Christ communities he founded in Philippi and beyond.

Keywords: New Testament, Pauline Literature, Philippians Dehumanizing rhetoric, Monster Theory

* * *

Introduction: Of Men and "Monsters"

Philippians is seen by many as a light-hearted, joy-filled letter, despite its often-dark themes of suffering, violence, death, martyrdom, and the dehumanizing appellations "the dogs" (τοὺς κύνας), "the evil workers" (τοὺς κακοὺς ἐργάτας), and "the mutilation" (τὴν κατατομήν) in Phil 3:2.[1] Such an a priori assumption regarding the motifs of joy and friendship in the secondary literature has become *de rigueur* in Pauline scholarship but may obfuscate Paul's rhetorical tactics and intent in debated passages like Phil 3:2.[2] While much ink has been

---

[1] Unless otherwise noted, all translations of the biblical and extrabiblical primary sources are my own. Translations of the Greek New Testament derive from Barbara Aland et al., eds., *Nestle-Aland Novum Testamentum Graece*, 28th ed. (Stuttgart: Deutsche Bibelgesellschaft, 2012).

[2] Representative of those emphasizing the centrality of the motif of joy in Philippians is Anke. Inselmann, who writes of Paul's focus on joy in Philippians: "*In keinem anderen Zeugnis des Paulus wird das Motiv der Freude so häufig aufgenommen und complex thematisiert*". Inselmann bases his observation on the occurrences of joy/rejoicing nomenclature in Philippians: "*Das Substantiv* χαρά *begegnet in diesem Brief fünfmal, das Verb* χαίρειν *elfmal*". Anke Inselmann, "Zum Affekt der Freude im Philipperbrief: Unter Berücksichtigung pragmatischer und psychologischer Zugänge", in *Der Philipperbrief des Paulus in der hellenistisch-römischen Welt*, ed. Jörg Frey and Benjamin Schliesser, WUNT 1, Reihe 353 (Tübingen: Mohr Siebeck, 2015), 255 n. 2. Regarding epistolary approaches taking Philippians as being an exemplary model of a Greek friendship letter, see Heikki Koskenniemi, *Studien zur Idee und Phraseologie des griechischen Briefes bis 400 n. Chr.* (Helsinki: Suomalainen Tiedeakatemia, 1956), 115–27; Stanley K. Stowers, *Letter Writing in Greco-Roman Antiquity*, ed. Wayne A. Meeks, Library of Early Christianity 5

spilt by scholars in attempts to identify Paul's referents in Phil 3:2 and to argue that Paul's abrupt shift in tone in Phil 3:1–2—from irenic to polemical—betrays the editing effects of a later redactor, there is no scholarly consensus.

Scholarship remains divided regarding the literary integrity of Philippians.[3] John Reumann et al. see Philippians as a composite document, whereas Joseph Hellerman et al. argue for the literary integrity of the epistle.[4] Reumann cites both external and internal factors in support of his partitioning position. Externally, Reumann notes Polycarp's attestation of Paul's having written multiple "letters" (ἐπιστολάς) to the Philippians, which could have been later stitched together to form canonical Philippians.[5] Internally, Reumann notes the severe shift in tone and content between Phil 3:1–2 as well as the odd placement of Paul's supposed "thanks" to the Philippians near the end of the letter in Phil 4:10–20.[6] Conversely, while conceding the possibility of the non-Pauline authorship of the *Carmen Christi*,[7] Hellerman notes that a partition theory cuts both ways: scholars would need a plausible theory as to why the supposed redactor(s) "would retain the troublesome transitions".[8] Thus, a seeming scholarly impasse remains.

(Philadelphia: Westminster, 1986), 50–70; L. Michael White, "Morality between Two Worlds: A Paradigm of Friendship in Philippians", in *Greeks, Romans, and Christians: Essays in Honor of Abraham J. Malherbe*, ed. David L. Balch, Everett Ferguson, and Wayne A. Meeks (Minneapolis: Augsburg Fortress, 1990), 206–15; Ben Witherington III, *Friendship and Finances in Philippi* (Valley Forge, PA: Trinity International, 1994), 118–20; and Gordon D. Fee, *Paul's Letter to the Philippians*, NICNT (Grand Rapids: Eerdmans, 1995), 12.

[3] For a discussion of the debates surrounding the literary integrity of Philippians, see F. W. Beare, *The Epistle to the Philippians*, 3rd ed., BNTC (Edinburgh; London: Black, 1973), 1–5; David E. Garland, "The Composition and Literary Unity of Philippians: Some Neglected Factors", *NovT* 27.1 (1985): 141–73; Fee 21-23; Wolfgang Schenk, *Die Philipperbriefe des Paulus: Kommentar* (Stuttgart: Kohlhammer, 1984), 1–28; and John Reumann, *Philippians*, AB 33B (New Haven: Yale University Press, 2008), 8–13.

[4] See Joseph H. Hellerman, *Philippians*, Exegetical Guide to the Greek New Testament (Nashville: Broadman & Holman, 2015), 3; and Carolyn Osiek, who writes, "The rhetorical function of the passage [i.e., Phil 3:1–8] needs also to be taken into account. If it really is an abrupt departure from what went before, the quick turnabout is a device to create 'shock value,' a startling interlude between two heavy points". Osiek, *Philippians, Philemon*, Abingdon New Testament Commentaries (Nashville; New York: Abingdon, 2000), 81. Thus, for Osiek, Paul's sharp change of tone in 3:1–2—moving from peace to polemic—does not betray the mark of different letters being "stitched" together by a later redactor but evinces Paul's rhetorical tactics in shocking his audience's senses.

[5] See Polycarp, *Phil.* 3.2; 13.2; and Reumann, *Philippians*, 8–9.

[6] Reumann, *Philippians*, 9.

[7] Phil 2:5–11.

[8] Hellerman, *Philippians*, 3.

Regarding the identities of Paul's referents in Phil 3:2, post-*Shoah* scholarship has recently tried to overturn the commentary tradition that has—since Chrysostom—suggested that Paul is here arguing against "Jewish Judaizers" and is reversing a so-called Jewish invective against gentiles by calling these Judaizers "dogs".[9] Some still argue that Phil 3:2 refers to either Jewish or gentile "Judaizers",[10] while others—focusing primarily on external evidence— propose pagan groups such as the "Cynics"[11] or the temple cults of Diana as Paul's intended target.[12] Given this disparity of scholarly opinion, pause rather than dogmatism is required regarding the identity of the group(s) in Phil 3:2. Rather than "Who?" a better question might be "Why?"—why does Paul use these specific negative descriptors in Phil 3:2? Comparatively, little scholarly discussion has ensued regarding the demarcating aspects of the monstrous, dehumanizing terms Paul uses in 3:2 as boundary markers denoting outsiders to the nascent Christ community(-ies) in Philippi.[13]

One helpful attempt at investigating Paul's boundary marker language in Phil 3:2–9 is by Christopher Porter, who employs a "socio-cognitive approach"—that is, social identity theory (SIT).[14] Porter posits that in Phil 3:2–9, Paul employs a

---

[9] For a detailed explanation of this argumentation, see Mark D. Nanos, "Paul's Reversal of Jews Calling Gentiles 'Dogs' (Philippians 3:2): 1600 Years of an Ideological Tale Wagging an Exegetical Dog?" *BibInt* 17.4 (2009): 448–82; and Matthew Thiessen, "Gentiles as Impure Animals in the Writings of Early Christ Followers", in *Perceiving the Other in Ancient Judaism and Early Christianity*, ed. Michel Bar-Asher Siegal, Wolfgang Grünstäudl, and Matthew Thiessen, WUNT 394 (Tübingen: Mohr Siebeck, 2017), 26–32.

[10] See Mark J. Keown, *Philippians*, Evangelical Exegetical Commentary, 2 vols. (Bellingham, WA: Lexham, 2017), 2:102; and Thiessen, "Gentiles as Impure Animals", 28.

[11] See Mark D. Nanos, *Reading Corinthians and Philippians within Judaism: Collected Essays of Mark D. Nanos Vol. 4* (Eugene, OR: Cascade, 2017), 111–85.

[12] See Kathy Ehrensperger, "'Join in Imitating Me' (Phil 3:17): Embodying Christ in the Face of 'the Enemies of the Cross'" (paper presented at the Annual Meeting of the Society of New Testament Studies, Pretoria, South Africa, 10 August 2017).

[13] In this vein, Sergio Rosell Nebreda writes, "Ancient Christian texts played an important role as constructors of identity. The characters portrayed in both narratives and theologically charged letters—be they heroes or villains—embodied values and social practices for individuals and groups to adhere to or reject". Nebreda, "Echoes of Paul's Philippians in Polycarp: Texts that Create Identity", in *T&T Clark Handbook to Social Identity in the New Testament*, ed. J. Brian Tucker and Coleman A. Baker (London; New Delhi; New York; Sydney: Bloomsbury, 2016), 347.

[14] Christopher Porter, "Which Paul? Whose Judaism? A Socio-Cognitive Approach to Paul within Judaism", in *Paul within Judaism*, ed. Michael F. Bird et al., WUNT 1, Reihe 507 (Tübingen: Mohr Siebeck, 2023), 94–96, 99–101. Founded by Henri Tajfel in 1978, SIT was based upon a seminal experiment performed by Tajfel et al. in 1971, which highlighted how group categorization affected intergroup behaviors. Such social categorization led to intergroup behaviors that discriminated against outsiders and favored the in-group.

"*qal wa-homer* argument" from the lesser (Paul's "fleshly resume") to the greater (his "super-ordinate 'in-Christ' identity").[15] In his brief sketch of 3:2, however, Porter focuses on identifying Paul's opponents as "Judaizers" and omits from his discussion Paul's triadic, imperative warning (βλέπετε), Paul's description of the "evil workers" and the dehumanizing aspects of Paul's terminology.[16] These omissions, as will be demonstrated below, betray the complexity of the discussion, which transcends issues of opponent identification and simplistic insider/outsider distinctions.[17] Moreover, these omissions obscure Paul's rhetorical and apocalyptic intent in Philippians and require further exploration.[18]

Paul has previously used dehumanizing epithets often associated with "deformed monsters" (ἔκτρωμα) in the *crux interpretum* of 1 Cor 15:8 in reference to his own "abnormal, untimely birth" and unlikely inclusion as an apostle of Christ due to his former persecution of Christ's church.[19] Monsters

---

This discriminatory behavior fostered rivalry and competition between the outsiders and in-group. Related to SIT is self-categorization theory (SCT), which focuses primarily on intragroup mobility whereas SIT focuses primarily on intergroup processes and dynamics. See Philip Esler, "An Outline of Social Identity Theory", in *T&T Clark Handbook to Social Identity in the New Testament*, ed. J. Brian Tucker and Coleman A. Baker (London; New Delhi; New York; Sydney: Bloomsbury, 2016), 13–15, 22–23; Henri Tajfel et al., "Social Categorization and Intergroup Behaviour", *European Journal of Social Psychology* 1.2 (1971): 149–78; and Tajfel, ed., *Differentiation between Social Groups: Studies in the Social Psychology of Intergroup Relations*, European Monographs in Social Psychology (London: Academic Press, 1978).

[15] Porter, "Which Paul?" 100–01. In SIT, the "superordinate identity" can be described as that identifying factor uniting the insider group in shared solidarity and supersedes all other (personal) identifiers and identity markers, which are subordinated under the supreme, superordinate identity. Coleman A. Baker, "Social Identity Theory and Biblical Interpretation", *BTB* 42.3 (2012): 130.

[16] Porter, "Which Paul?" 100–01.

[17] On the complexity of Paul's choice of terminology in Philippians 3, see Jennifer Eyl, "'I Myself am [*sic*] an Israelite': Paul, Authenticity, and Authority", *JSNT* 40.2 (2017): 148–68, here 160–62.

[18] On Paul's apocalyptic imagery in Philippians, see Angela Standhartinger, "Apocalyptic Thought in Philippians", in *The Jewish Apocalyptic Tradition and the Shaping of New Testament Thought*, ed. Benjamin E. Reynolds and Loren T. Stuckenbruck (Minneapolis: Augsburg Fortress, 2017), 233–43, here 235–37.

[19] In addition to the commentaries, see e.g., George W. E. Nickelsburg, "An Ἔκτρωμα, Though Appointed from the Womb: Paul's Apostolic Self-Description in 1 Corinthians 15 and Galatians 1", *HTR* 79.1–3 (1986): 198–205; H. W. Hollander and G. E. van der Hout, "The Apostle Paul Calling Himself an Abortion: 1 Corinthians 15:8 within the Context of 1 Cor 15:8–10", *NovT* 38.3 (1996): 224–36; and Andrzej Gieniusz, "As a Miscarriage': The

are liminal creatures that exude "otherness" yet threaten to infiltrate and blur the lines of difference. Monsters defy categorization and simultaneously repel, fascinate, and attract. In describing monster theory, Jeffrey Cohen suggests that "the monster threatens to destroy not just individual members of a society, but the very cultural apparatus through which individuality is constituted and allowed".[20] The Hebrew Bible often characterizes certain nations and figures as "monsters" that threaten Israel. For example, Safwat Marzouk argues that Egypt is portrayed as a "monster" in Ezekiel because of Egypt's threat to destroy the religious boundaries separating Israel from paganism via religio-cultural assimilation and syncretism.[21] As a zealous Pharisee steeped in the religious traditions and Scriptures of his Jewish ancestors,[22] Paul was keenly aware of the dangers of assimilation and syncretism, as evinced in his intense persecution of the Jesus movement, which he once perceived to be a religious threat.[23] In Phil 3:2, it appears that Paul similarly uses dehumanizing terminology to identify enemy outsiders of the Jesus movement who, like Saul of Tarsus, sought to derail and destroy the Christ communities in Philippi and throughout the first-century Mediterranean world. Thus, Paul—a redeemed "*Jekyll and Hyde*" figure having once embodied threatening and monstrous traits against the Jesus movement but now bearing "the stigmata" of Christ[24]— refers to these outsiders in Philippians as subhuman "monsters": deformed, mutilated beings, who live unworthily of Christ's gospel, whose allegiances are to their selfish desires and this world, and whose eschatological end is destruction. Furthermore, Paul "rehumanizes" Christ's enemies by lamenting rather than gloating over their eschatological destruction.[25]

In this essay, I argue that a more fruitful approach to Phil 3:2 is found in understanding Paul's repeated threefold warning to "Beware!" (βλέπετε) as a rhetorical boundary marker vividly and apocalyptically highlighting outsiders who hold worldly rather than heavenly citizenship[26] and are to be avoided at all costs by the Philippian saints. Such an approach fills at least two lacunae in

---

Meaning and Function of the Metaphor in 1 Cor 15:1–11 in Light of Num 12:12 (LXX)", *The Biblical Annals* 3 (2013): 93–107.

[20] Jeffrey J. Cohen, ed., "Monster Culture (Seven Theses)", in *Monster Theory: Reading Culture* (Minneapolis: University of Minnesota Press, 1996), 3–25, here 12.

[21] Safwat Marzouk, *Egypt as a Monster in the Book of Ezekiel*, ed. Konrad Schmid, Mark S. Smith, and Hermann Spieckermann, FAT II/ 76 (Tübingen: Mohr Siebeck, 2015), 3, 238.

[22] Phil 3:5–6.

[23] Gal 1:13; Phil 3:6.

[24] Gal 1:13–17, 23; 6:17.

[25] Phil 1:27; 3:18–19.

[26] Phil 3:20.

biblical studies: (1) it moves discussions of Phil 3:2 away from the seeming scholarly stalemates of opponent identification and literary integrity, and (2) it moves discussions forward in terms of Paul's conception of insider and outsider groups amongst the Christ communities he founded in Philippi and elsewhere throughout his first-century Mediterranean world.[27] While Paul's letters do not reveal a monolithic, one-size-fits-all approach regarding insiders, outsiders, and the differences delineating the potentiality of inclusivity from one group to another, Paul's rhetorical use of boundary marker terminology in Phil 3:2 *et passim* offers windows of illumination into his epistles. The remainder of this essay shall outline my methodology and succinctly sketch Paul's boundary marker terminology in Philippians, specifically, as well as in the rest of his seven-letter corpus. It will conclude with a comparison of the law of the neighbour, Jesus tradition, and Paul's pejoratives in Phil 3:2, as well as the implications for Pauline's studies.

Methodology and Sketch of Paul's Dehumanizing and Boundary Marker Terminology

In the brief survey examining Paul's writings and his insider/outsider terminology below,[28] I organize Paul's boundary marker terminology into three increasingly intense categories utilizing monster theory and SIT. More specifically, I build

---

[27] Such discussions are impeded by the tendency within and without biblical studies to attribute to the writings of the New Testament, *vox Jesu*, and *vox Pauli* a mostly irenic, universalizing tone of peace, love, acceptance, and inclusion despite the numerous New Testament texts that demarcate boundary lines for the nascent Christ communities and polemical insider/outsider language as in 3:2 *et passim*. Jeremy Punt elucidates, "[T]he New Testament can be seen to tolerate violence and, even worse, at times promote and incite animosity if not violence. The violent element is related to various sociohistorical and theological factors, determined by interests of communities, ideologies, and others. The reluctance to deal with the entanglement of the New Testament in violence may be appreciated; both, however, require investigation. Could the reluctance be related to the New Testament's strong calls for peace, which are more easily explained within theological perimeters and are more palatable than its malevolent tenor? Could it be that the New Testament's ambivalent attitude on both peace and violence is simply subsumed in a rather facile, spiritualized notion of peace?" Punt, "Paul and the Others: Insiders, Outsiders, and Animosity", in *Animosity, the Bible, and Us: Some European, North American, and South African Perspectives*, ed. John T. Fitzgerald, Fika J. van Rensburg, and Herrie F. van Rooy, Global Perspectives on Biblical Scholarship 12 (Atlanta: SBL Press, 2009), 138. While Christ's gospel promotes eternal peace and serves as an antithesis against injustice, violence, and abuse throughout the world—past, present, and future—to flatten Philippians and the rest of the New Testament documents into a monolithic theme ("joy" or "friendship", for example) risks misinterpreting, misunderstanding, or worse still, ignoring the theological and rhetorical complexity and depth within Scripture.

[28] An exhaustive exploration of this nomenclature in the *Corpus Paulinum* is far beyond the scope of this essay. Thus, I have limited my survey to some of the most salient examples within the scholarly consensus of Paul's seven "authentic" letters.

upon Valérie Nicolet's 2019 article that proffers a reading of Galatians and Paul through the lens of monster theory[29] and Paul Trebilco's 2017 work denoting outsider designations in the New Testament (NT).[30] Nicolet sees monster theory as a useful lens which illuminates Paul's reversal of certain Jewish expectations and the "fragility of constructions of normalcy" that challenge "the notion of ideal bodies and perfect communities" in first-century Philippi and beyond.[31] Whereas Nicolet's methodology mostly aims to show Paul's acceptance, inclusivity, relatability, and normalization of those in Galatia who have been marginalized and monstrified by others,[32] I employ monster theory in an attempt to reveal how Paul, himself, can *exclude* and distance outsider groups using monstrous and dehumanizing terminology. Indeed, Paul can construct "his own monsters in order to convince his audience of his position".[33] Hence, there appears to be a broad spectrum and polyvalence of monstrosity in the way Paul employs these dehumanizing, boundary marker concepts and terms throughout his corpus.[34]

Trebilco lists three categories for these boundary marker terms[35]: Category One delineates outsiders contemporaneous with a particular audience; Category Two denotes the former, sinful lives of saints within the Christ communities;[36] and Category Three describes those who may perceive or portray themselves as insiders but whom the author considers to be outsiders— malevolent, misguided, and potentially dangerous to the insider group(s). For Trebilco, such outsiders are the most proximate to the insider group and, therefore—like a Trojan horse—can infiltrate, deceive, and destroy the insider movement. Trebilco describes this third category of outside deviants in ideological terms:

---

[29] Valérie Nicolet, "Monstrous Bodies in Paul's Letter to the Galatians", in *Bodies on the Verge: Queering Pauline Epistles*, ed. Joseph A. Marchal, SemeiaSt 93 (Atlanta: SBL Press, 2019), 115–42.

[30] Paul Trebilco, *Outsider Designations and Boundary Construction in the New Testament: Early Christian Communities and the Formation of Group Identity* (Cambridge; New York: Cambridge University Press, 2017).

[31] Nicolet, "Monstrous Bodies", 116, 120, 127.

[32] Nicolet, "Monstrous Bodies", 120–22.

[33] Nicolet, "Monstrous Bodies", 125.

[34] Paul's polyvalence of monstrosity and desire to deploy monsters to "create or maintain boundaries" in his letters are points, which Nicolet concedes. Nicolet, "Monstrous Bodies", 132, 135.

[35] Specifically, Trebilco features chapters on "the unbelievers", "the outsiders", "the sinners", "the gentiles", and "the Jews". Trebilco, *Outsider Designations*, viii–ix, 3–5.

[36] cf. Rom 5:6–10; Eph 2:1–7.

These 'opponents' are often the most strongly 'othered' groups in our [NT] texts—that is, the most maligned, or most polemically attacked, with the most pejorative language in the books concerned being used for them. There is also often a strong sense of vilification of such opponents. This reflects the point that social groups are often most strongly in conflict with those who are perceived to be closest to them ideologically. It is the most proximate other who poses the greatest threat and about whom authors are most concerned.[37]

However, I will survey some key Pauline designations not featured or adequately covered in Trebilco's broader work that highlight the following three progressively polemical categories of "otherness" Paul specifically uses to distance outsiders: (1) low boundary markers denoting Paul's generalized "others" and "outsiders" (such as the gentiles);[38] (2) high boundary markers describing Paul's "opponents" and "enemies" (both Jewish and gentile); and (3) Paul's dehumanized and "monstrified" enemies (the most threatening and vilified groups).[39]

In surveying Paul's outsider designations, at least four notable characteristics emerge. First, Paul's boundary marker terminology is variegated and progressively more scathing throughout his different letters, as there is a vast difference between referring to someone as a "gentile" or "unbeliever" and an "abortion". Yet, Paul does utilize some key repeated terms and themes such as "the gentiles", "the world", "sinners", "the uncircumcision", and sundry others.[40]

Second, in order to highlight the contrast between insider and outsider groups, Paul often uses antithetical terms and concepts in juxtaposition and proximity. For example, Paul often contrasts groups such as "the unrighteous" with "the saints;" and "slaves of sin" with those considered to be "slaves of righteousness" or "free"; Paul contrasts the dehumanizing concept of a clay "vessel of wrath" with those considered to be "vessels of honour"; and those "walking in the flesh" or in "darkness" with those who "walk in the Spirit".[41]

Third, Paul's inclusivity toward outsiders seems to vacillate from one letter to another and even appears to fluctuate within individual letters. Paul's inclusivity is apparent in texts like Rom 11:17–24, where both "natural" and

---

[37] Trebilco, *Outsider Designations*, 4–5.

[38] While my first category may resemble that of Trebilco's, Trebilco fails to highlight some of the specific terms Paul uses in his letters to denote generalized "outsiders" (e.g., "slaves" and "the dead").

[39] In addition to Trebilco's outsider designations, my brief survey below highlights, among others, the dehumanizing language Paul uses towards outsiders such as the "mutilation", "dogs", "abortion", and "leaven".

[40] Rom 2:26, 3:6, 5:19, 2:26; Gal 2:7–15; 1 Cor 6:2.

[41] 1 Cor 6:1; Rom 6:20, 8:4, 9:21–22; Gal 4:22–26, 5:16.

"unnatural branches" have the potential to be "grafted into" the "olive tree"—that is, the family and kingdom of God—through faith. Paul also supports Jesus tradition of love for enemy and neighbour[42] and the Mosaic injunction of the law of the neighbour[43] in texts like Rom 13:9 and Gal 5:14. However, even within Romans, perhaps Paul's most inclusive letter to outsiders,[44] we see Paul's command to "turn away" from those causing "the dissensions and stumbling blocks antithetical to the teaching which you all learned [from Paul et al.]".[45]

Fourth, there also appears to be a diachronic difference in the way Paul employs dehumanizing, boundary marker terminology when comparing his earliest letters (Galatians and 1 Thessalonians) with his later letters (Romans, Philippians, and Philemon) in Paul's generally accepted, seven-letter corpus.[46] In Paul's earlier letters, he sometimes employed harsh terminology to distance himself and his audience from certain outsider groups—see, for example, Paul's shocking statement against opponents in Gal 5:12: "Oh that those who are troubling you all would even mutilate themselves"—but these were seemingly intra-Jewish conflicts regarding the inclusion of gentiles within the nascent Christ communities.[47] However, in Philippians, which was perhaps Paul's last letter,[48] Paul escalates his polemical warnings and dehumanizing

---

[42] Matt 5:43–44; Luke 10:25–37.

[43] Lev 19:17–18.

[44] Paul presents the possibility of outsiders becoming insiders in Romans via God's calling (9:24), through faith (9:30), by belief in Christ's gospel (10:1–15), and by their "ingrafting" into God's family (11:11–24). T. L. Carter suggests that in Romans, Paul presents sin as the all-pervasive enemy of humanity regardless of ethnicity and religious tradition, and that Paul presents true Jewishness as being internal—"circumcised hearts"—rather than external. Carter, *Paul and the Power of Sin: Redefining "Beyond the Pale"*, ed. Richard Bauckham, SNTSMS 115 (Cambridge; New York: Cambridge University Press, 2004), 146, 163. Thus, for Carter, Christ's gospel levels the playing field for all as outward circumcision and torah-keeping are no longer the primary boundary markers for God's children. Carter, *Paul and the Power of Sin*, 162–64.

[45] Rom 16:17.

[46] On the dating of the *Corpus Paulinum*, see Jonathan Bernier, *Rethinking the Dates of the New Testament: The Evidence for Early Composition* (Grand Rapids: Baker Academic, 2022), 170–71.

[47] For Eung Chun Park, Pauline texts like the *Hauptbriefe* present two different and seemingly competing gospels: a "gospel of circumcision" by Peter that was thoroughly Jewish in nature and praxis, and Paul's "gospel of uncircumcision" that inclusively invites all to become in-Christ insiders while retaining their ethnic and cultural distinctions (Gal 2:7). Park, *Either Jew or Gentile: Paul's Unfolding Theology of Inclusivity* (Louisville: Westminster John Knox, 2003), ix.

[48] Though, I disagree with Bernier's Caesarean provenance for Paul's penning of Philippians, I concur with Bernier that Philippians was likely the last of the seven authentic Pauline letters Paul penned. Bernier, *Rethinking*, 170.

language against outside groups without offering any possibility or hope of their future reconciliation with God or inclusion into the insider group. These groups are merely contrasted with those in Christ, and their eschatological fate is sealed: "Their end [is] destruction".[49]

Category One (Low Boundary Markers): Paul's Generalized "Others" and "Outsiders"

Paul's letter to the Romans brims with "high" and "low" boundary marker language, distancing outsiders from the inside group.[50] As James Barr has aptly critiqued, a study of the range of concepts in Paul's linguistic repertoire regarding these subjects in their proper contexts is needed beyond mere individual words.[51] In Romans, Trebilco highlights concepts such as "the sinners", "the gentiles", "the Jews", and "the world", among others.[52] In addition to these concepts/phrases, Paul employs other concepts, synonyms, and antonyms to demarcate low boundary lines between insiders and outsiders of the Roman Christ communities.

In Rom 1:13–16, Paul makes the ethnic distinctions between "Greeks", "barbarians", and "Jews"—"the wise" and "the foolish"—yet shows the inclusive power of the gospel as the "power of God", transforming outsiders into insiders. The key to such a holistic transformation for Paul is the presence of continued, quotidian belief in the gospel and its power since "the righteous will live by faith".[53] Thus, for Paul, there remains a sense of potential inclusivity regarding these generalized outsiders in Christ.

In Rom 11:16–25, Paul employs metaphors of a mixed lump of dough (τὸ φύραμα), natural and grafted branches, and wild olive trees vis-à-vis cultivated trees. To remain or to become in-Christ insiders requires the person to act commensurately as citizens within the Christ community by "continuing in his [God's] kindness" (v. 22) and to not "continue in unbelief" (v. 23). There is still

---

49 Phil 3:19.

50 Trebilco explains the differences between "high" and "low" boundary markers in that a high boundary marker "*excludes* the outsider through its negativity, and thus creates a 'high' boundary for the group…. A low boundary term can be thought of as a term that is neutral or positive toward outsiders and emphasizes *commonality* between insiders and outsiders, in contrast to a high boundary term that emphasizes *difference* and powerfully *demarcates* and *distinguishes*". Trebilco, *Outsider Designations*, 25, emphasis original.

51 James Barr, *The Semantics of Biblical Language* (Oxford; London; New York: Oxford University Press, 1961), 1–4, 207.

52 Trebilco, *Outsider Designations*, 132–33, 155, 182, 210.

53 Rom 1:16–17.

hope—both temporally and eschatologically—for outsiders willing to heed Paul's message in that they will be "grafted in" (ἐγκεντρισθήσονται) to this seeming "tree of life".

Paul mixes both out-group terms and upholds Mosaic and Jesus traditions in Rom 12:14–14:9. Regarding the outsider concepts, Paul contrasts "the ones doing/practising evil" with those considered "servants of God" in Rom 13:4, and Paul juxtaposes "the living" and "the dead" (νεκρῶν καὶ ζώντων) in Rom 14:9. Regarding the Mosaic and Jesus traditions, Paul cites the law of the neighbour to show the warm, inclusive treatment of neighbouring outsiders in proximity to the Christ community. It appears that Paul employs here what Trebilco refers to as "low boundary markers"[54] rather than seeing these groups as dangerous threats to be avoided and excluded. Paul echoes Jesus's commands in the Sermon on the Mount to "bless" (εὐλογεῖτε) rather than curse such outsiders persecuting them[55] and to "love" (ἀγαπήσεις) those neighbouring outsiders as the insiders love themselves.[56]

However, in Rom 16:17–18, Paul's warm and irenic invocation quickly devolves into a warning to "turn away from them" (ἐκκλίνετε ἀπ' αὐτῶν). These particular outsiders apparently pretend to be "insiders", intentionally perverting Paul's teachings with erroneous religious instructions that deceive actual insiders.[57] Paul refers to these insidious outsiders as being "slaves" not to Christ" (Χριστῷ οὐ δουλεύουσιν), but to "their own fleshy appeties" (τῇ ἑαυτῶν κοιλίᾳ; v. 18). Thus, much contrast can be seen within Romans in how

---

[54] Trebilco, *Outsider Designations*, 25.

[55] Rom 12:14.

[56] Rom 13:9.

[57] Paul's sharp break in tone in Rom 16:17–20 has led some scholars (so Robert Jewett) to see these verses as a non-Pauline interpolation. Jewett writes, "While most commentators view this passage as a peculiar Pauline postscript, a small group of scholars has correctly identified it as a non-Pauline interpolation…. These verses contain direct contradictions to the proceeding argument of Romans. Whereas 6:17 acknowledges that the Roman Christians were 'obedient to the form of teaching with which you were entrusted,' 16:17 warns against a group within Rome that opposes such teaching". Jewett, *Romans*, Hermeneia (Minneapolis: Augsburg Fortress, 2007), 986–87. As is the case with Phil 3:2, Paul's sharp change in subject and tone in Rom 16:17–20 do not a priori suggest a non-Pauline interpolation by a later redactor. Rather, these shifts can, perhaps, be better explained as Paul's rhetorical use of insider, outsider, and boundary marker concepts and terminology, which help Paul's audience to focus on the exigences Paul addresses in these letters: namely, that dangerous outside groups have infiltrated—or are attempting to infiltrate—the Christ communities that Paul and other in-Christ saints have founded with erroneous, contradictory teachings (e.g., the ἕτερον εὐαγγέλιον Paul references in Gal 1:6), and such dangerous outsiders should be avoided at all costs.

Paul uses inclusive, low boundary markers for some outsiders, with higher, more severe and dehumanizing lines of demarcation (slavery) to separate the developing Christ communities from outsiders Paul deems as more dangerous threats to insiders.[58] What are the low boundary markers in the Corinthian correspondence?

Like Romans, the Corinthian correspondence is replete with insider, outsider, and boundary marker terminology. In 1 Cor 1:18, we see Paul's contrast between the outsiders who are "perishing" (τοῖς... ἀπολλυμένοις) and the insiders "being saved" (τοῖς... σῳζομένοις). Paul heightens this division between outsiders and insiders by his use of the contrastive conjunction δὲ. To the rescued insiders, Paul's gospel—his *theologia crucis*—is a "message of the cross [of Christ]" and "the power of God". Yet, to the perishing outsiders, such a cruciform message is "moronic foolishness" (μωρία). In 1 Cor 2:14–15, another Pauline contrast is seen between the outsider deemed a "natural person" (ψυχικὸς... ἄνθρωπος) and the in-Christ insider considered a "spiritual person" (ὁ... πνευματικὸς). The former cannot discern spiritual things since they are not "in Christ"[59] and remain in their natural, unregenerate state. They also consider spiritual matters to be μωρία.

Paul's inclusivity toward outsiders is shown in 1 Cor 4:12 in his willingness to "bless" and "endure" (εὐλογοῦμεν... ἀνεχόμεθα) those enemies reviling and persecuting him. Paul's warm words hark back to Rom 12:14 and further echo the Jesus tradition in the Sermon on the Mount/Plain (Matt 5:44; Luke 6:28). Paul's words are inclusive not only toward the outsiders but also his insider companions and audience as he uses the first-person plural and reflexive middle ("We bless... we, ourselves, endure") to highlight the inner attitude and outward actions commensurate with being in Christ.

A contrast of morality is seen in 1 Cor 6:1–2, in which Paul contrasts "the unrighteous" (τῶν ἀδίκων) with the insider "saints" (τῶν ἀγίων) who "will judge the world" rather than be judged and condemned. In 1 Cor 7:22–23, Paul makes a low boundary marker distinction—in contrast to the high boundary marker use of δουλεύουσιν in Rom 16:18—between outsiders, who are "slaves of men" (δοῦλοι ἀνθρώπων) and those insiders described as "the freed person" (ἀπελεύθερος) and as a "slave of Christ" (δοῦλός... Χριστου). Thus, Paul's gospel reverses one's ultimate allegiance from being horizontal (as an enslaved person serving a mere human master) to vertical (being submissive and subservient primarily to God/Christ alone).

---

[58] Trebilco, *Outsider Designations*, 25.
[59] 1 Cor 1:30.

The last Pauline comparison I will discuss in 1 Corinthians involves outsiders descending from the "first man", Adam, and are known as "the earthy ones".[60] Using apocalyptic imagery, Paul contrasts these Adamic outsiders vis-à-vis insiders descending from Christ, the Second Man, who is considered "the heavenly ones" (οἱ ἐπουράνιοι) since Christ descended from heaven.[61] Those outsiders born of the dusty earth return to the dust when they perish. Similarly, heavenly insiders never perish in the ultimate sense but ascend to the heavens as they bear the image of the heavenly Man [Christ].

Second Corinthians repeats many of the same outsider designations seen in Romans, 1 Corinthians, Galatians, and Philippians, such as: "the perishing", "the unbelieving", "the world", "the gentiles", "false brethren",[62] and others. Of interest to this discussion is Paul's warm inclusivity and restoration of the "one punished" and formerly treated as an outsider to the Corinthian insider group. Paul exhorts the Corinthian insiders "to reaffirm their love to him" and to "forgive and comfort him".[63] Paul does not hold animosity or distance toward the offending party but offers open arms of reconciliation.

In 2 Cor 6:14–15, Paul contrasts the insider Corinthian "believers" (πιστῷ), whom he metaphorically considers to be "righteousness" and "light" (δικαιοσύνη... φωτὶ) with the "unbelievers", (ἀπίστοις/ἀπίστου) who, according to Paul, personify "lawlessness" and "darkness" (ἀνομίᾳ... σκότος). Paul explains that the Corinthian insiders are not to "be yoked together" (ἑτεροζυγοῦντες) or to intermingle with such outsiders since they are deemed "unclean" (ἀκαθάρτου) and must be "separate" (ἀφορίσθητε; 6:17). Thus, in 2 Corinthians, Paul perceives outsiders differently depending on the level of threat he sees in them. Some (so the reconciled offender of 2 Corinthians 2) are to be forgiven and restored, whereas other outsiders are treated xenophobically with contempt and separation at all costs. We now turn to Galatians, perhaps Paul's earliest epistle.

In Galatians, Paul also employs many contrastive elements to emphasize the religious and ideological lines of demarcation between outsiders and insiders within Christ communities. In addition to the aforementioned "circumcision" and "uncircumcision" distinction,[64] we see Paul contrasting slaves with sons,[65] slaves of Christ (Χριστοῦ δοῦλος) with those serving man,[66] and slaves of man

---

[60] That is, οἱ χοϊκοί; 1 Cor 15:48.

[61] 1 Cor 15:46–49.

[62] 2 Cor 4:3–4, 5:19, 11:26.

[63] 2 Cor 2:5-10.

[64] Gal 2:7.

[65] Gal 4:7.

[66] Gal 1:10.

contrasted with God's children and heirs (υἱός, καὶ κληρονόμος διὰ θεοῦ in Gal 4:7). But what of Paul's boundary marker language in Philippians?

Paul's brief letter to the Philippians contains, perhaps, Paul's most clearly defined insider, outsider, and boundary marker language out of the seven letters surveyed. Such an estimation may be surprising to some since much scholarly ink has been spilt describing Philippians as Paul's "most joyful, warm, and friendly" letter.[67] However, the expected friendship terminology (φίλος and φιλία) is absent from Philippians' four chapters[68] and the entire *Corpus Paulinum.* Moreover, to other scholars, a much different picture emerges upon a close reading of Philippians' rhetoric. For instance, Joseph Marchal writes,

> The first time I sat down to read…. Philippians…. I was struck by how intensely infused most of those 104 verses were with dynamics and declarations of power. Sometimes, they were subtle, but more frequently, they appeared rather obvious to me as I saw Paul try to construct certain kinds of relationships within and through his arguments about Christ and the community, about himself and others…. When I turned to the secondary literature, though, I had a second (but hardly less significant) striking experience. It was as if these scholars and I had read a completely different letter! What warmth and joy they saw in Philippians.[69]

Examples of Paul's hierarchical, boundary marker language are presented in the very first verse of Philippians: "Paul and Timothy *slaves of Christ Jesus* (δοῦλοι) to all *the saints in Christ Jesus* (τοῖς ἁγίοις ἐν Χριστῷ Ἰησου)—those being in Philippi together with [the] *overseers* and *deacons* (ἐπισκόποις…

---

[67] Philippians' warm, friendly tone is assumed in the title of Witherington III, *Friendship and Finances in Philippi,* and in his later commentary where Witherington attempts to distance himself from the scholarly "straitjacket" that Philippians exemplifies the traits of pagan "friendship letters" (φιλικαὶ), but nonetheless repeats his earlier assumptions that Philippians is a warm, "friendly" letter. See Witherington, *Philippians,* 14. On "friendship letters" in antiquity see e.g., Stanley K. Stowers, *Letter Writing in Greco-Roman Antiquity,* ed. Wayne A. Meeks (Philadelphia: Westminster, 1986), 58–70. Stowers baldly states, "[T]here are no letters of friendship in the New Testament". Stowers, *Letter Writing,* 60.

[68] See Markus Bockmuehl, *The Epistle to the Philippians,* BNTC (Grand Rapids: Baker Academic, 2013), 35.

[69] Joseph A. Marchal, *Philippians: Historical Problems, Hierarchical Visions, Historical Anxieties,* ed. Tat-siong Benny Liew, T&T Clark Study Guides to the New Testament (London; New Delhi; New York; Sydney: Bloomsbury, 2017), 1.

διακόνοις)".[70] Thus, Paul reimagines slavery to man with that of servility to Christ and distinguishes the Philippian believers as "holy ones/saints", in light of their boundary marker status of being "in Christ" (ἐν Χριστῷ ['Ιησοῦ])—an insider phrase so important to Paul in Philippians that he repeats this concept ten times throughout the letter.[71] Paul then highlights the hierarchical distinctions of "saints", "overseers", and "deacons", amongst the inside group with their shared, common identifying marker of being "in Christ".

While there appears to be more high boundary markers than low ones, a few related Pauline contrasts will be mentioned here. First, in Phil 1:15–17, Paul contrasts those preaching Christ with "envy and strife" (φθόνον καὶ ἔριν) and those with "goodwill" (εὐδοκίαν). The former group, Paul says, displays "selfish ambition" (ἐξ ἐριθείας), whereas the latter displays "selfless love" (ἐξ ἀγάπης). Yet, Paul rejoices and does not denounce the former group as outsiders since Christ is proclaimed, which is what matters most to him.[72] Next, in Phil 2:4, Paul contrasts those with only self-interests (τὰ ἑαυτῶν) and those who also seek the interests of others (τὰ ἑτέρων). This contrast is later repeated in Phil 2:21, with Timothy's example of selflessness being contrasted with "all the ones seeking their own interests [τὰ ἑαυτῶν], not those of Christ". Lastly, in Phil 4:15, Paul contrasts the generosity of the Philippian saints with other supposed Christ communities who failed to give Paul support. The shared negative trait in all these contrasted groups is myopic self-absorption: the failure to consider the needs of others above their own. This appears to be a pervasive problem given the repetition of this theme in Philippians and the fact that Paul does not rebuke them as outsider enemies. Paul's solution is conformity to Christ.[73]

Like Galatians and unlike Philippians, 1 Thessalonians represents one of Paul's earliest (if not the earliest) letters. The boundary marker terms in 1 Thessalonians deal with religio-social distinctions amid persecution. Paul employs the fictive kinship term "brethren" (ἀδελφοί) to contrast the Thessalonian Christ community with "the gentiles" (τοῖς ἔθνεσιν). Yet, these Thessalonian saints are more proximate ideologically—given their ethnicity—

---

[70] Not all agree with Marchal's assessment of hierarchical language in Philippians, however. For instance, Isaac D. Blois downplays hierarchical arrangements in the relationships Paul presents in Philippians—favoring instead to use language of "mutuality" and "Paul's friendship rhetorics" in Philippians. Blois, *Mutual Boasting in Philippians: The Ethical Function of Shared Honor in its Biblical and Greco-Roman Context*, ed. Chris Keith, LNTS 627 (London; New Delhi; New York; Sydney: Bloomsbury, 2020), 29–31.

[71] See Phil 1:1, 13, 26; 2:1, 5; 3:3, 14; 4:7, 19, 21.

[72] Phil 1:18.

[73] Phil 2:5.

to the outsider gentiles whom Paul wishes to evangelize than to their Jewish neighbours (τῶν Ἰουδαίων), whom Paul vilifies. In Trebilco's schema, we would expect the more proximate gentiles to be vilified using high boundary markers, not the Jews. Thus, if 1 Thess 2:14–16 is not a later, anti-Semitic interpolation as some suggest,[74] there seems to be fluidity in the way Paul employs low and high boundary markers to describe insiders and outsiders in his corpus. By using high boundaries for the less ideologically proximate Jewish group, Paul highlights in 1 Thess 2:15–16 the violent persecution and malicious intent these outsiders have in seeking to prevent Paul and his people from speaking to the pagans' so that the gentails' ethnic and religious differences might be set aside in hoping they might be included as insiders and experience eschatological salvation.

In 1 Thess 4:12, Paul contrasts the Thessalonian Christ-allegiants (τοὺς ἀδελφοὺς) with the out-group phrase τοὺς ἔξω ("the outsiders"), "the gentiles, who have not [yet] come to know the God" (τὰ ἔθνη τὰ μὴ εἰδότα τὸν θεόν) and are not part of the inside group. The way Paul uses the phrase "the outsiders" is reminiscent of the way the author of Beowulf describes the monstrous Grendel—as an "outsider" or *mearcstapa.*[75] *Mearcstapan* were oft-considered "border-walking" monsters, marginalized outsiders distantly lurking on the fringes of society. However, a close reading attuned to the author's intent realizes that *mearcstapan* were more human and beneficial than monstrous and malevolent—cross-cultural border-walkers that were essential to the flourishing of societies.[76] Jesus and Paul were such border-walking "*mearcstapan*"—navigating from village to village between Jewish persons and

---

[74] While some scholars have argued that the outsider language Paul uses in 1 Thess 2:14–16 is the result of later, anti-Semitic interpolations, many others suggest that these terms and verses are original to Paul. See Carol J. Schlueter, *Filling Up the Measure: Polemical Hyperbole in 1 Thessalonians 2:14–16,* JSNTSS 98 (Sheffield: Sheffield Academic Press, 1994), 13–24; and Abraham J. Malherbe, *The Letters to the Thessalonians: A New Translation with Introduction and Commentary,* AB 32B (Garden City, NY; New York: Doubleday, 2000), 164–65. For a helpful discussion of some of the issues involved in light of Paul's own Jewishness and self-identification, see Trebilco, *Outsider Designations,* 182–91.

[75] Makoto Fujimura, *Culture Care: Reconnecting with Beauty for Our Common Life* (Downers Grove, IL: InterVarsity Press, 2017), 58–59.

[76] Though, most think of Grendel as a cinematically hideous, malignant monster, the author paints Grendel in more human, sympathetic hues—describing both Grendel and Grendel's mother as border-walking *mearcstapan.* Christopher Abram, "At Home in the Fens with the Grendelkin", in *Dating Beowulf: Studies in Intimacy,* ed. Daniel C. Reimin and Erica Weaver (Manchester: Manchester University Press, 2020), 127–28. In ancient tribal traditions, *mearcstapan* were necessary border-walkers, who traveled inside and outside various groups to bring vital information, supplies, and hope-filled news to their people. Fujimura, *Culture Care,* 58.

gentiles and between self-abasing "sinners" and self-promoting "saints" to bring the gospel of God.[77]

By presenting the gentiles as τοὺς ἔξω, Paul is perhaps not highlighting so much their eschatological exclusion but an urgent, missionary appeal for their potential inclusion as useful insiders in the family of God. Paul's clarion call is being impeded by the Judean persecutors who, in Paul's purview, stand further from the inside group than the pagans. Lastly, Paul contrasts the Thessalonian brethren as "sons of light" and "sons of the day" (υἱοὶ φωτός... υἱοὶ ἡμέρας) against those of "the night" and "darkness" (νυκτὸς... σκότους) in highlighting the eschatological urgency, which compels and propels Paul in his missionary travels and evangelistic endeavours.

Category Two (High Boundary Markers): Paul's "Opponents" and "Enemies"

In Category Two, we see many comparisons that further distance outsiders from the inside group. For example, in Rom 2:9–10, Paul sets up a contrast between those "who are continuously doing the good" (τῷ ἐργαζομένῳ τὸ ἀγαθόν) and those "who are continuously doing the bad" (τοῦ κατεργαζομένου τὸ κακόν). Paul explains that "every soul of humanity who continuously does evil" will reap "tribulation and calamity", whereas those insiders who are daily doing "the good", no matter their ethnicity (Jew or Greek), will be rewarded with "glory, honour, and peace", since God is impartial regarding one's exterior features and biological descent. Paul's inclusivity toward outsiders hinges upon volitional, active participation: doing the actions and requirements commensurate with being an insider in the community of God and not merely passively hearing the Torah without allowing it to transform the person from the inside out. "(Rom 2:13—15; cf. Jas 1:22—25)

Paul employs the high boundary marker phrase "the uncircumcision" (ἡ ἀκροβυστία) in Rom 2:25–26, which was typically used to denote gentile pagans in the NT and Second Temple Jewish literature.[78] Paul explains here that the outward, covenantal boundary marker of "circumcision" does not denote true insiders within the Christ communities. Rather, such a boundary marker is transformed into "uncircumcision" for those displaying the marker but failing to live up to the requirements of the Torah. Paul's statement here would likely have been startling and offensive to those placing such a high

---

[77] Mark 1:14–15; Rom 1:1.
[78] See e.g., Jdt 14:10; 1 Macc 1:15; Acts 11:3; Rom 2:26; Gal 2:7; Eph 2:11; Col 3:11; and cf. Jub. 15:26.

priority on physical, outward signs of "Jewishness".[79] Thus, for Paul, being an insider in God's family requires a transformation from the inside out: the Spirit forms "Jews inwardly" (ἐν τῷ κρυπτῷ)–by circumcising the heart—not "outwardly" (τῷ φανερῷ) by removing the foreskin.[80]

Romans 5:6–10 reveals Paul's reminiscence of his former life as an outsider to the Christ community and inclusivity toward the possibility of other outsiders progressively deemed to be "ungodly" (ἀσεβῶν), "sinners" (ἁμαρτωλῶν), and "enemies" (ἐχθροὶ) of God to be "made justified" (δικαιωθέντες), "saved" (σωθησόμεθα), "reconciled" (κατηλλάγημεν/καταλλαγέντες) to God, spared from YHWH's eschatological "wrath" (ὀργῆς), and accepted and welcomed as insiders into the Christ community. Such inclusion of outsiders is made possible, in Paul's purview, through the blood and sacrificial death of Christ.

In Rom 9:21–10:15, Paul contrasts outsider "vessels of dishonour" (ἀτιμίαν [σκεῦος]) with insiders, who are deemed "vessels of honour" (τιμὴν σκεῦος). These outsiders are "objects of wrath" (σκεύη ὀργῆς) and headed for eschatological "destruction" but are shown "much longsuffering" (πολλῇ μακροθυμίᾳ) by YHWH, so that they, too, might become "objects of mercy" (σκεύη ἐλέους). Paul's optimistically inclusive language continues in Rom 10:12–15, in which Paul invokes Isaianic overtones[81] to describe the inclusive ministry of in-Christ insiders to those outside Christ. Insiders are to be "bringing the good news of great things" (τῶν εὐαγγελιζομένων τὰ ἀγαθά) to outsiders—a kerygmatic process Paul heralds as "beautiful" (ὡραῖοι) in Rom 10:15. Galatians continues Paul's high boundary marker comparisons.

A prime contrast Paul makes in Galatians is between those outsiders whom he considers "false brethren" (ψευδαδέλφους) and the in-Christ insiders. Paul accuses these outsiders in Gal 2:4 of being "those secretly smuggled in" (τοὺς παρεισάκτους), "who snuck in to spy out [οἵτινες παρεισῆλθον κατασκοπῆσαι] the freedom we have in Christ Jesus in order that they might enslave us [καταδουλώσουσιν]". These outsiders desire to infiltrate and enslave the

---

[79] Numerous relevant Second Temple Jewish texts equate circumcision with "Jewishness". One of the most salient examples is found in Jub. 15:26 in which the writer explains, "Anyone ... whose own flesh is not circumcised on the eighth day is not from the covenant sons which the Lord made for Abraham since [he is] from the children of destruction". In considering such texts, Andreas Blaske surmises that "the high estimation of circumcision corresponds to the low estimation of uncircumcision", which was in the Second Temple Jewish literature, "a synonym for what is lawless, alien, hateful and detestable". Blaske, *Beschneidung: Zeugnisse der Bibel und verwandter Texte*, TANZ 28 (Tübingen: Francke, 1998), 321.

[80] Rom 2:28–29.

[81] Isa 28:16, 52:7.

saints secretly—thus, Paul erects high boundaries to distance these false brethren. What of Philippians?

Unity is a leitmotif throughout Philippians, as many scholars have noted. For example, Dave Black argues that,

> Philippians is an integral composition whose primary rhetorical function is deliberative, that is, the bulk of the letter is directed toward solving the issue of disunity arising from the exigence reflected most clearly in 4:2-3[.] 'Unity for the sake of the gospel' provides the overarching framework and motif within which the other themes and concerns are introduced and elucidated.[82]

Unity for the sake of the gospel is required for Paul and the Philippians in a world where increasingly intense persecution by outsiders is the norm. Indeed, Paul writes Philippians from prison and notes the fearlessness that his chains inspire in other gospel preachers (Philippians 1:12—14). While at times Paul writes Philippians from the standpoint of a tender-hearted, missionary pastor edifying and admonishing his saintly sheep, he simultaneously writes as a seasoned and salty "general" in a spiritual warfare in which Paul feels the *missio Dei*, his missionary ambit, and the progress of the Jesus movement are at stake. While Paul may at times speak softly and tenderly to the Philippian saints, he nonetheless bears the responsibility and weight of his God-given apostolic "stick" and remains *primus inter pares* as the "superior family member" to his Philippian siblings—fiercely warning them against outsiders seeking to disrupt, derail, and destroy the work that Paul is doing amongst the Christ communities in Philippi and beyond.[83]

Three examples in Philippians reveal how Paul uses contrast to distinguish high boundary markers separating insiders from outsiders. First, Paul's dual imperative commands in Philippians are seemingly political, militaristic calls for the Philippian Christ-allegiants to "live as good citizens [πολιτεύεσθε] worthy of the gospel of Christ" and to "stand firm" (στήκετε) in unity.[84] Paul

---

[82] David A. Black, "The Discourse Structure of Philippians: A Study in Textlinguistics", *NovT* 37.1 (1995): 16.

[83] Gregory E. Lamb, review of *Mutual Boasting in Philippians: The Ethical Function of Shared Honor in its* [sic] *Biblical and Greco-Roman Context*, by Isaac D. Blois, *RBL* 24 (2022): n.p.

[84] On the political and militaristic metaphors in Philippians, see e.g., Edgar M. Krentz, "Military Language and Metaphors in Philippians", in *Origins and Methods: Toward a New Understanding of Judaism and Christianity: Essays in Honour of John C. Hurd*, ed. Bradley H. McLean, JSNTSup 86 (Sheffield: Sheffield Academic, 1993), 105–27; Timothy C. Geoffrion, *The Rhetorical Purpose and the Political and Military Character of Philippians: A Call to Stand Firm* (Lewiston, NY: Mellen, 1993); and Dierk Mueller, "Military Images in Paul's Letter to the Philippians", (PhD diss., University of Pretoria, 2013).

also highlights at the end of Phil 1:27 the necessity of "striving together [συναθλοῦντες] for the faith of the gospel", which would have also likely carried militaristic undertones to Paul's first-century Philippian audience.[85] Paul continues his military imagery in Phil 1:28 and contrasts these supposed-to-be united and standing-firm "soldier-saints" with outsiders, whom Paul considers "the opposing ones" (τῶν ἀντικειμένων) to be fought rather than as neighbouring friends and potential converts to be "won".[86] The eschatological end of these outsider enemies is vastly different from the inside group: their end is "destruction" (ἀπωλείας), whereas insiders will ultimately experience eschatological "salvation" (σωτηρίας) from God.

Second, in Phil 2:15, Paul vividly contrasts those outsiders whom he deems to be the "crooked and perverse generation" against whom Paul's Philippian insiders "shine like stars in the cosmos". Paul's exemplary shining saints are the "children of God"—"blameless and pure"—since they are in Christ. However, the disunity amongst the insider Philippians—most vividly expressed in Phil 4:2–3[87]—gives Paul at least some pause, as indicated by his use of the subjunctive mood in Phil 2:15 (γένησθε) and Paul's introspective consideration of having run his ministry to the Philippians in "vain" (κενὸν) in Phil 2:16.

---

[85] On the militaristic connotations embedded within the participle συναθλοῦντες, Thomas Moore argues that the term "suggests a military image of fighting side-by-side" similar to the phalanx formation of the Greeks, which was later adopted and modified by the Romans. Moore, *Philippians: An Exegetical Guide for Preaching and Teaching*, Big Greek Idea Series (Grand Rapids: Kregel, 2019), 107. Hellerman also notes the familiarity that the Philippians would have likely had with Paul's militaristic metaphors when he writes, "Philippi had been founded as a veteran colony.... The settlement's location along the Egnatian Way would have exposed residents to Roman armies traveling east or west across the empire.... It is not unreasonable to see a military *topos* here". Hellerman, *Philippians*, 79, emphasis original.

[86] Paul Holloway remarks regarding Paul's seeming war against outsiders in 1:27–28: "the language Paul employs evokes the battlefield ... and, as such, stands at the head of a long tradition of martial imagery used to characterize the church's relationship to outsiders, what Tacitus called Christ-believers' *odium humani generis* ("hatred for the human race"; *Ann.* 15.44) ... To resist the gospel's enemies the Philippians must do two things: They must ... fight as a unit ... And they must remain calm in the battle". Paul A. Holloway, *Philippians*, Hermeneia (Minneapolis: Augsburg Fortress, 2017), 106.

[87] Some scholars have suggested that Phil 4:2–3 does not suggest a quarrel between Euodia and Syntyche but a call to "to pursue the vision of unity that Paul expounds throughout the letter". See Tyler Allred, "Philippians 4:2–3: An Alternative View of the Euodia-Syntyche Debate", *Priscilla Papers* 33.4 (2019): 4–8, here 4. Cf. Richard G. Fellows and Alistair C. Stewart, "Euodia, Syntyche and the Role of *Syzygos*: Phil 4:2–3", *ZNW* 109.2 (2018): 222–34.

Third and last, Paul uses apocalyptic imagery to describe the spiritual warfare between heavenly citizens,[88] whose ultimate allegiance is to Christ, and the citizens of this world, whose ultimate allegiance is to Caesar and self. These outsider citizens are fixated on "earthly" thoughts and desires (οἱ τὰ ἐπίγεια φρονοῦντες) and are deemed the "enemies of the cross of Christ" (τοὺς ἐχθροὺς τοῦ σταυροῦ τοῦ Χριστου). Their eschatological end—like the opponents in Phil 1:28—is "destruction" (ἀπώλεια). Ἀπώλεια only appears thrice in the seven letters surveyed: twice in Philippians and once in Rom 9:22. In Rom 9:22, however, Paul presents a hypothetical situation in which God may have "endured with much patience" (ἤνεγκεν ἐν πολλῇ μακροθυμίᾳ) those "vessels of wrath [σκεύη ὀργῆς] prepared for destruction". Whereas in Philippians, ἀπώλεια represents the seemingly unchanging eschatological reality for these outsider enemies. Thus, Phil 1:28 and 3:19 present a bleaker outlook regarding the concrete eschatological reality of outsiders than the imagined situation sketched by Paul earlier in Rom 9:22. Interestingly, it seems that there may be a contrastive link between the positive description of "the circumcision" in Phil 3:3 and the negative description of "the enemies of the cross of Christ" in Phil 3:19. The parallels are seen in Table 2.1.

Table 2.1. Contrast between the Group Descriptions of Phil 3:3 and 3:19

Insider Group Description ("The Circumcision;" 3:3)	Outsider Group Description ("The Enemies;" 3:19)
"the ones worshipping in God's Spirit"	"the ones whose end is destruction"
"those boasting in Christ Jesus"	"whose god is their stomach and whose glory [is] their shame"
"and have not been placing confidence in [the] flesh"	"those who are setting their minds [on] earthly things"

In Phil 3:3 and 3:19, Paul contrasts the characteristics of insiders, who are "celestial citizens"—having the goal of resurrection from the dead and eschatological salvation[89]—with enemy outsiders, who are worldly citizens— reaping eschatological destruction in their earthly/fleshly thinking and idolatry. Thus, Paul appears to be less inclusive, less eschatologically optimistic, and more polemical toward these opposing outside groups in Philippians than in his earlier letters. Paul's appeal to unity in Philippians appears to be a call to solidarity in the midst of threat and spiritual warfare against the

---

[88] Phil 1:27, 3:20.
[89] Phil 1:28; 2:12; 3:10–14.

outside group(s), whom Paul considers to be "opponents" and "enemies of Christ's cross".

Category Three (Highest Threats):
Paul's Dehumanized and "Monstrified" Enemies

Category Three evinces Paul's highest boundary marker language in his epistles, which creates the furthest distance between insider and outsider groups through the dehumanization and monstrification of Paul's/Christ's enemies. At the outset of this section, a brief sketch of what I mean by the slippery term "dehumanization"—as well as its linkage to monstrification—is necessary.

At the most basic level, "dehumanization" means to "conceive of others as less than human".[90] This often involves ethics and making moral judgments about an outsider's inferiority in contrast to the insider's superiority. Many of the most memorable monstrous myths and legends—Mary Shelley's *Frankenstein* and Bram Stroker's *Dracula*, for example—highlight the dehumanization of their characters, which results from their or their agents' moral defects.[91] Thus, their morality—or lack thereof—is inextricably linked to their monstrosity. Moreover, monstrosity is often linked to physical deformity or "otherness", which physiognomy caricatures in dehumanizing ways and traces to inner, moral flaws.[92] This can be seen in the Hebrew Bible as Job's three "friends" made inner character judgments about him due to his exterior appearance, as well as in the NT, where those with deformities or handicaps were often stereotyped as "sinners".[93]

Monstrification is a process, the result of dehumanization. The abnormality in the monstrous "other" highlights what is to be normative for insiders.[94] This is not to say that the dehumanized are always monstrified. Monsters are

---

[90] David Livingstone Smith, *On Inhumanity: Dehumanization and How to Resist It* (Oxford; London; New York: Oxford University Press, 2020), 6. Cf. Hal Brunson, *Lesbos, Narcissus, and Paulos: Homosexual Myth and Christian Truth* (New York; Lincoln; Shanghai: iUniverse, 2006), 21.

[91] In the case of Frankenstein's monster, its amalgam of body parts consisted either of the worst criminals themselves or were stolen by other thieves. In either case, both the mal-intent of Victor von Frankenstein and his creature's criminalized, scandalous body lead to the audience's perception and assumption of the creature's criminality even before it had committed any crime.

[92] Nicolet, "Monstrous Bodies", 115.

[93] See Gregory E. Lamb, "Sinfully Stereotyped: Jesus's Desire to Correct Ancient Physiognomic Assumptions in the Gospel according to Luke", *WW* 37.2 (2017): 178 n. 4. Cf. Job 2:11–12; 4:7–8; 8:1–6; 15:1–16; 18:1–21; 22:5–8; John 9:2.

[94] Smith, *On Inhumanity*, 158.

powerful, threatening, terrifying, and cannot be trusted.[95] Monsters are border-walkers living in the proverbial shadows, at the edge of society and desiring to demolish boundaries.[96] Monsters also serve as intermediaries—as messengers that seek to change and disrupt the inside group.[97] We *need* monsters in order to establish what is "good", "normative", and "ideal" in relation to our behaviours, beliefs, bodies, and being.[98] Indeed, monster theory reminds us that the "ideal" body or community (utopia) on this fallen earth is a mythical *chimaera*—it does not exist.[99] Consider Christ's crucified and broken body or Paul's battered, stigmatized body. Scripture reveals "perfect" bodies and "communities" using apocalyptic, resurrection, and heavenly (afterlife) imagery.[100] In this present life, according to the NT writers, humanity can expect dystopia along with dying, blemished bodies.[101] However, Paul explains that there are boundaries to be maintained and norms commensurate with having an in-Christ identity for these insider saints. Such boundaries and norms require obedience and conformity to Christ[102] and seem to be what Paul is protecting in Phil 3:2—hence, Paul's language of "safeguarding" (ὑμῖν δὲ ἀσφαλές) in Phil 3:1.

In this sense, I feel that monster theory and SIT serve as helpful handmaidens in illuminating Phil 3:2 and, indeed, the rest of the NT, as Paul sought to shield and protect the Philippian saints from outsider groups threatening their flourishing and very existence. While Paul may not have so explicitly crafted literary "monsters" in quite the obvious way that Shelley or Stoker did, he nevertheless invokes *ekphrastically* dehumanizing and monstrous descriptors toward outsiders in his epistles.[103] A few notable examples of Paul's dehumanizing

---

[95] Smith, *On Inhumanity*, 158–60; and Nicolet, "Monstrous Bodies", 115–16.

[96] Nicolet, "Monstrous Bodies", 117.

[97] Nicolet, "Monstrous Bodies", 118.

[98] Nicolet, "Monstrous Bodies", 119–20. Cf. Judith Halberstam, *Skin Shows: Gothic Horror and the Technology of Monsters* (Durham, NC: Duke University Press, 1995), 27.

[99] Nicolet, "Monstrous Bodies", 136–37.

[100] Phil 3:10–14, 20 *et passim*.

[101] John 16:33; Phil 1:20–24.

[102] Phil 2:5–11, 3:10–17.

[103] The term "*ekphrasis*" denotes a vivid, rhetorical effect that gives the visceral impression to the audience that they are experiencing what the author describes. Theon authors the *Progymnasmata* containing the earliest extant usage of the term *ekphrasis* (ἔκφρασις). Theon defines *ekphrasis* as, "descriptive language, bringing what is portrayed clearly before the sight". Aelius Theon, *Progymnasmata* 7.118. Cf. Ruth Webb, *Ekphrasis, Imagination and Persuasion in Ancient Rhetorical Theory and Practice* (Burlington, VT; Farnham, Surrey, UK: Ashgate, 2009), 39.

language from 1 Corinthians, Galatians, Philippians, and Philemon shall be discussed here.

In 1 Cor 5:6–8, Paul contrasts outsiders dehumanizingly described as "leavened" (ζύμη/ζυμοῖ) with insiders, who are "unleavened" (ἄζυμοι). While Paul's use of "mixed-up dough" in Rom 11:16 was deemed a low boundary marker in its intra-Jewish, soteriological context, Paul's contrast in 1 Cor 5:6–8 serves as a much higher boundary marker and threat. The "leavened" outsiders boast in the flesh and that which is "not good" (οὐ καλὸν); they risk corrupting the Christ communities of Corinth; and they display "wickedness and depravity" (κακίας καὶ πονηρίας). In stark contradistinction, the "unleavened" insiders boast in Christ and are marked by "purity and truth" (εἰλικρινείας καὶ ἀληθείας).

In 1 Cor 15:8, Paul speaks of his former life as an outsider—before obtaining his in-Christ identity and apostolic status—in dehumanized, monstrous terms. However, the English translations mostly obscure the monstrous severity of Paul's Greek.[104] Paul writes, "And last of all, he [the resurrected Christ] appeared to me also, the aborted fetus [τῷ ἐκτρώματι], as it were".[105] The articular term Paul uses here (ἔκτρωμα) is a NT *hapax legomenon* but does appear elsewhere in the Greek Old Testament (LXX),[106] in the Second Temple Jewish literature in Philo,[107] and ancient pagan literature as early as the fourth-century BCE writings of Aristotle, according to searches within the *Thesaurus Linguae Graecae* (*TLG*) database.[108] In each case, the authors employ ἔκτρωμα to denote death: an abortive process in which the unborn creature never sees the light of life and is ejected from its mother as an abortion. The mother cannot bring the birth to completion, and the unborn is discharged and perishes as an immature, stillborn miscarriage. Aaron, Moses's brother, intercedes to Moses (and implicitly to God) for their diseased and leprous sister, Miriam, in Num 12:12 and highlights the monstrous, dehumanizing, and destructive effects of the ἔκτρωμα: "Do not let her [Miriam] become as equal to death like an abortion [ἔκτρωμα] coming out of its mother's womb and whose flesh is half-eaten away".[109] In *Leg.* 1.24.76, Philo offers commentary on the

---

[104] Some of the most popular English translations of ἔκτρωμα include: "as to one untimely born" (ESV); "as to one abnormally born" (NIV, HCSB); "to one untimely born" (NASB, NRSV); and "as of/by one born out of due time" (KJV, NKJV).

[105] 1 Cor 15:8.

[106] See Num 12:12; Eccl 6:3; and Job 3:16.

[107] Philo, *Leg.* 1.24.76.

[108] Aristotle, *Gen. an.* 773b.18.

[109] My translation derives from the Greek text of Alfred Rahlfs et al., eds., *Biblia Graeca: Septuaginta, Novum Testamentum Graece* (Stuttgart: Bibelgesellschaft, 2013), 236.

futility of folly in the foolish mind and cites the monstrously *ekphrastic* sight in Num 12:12 to support his argument.

Paul likewise describes the nature of his apostleship in monstrous, abortive terms. Andrzej Gieniusz concludes that Paul intends a double entendre in using ἔκτρωμα to connote "death" and something "deadly". Gieniusz writes, "In this double meaning, the term utilized by Paul in 1 Cor 15:8 [ἔκτρωμα] describes the pre-Christian past of the Apostle as both lacking life (as being without Christ) and lethal (as a persecutor of the church of God)".[110] George Nickelsburg explains the monstrous connotations embedded in Paul's term:

> *Ektrōma* denotes monster or monstrous birth. The term originated not with Paul but with his opponents. Hinted at are the demonic nature of Paul's persecution of the church; the abnormal manner in which he became an apostle; [and] the inability of his baptism (ἀναγέννησις, 'rebirth)' [*sic*] to form him in Christ's image.[111]

Paul also employs dehumanizing language in Galatians.

Given Paul's concern with infiltrators, who were "bewitching" the Galatians with seductive, erroneous teachings that distorted Paul's gospel,[112] Paul saves his severest comments for these outsiders masquerading as spies within the insider group. In Gal 1:8, Paul exclaims regarding the outsiders, "Let him be accursed [ἀνάθεμα ἔστω]!" In the rebuke mentioned above to troublemaking outsiders in Gal 5:12, Paul invokes the dehumanizing and emasculating language of "mutilation" by employing a vividly *ekphrastic* term (ἀποκόψονται) that suggests that the outsiders were using the wrong missionary tactics—Peter's gospel to the circumcised[113]—on the gentiles. The boundary marker ἀποκόψονται is dehumanizing in the sense that Paul's irritated sense of dark humour removes the very reproductive aspect of his opponents' humanity and renders them outside the sphere of God's worshipping, covenantal people

---

[110] Gieniusz, "'As a Miscarriage,'" 93.

[111] Nickelsburg, "An Ἔκτρωμα", 199. Hollander and van der Hout add: "[Paul] employed the term to depict himself as one who is in a most deplorable situation, who is the most miserable and worthless man on earth. As a former persecutor of the Church Paul felt that he was the most worthless man on earth, but in spite of his insufficiency he was appointed by God to be his apostle". Hollander and van der Hout, "The Apostle Paul Calling Himself an Abortion", 236.

[112] See J. Louis Martyn, *Galatians: A New Translation with Introduction and Commentary*, AB 33A (New Haven: Yale University Press, 1997), 447–48.

[113] On the differing "Petrine" and "Pauline" gospels hypothesis, see n. 47 above.

and more akin to the pagan (Cybele) cults in Galatia and beyond in *colonia* such as Philippi.[114]

In considering Paul's highest boundary markers in Philippians, a possible dehumanizing clause connoting "monsters" or the "monstrous" appears in the so-called *Carmen Christi* ("Christ Hymn") of Phil 2:10, which reads: "so that, at the name 'Jesus,' every knee should bend in heaven and of those upon the earth and under the earth". Phil 2:10 is a loose translation of the LXX text of Isa 45:23 in which either Paul or another writer has added to the *Carmen Christi* the apocalyptic descriptors "in heaven and of those upon the earth and under the earth" to denote the cosmic sphere and totality of Christ's powerful Lordship, superiority, and reign. The last phrase, "and under the earth" (καὶ καταχθονίων), is absent from Isaiah's text and is a scriptural *hapax legomenon*. Yet, the phrase may have invoked monstrous connotations to pagans and former pagans in Philippi since καταχθόνιος (*katachthonios*) comprises, in a generalized, cosmological and theological sense, the subterranean monsters,[115] gods (*chthonic*), and netherworld within the Greco-Roman pantheons and appears in the pagan literature (and implicitly in art) as early as the Homeric epics (ca. eighth century BCE).[116] While much debate exists regarding the

---

[114] See Deut 23:1; cf. Lev 21:20; and 22:24. James Dunn quips regarding Paul's darkly humorous wish, "The wish then is a savage one: would that the knife might slip in the hand of those who count circumcision indispensable to participation in the assembly of the Lord, so that they might find the same rules excluding themselves". James D. G. Dunn, *The Epistle to the Galatians*, BNTC 9 (Peabody, MA: Hendrickson, 1993), 282–83. Moreover, eunuchs were among the most despised groups in the ancient world according to Josephus (*Ant.* 4.290–91) and Lucian (*Eunuch.* 6). Dieter Lührmann sees a boundary marker connection between Paul's slur in Gal 5:12 and Phil 3:2. Lührmann, *Galatians: A Continental Commentary*, trans. O. C. Dean, Jr. (Minneapolis: Augsburg Fortress, 1992), 98. Regarding the Cybele cults, their priests were known to castrate themselves. One of the major temples of this castration cult was located in Pessinus and was, according to Martyn, quite possibly in the same city as one the Pauline Christ communities of Galatia. Martyn, *Galatians*, 478. Thus, Paul's bloody image would have likely resonated with the pagan and formerly pagan Galatian peoples.

[115] The *Homeric Hymn to Apollo* and various extant Greek artworks portray such a subterranean *chthonic* monster in Python, a monstrous dragon-serpent creature, who was slain by the god Apollo with a volley of arrows. See *Hom. H. Ap.* 372–74. Cf. Christiane Sourvinou-Inwood, "Myth as History: The Previous Owners of the Delphic Oracle", in *Interpretations of Greek Mythology*, ed. Jan Bremmer, Routledge Revivals (London; New York: Routledge, 2014), 227.

[116] Based on lexical searches in the *TLG* database. See e.g., Homer, *Il.* 9.457; and the first-century CE philosophical/theological writings of the Stoic Lucius Annaeus Cornutus *Nat. d.* 72.18 (καὶ χθονίαν ἐκάλεσαν καὶ τοῖς καταχθονίοις θεοῖς ἤρξαντο συντιμᾶν), which were contemporaneous with Paul and his Philippian audience.

Pauline authorship of the *Carmen Christi*,[117] Paul either penned or at least *included* the additions to LXX Isa 45:23 in canonical Philippians to show the universal supremacy of Christ above all other gods, goddesses, titans, monsters and the monstrous, and human rulers throughout the cosmos.

The last example of boundary markers discussed in Philippians derives from Phil 3:2-3. Here, Paul contrasts the dehumanized outsider group(s) he calls "dogs", "evil workers", and the "mutilation" with those insiders Paul describes as "the circumcision" (ἡ περιτομη). Scholars have taken the phrase "evil workers" as a deliberate pun or "terminus technicus", referring to Judaizing missionaries wishing to force the "works of the Law" upon the Philippian saints.[118] Others suggest an apocalyptic reading of "evil workers" that harks back to the Greek Psalter.[119] While some object that the Psalms do not reflect "exact parallels",[120] this can be explained in Paul's rhetorical emphasis in Phil 3:2 on alliteration (κύνας... κακοὺς... κατατομήν).[121] Moreover, the Psalter's apocalyptic imagery of YHWH's destruction of these evildoers comports well with Paul's apocalyptic language of destruction in Phil 1:28 and 3:19. Regarding "the mutilation", the NASB translation highlights the contrast and seeming pun (τὴν κατατομήν ... ἡ περιτομή) by adding the descriptor "true circumcision" in Phil 3:3a. Paul rhetorically reimagines the articular phrase ἡ περιτομη in terms of inward, spiritual circumcision of the heart that results in obedience,[122] which is representative of being in Christ and being the true spiritual children of God and Abraham. Lastly, we turn to Philemon.

---

[117] For a fulsome discussion of the arguments for and against Pauline authorship of the *Carmen Christi*, see the classic study of Ralph P. Martin, *Carmen Christi: Philippians ii. 5–11 in Recent Interpretation and in the Setting of Early Christian Worship*, SNTSMS 4 (Cambridge; New York: Cambridge University Press, 1967), 42–62.

[118] See Reumann, *Philippians*, 461–62.

[119] LXX Ps 5:6; 6:8; 63:3 *et passim*.

[120] Reumann, *Philippians*, 461.

[121] The longer terminology in LXX Ps 5:6 (τοὺς ἐργαζομένους τὴν ἀνομίαν) or even the shorter reading in LXX Ps 63:3 (ἐργαζομένων τὴν ἀνομίαν) would not have flowed off the tongue as easily as Paul's possible rhetorical adaptation in Phil 3:2 (τοὺς κακοὺς ἐργάτας). Paul's letters were oral documents to be heard as well as literary documents to be read.

[122] Rom 2:28–29; 1 Cor 7:19.

Given its brevity and deeply personal,[123] ministerial focus, it might be expected that Philemon would be absent of such insider, outsider, and boundary marker terminology. However, that assumption would be false. Paul writes Philemon to address his divisive treatment of Onesimus—Philemon's runaway slave—as his inferior, marginalized other. Paul uses warm, affectionate, insider and familial language to describe his relationship with Philemon and Onesimus. Paul refers to these men in fictive kinship/sibling terms with God as "our Father", with Philemon as Paul's spiritual "brother", and Onesimus as Paul's "child" in the faith. He feels it necessary to remind Philemon of Paul's own ministerial and apostolic authority. Furthermore, Paul explains that Philemon must begin to willingly identify Onesimus not merely as his slave, "but more than a slave" (ἀλλ᾽ ὑπὲρ δοῦλον): as Philemon's "beloved brother" (ἀδελφὸν ἀγαπητόν), insider, and most poignantly, as Philemon's equal.[124] Additionally, Onesimus is a useful brother and partner to Paul, Philemon, and the nascent Jesus movement.

Slavery in Paul's first-century Mediterranean world was a demeaning, dehumanizing, divisive, and often destructive industry, with enslaved peoples' treatment often being determined by the whims of their masters.[125] They were dehumanized, animalized commodities—like livestock—to be bought and sold.[126] Their body were not their own but existed merely to please their master through forced labour and often forced sexual acts and prostitution.[127] Enslaved peoples were often regarded as "indispensable outsiders ... morally

---

[123] The depth of Paul's personal and ministerial tenor in Philemon is displayed in Paul's triadic use of σπλάγχνον (Phlm 7, 12, 20), which only occurs eight times in the *Corpus Paulinum* and is one of the most *ekphrastically* intimate, heartfelt, and affectionate terms in all of Paul's letters—conveying an object of deep affection, love, the heart, or inner seat of human emotions. Moreover, Paul's warm relationship with Philemon is seen in Paul's command for Philemon to prepare him a guest room in likely Philemon's own home (v. 22). On Paul's personal tone and artful use of rhetoric in Philemon, see Panayotis Coutsoumpos and Panagiotis L. Kampouris, *Reading Philemon: Christianity and Slavery in the First-Century Roman Empire* (Eugene, OR: Wipf & Stock, 2022), 72–73.

[124] Troels Engberg-Pedersen suggests that for Onesimus to truly become Philemon's "beloved brother" that Philemon must manumit Onesimus and release him from his servility to man so that Onesimus can become an equal to Paul and Philemon as a slave to Christ. Troels Engberg-Pedersen, *Paul on Identity: Theology as Politics* (Minneapolis: Augsburg Fortress, 2021), 110–11.

[125] Coutsoumpos and Kampouris, *Reading Philemon*, 86.

[126] See Joseph A. Marchal, ed., "Slaves as Wo/men and Unmen: Reflecting Upon Euodia, Syntyche, and Epaphroditus in Philippi", in *The People beside Paul: The Christian Assembly and History from Below*, ECL 17 (Atlanta: SBL Press, 2015), 147; and Tyler M. Schwaller, "'A Slave to All': The Queerness of Paul's Slave Form", in *Bodies on the Verge: Queering Pauline Epistles*, ed. Joseph A. Marchal, SemeiaSt 93 (Atlanta: SBL Press, 2019), 168.

[127] Schwaller, "'A Slave to All,'" 166.

deficient and potentially dangerous".[128] First-century pagans did not praise subservience. Plutarch recorded the story of a Spartan boy enslaved by King Antigonus, who—when asked to bring their owner a chamber pot—replied, "I will not be [a] slave" and threw himself off the owner's roof in suicide.[129] Plato also highlights ancient cultural aversions to slavery when he asks the rhetorical question, "For how can [a] man flourish if he is being a slave to anyone?"[130]

Hierarchical distinctions also occurred amongst freed siblings in the first century, with brothers differing in "age, nature, roles, ability, and social position".[131] Plutarch classifies siblings in terms of superiority (ὁ ὑπερέχων) and inferiority (ὁ λειπόμενος) with clearly demarcated differences of status through such nomenclature.[132] Yet, Plutarch, the pagan, knew that such discordant inequality in speech and culture should be guarded against and cured for the flourishing health of society.[133] Paul feels compelled to remind Philemon of this truth in his letter and break the yoke of the alienating boundary marker of slavery between his two equal brothers, Philemon and Onesimus. Thus, the concept of "slavery" in Paul's letters can serve both as insider—when describing those called "slaves of Christ"—and outsider language with varying degrees of "otherness". "Slave" is a low boundary marker concept for Paul when describing general humanity in its natural state as "slaves to men" in 1 Cor 7:22–23 and "slaves to sin" in Rom 6:20 and Gal 4:22–26, but can also serve as a dehumanizing, high boundary marker when enslavement threatens to destroy unity and flourishing within the Christ communities.

Philippians 3:2 as Paul's Rhetorical Boundary Markers?

The commentary tradition surrounding Phil 3:2 has persistently, though not monolithically, portrayed these outsiders as Jewish or Judaizers. One of the greatest contributions that the Paul within Judaism (PWJ) movement has made to Pauline studies is to highlight this pernicious anti-Semitism. This a priori assumption is parroted by pastors and professors preaching and teaching these texts. Many different Jewish and gentile identities have been ascribed to Paul's opponents in Phil 3:2, which has led to a seeming scholarly stalemate with little hope of definitive determinations regarding the opponents' identity(-

---

[128] Sandra R. Joshel and Sheila Murnaghan, eds., *Women and Slaves in Greco-Roman Culture: Differential Equations* (London; New York: Routledge, 1998), 3. Cited in Marchal, ed., "Slaves as Wo/men and Unmen", 147.

[129] Plutarch, *Mor.* 234.c.38.

[130] Plato, *Gorg.* 491.e.6.

[131] Paul Trebilco, *Self-Designations and Group Identity in the New Testament* (Cambridge; New York: Cambridge University Press, 2012), 20.

[132] Plutarch, *Frat. amor.* 484D, 485C. Cf. Trebilco, *Self-Designations*, 20–21.

[133] Plutarch, *Frat. amor.* 484D.

ies) or moving the discussion forward. The value of approaching Phil 3:2 from the standpoint of Paul's boundary marker language and SIT is that is approach enables us to advance the discussion in, perhaps, more fruitful ways by comparing Paul's language and rhetoric in Phil 3:2 against the backdrop of his boundary marker, insider, and outsider language elsewhere in Philippians and the *Corpus Paulinum.*

In our age of pet superstores, where dogs are considered "children" or "fur-babies" and their owners are called "pet parents", it may be difficult for some to see canines as being "monstrous".[134] Yet Stephen King's *Cujo*, Joe Dante's *The Howling*, and the childhood folktale *Little Red Riding Hood* remind us that Canidae can be monstrous. The attitudes of a family living in the bush of Africa or Alaska toward packs of wild dogs and dog-like creatures (such as the hyena, which is technically a Hyaenidae, or wolf) would likely be much different than a urban family watching Disney's *Lion King*, where, interestingly, hyenas are also portrayed as sinister and "monstrous" at points in the film. Monstrified dogs can be seen in the ancient world in the λευκρόκοττας, κροκόττας (possibly hyenas), and the horrifying hybrid κυνόλυκος ("dog-wolf").[135] Homer's hounds were also depicted as monstrous beasts that devour corpses and strike terror in the hearts of characters like Priam, who fear being eaten by savage dogs,[136] a fate shared by biblical characters like Jezebel.[137]

The use of the negative descriptor "dogs" to denote outsiders is also common in biblical and extrabiblical Second Temple Jewish sources. Unlike contemporary domesticated canines treated as beloved pets and a part of one's "family", dogs in the Ancient Near East (ANE) were viewed much differently as

---

[134] When it comes to ancient perceptions of dogs, there is a complex spectrum of thought. Dogs served simultaneously as gods, sacrificial animals to the *chthonic* gods, underworld guides, beloved pets, guards, as faithful work and hunting companions, derogatory epithets, sexualized objects, food, and as feared and loathsome monsters—both on earth and in the afterlife. See Sonja Vuković and Mladen Jovičić, "Dog Burials from the Cemeteries of the Roman City of *Viminacium* (Moesia Superior, Kostolac, Serbia)", in *Proceedings of the 22nd International Congress of Roman Frontier Studies, Ruse, Bulgaria, September 2012*, ed. Lyudmil Ferdinandov Vagalinski and Nicolay Sharankov, Bulletin of the National Archaeological Institute 42 (Sofia: National Archaeological Institute with Museum at the Bulgarian Academy of Sciences, 2015): 687–702, here 687; and Kenneth F. Kitchell, Jr., *Animals in the Ancient World from A to Z* (London; New York: Routledge, 2014), 47–52.

[135] Kitchell, Jr., *Animals*, 34.

[136] See Homer, *Il.* 1.4–5; 22.66–76; and Kitchell, Jr., *Animals*, 47–48.

[137] 2 Kgs 9:10, 33–37.

filthy scavengers who could potentially do one harm.[138] To call someone a "dog" in the ancient world, as is still the case today, was a demeaning slur.

In the Greek text of 1 Sam 17:43, we see insults and outsider language being hurled from both combatants as David, the future Jewish king, and Goliath, the gentile warrior, face each other in lethal combat. The Greek text of 1 Sam 17:43 reads, "[A]nd the gentile [ὁ ἀλλόφυλος: Goliath] said to David, 'Am I myself as [a] dog [κύων] that you come to me with [a] stick and stones?' and David said, 'No, but worse than a dog [οὐχί ἀλλ᾽ ἢ χείρω κυνός],' and the gentile [ὁ ἀλλόφυλος] cursed David by his gods". C. T. R. Hayward suggests that David's derogatory slur represents an early (ca. late second-century BCE) stage of the tradition.[139]

Thus, similar to Paul in Philippians, by associating Goliath the gentile with the derogatory descriptor κυνός, David dehumanizes and distances Goliath from the insider Jewish group as a threatening enemy to be fought and destroyed. This negative association is clarified apocalyptically in Rev 22:14–15, where the writer cites Christ's final macarism in drawing the eschatological boundary lines between the insiders and outsiders in the eternal, heavenly city: "Blessed are those washing their robes, so that they, themselves, will have the right to the tree of life, and are the ones who may enter into the city by the gates. Outside [are] the dogs [ἔξω οἱ κύνες], the sorcerers, the sexually immoral persons, the murderers, the idolaters, and everyone loving and practising falsehood". The writer's sixfold use of polysyndeton in Rev 22:15 (καὶ ... καὶ ... καὶ ... καὶ ... καὶ ... καὶ) rhetorically highlights the distance of the dehumanized "dogs" et al. from the inside group.

The dehumanizing descriptor of "dogs" to denote outside groups is also seen in the extrabiblical Second Temple Jewish literature. Among the most salient texts is the Testament of Judah 23.3, where the writer equates the

---

[138] See Bockmuehl, *Philippians*, 185–86, who notes that dogs possessed a mostly negative connotation prior to Tobit in the ancient world, though there was at least some sympathy toward the beasts in ancient Phoenicia in the Persian period as is seen in the discovery of a cemetery at Ashkelon with 700 buried dogs. While evidence shows that the Greeks and Romans highly regarded domesticated dogs alike and coopted into human space, wild street beasts were especially feared for their violence and rabid, wolflike behavior. See Cristiana Franco, "Dogs and Humans in Ancient Greece and Rome: Towards a Definition of Extended Appropriate Interaction", in *Dog's Best Friend?: Rethinking Canid-Human Relations*, ed. John Sorenson and Atsuko Matsuoka (Montreal; Kingston, ON: McGill-Queen's University Press, 2019), 34–37.

[139] C. T. R. Hayward, "The Aramaic Song of the Lamb (The Dialogue between David and Goliath)", in *Old Testament Pseudepigrapha: More Noncanonical Scriptures, Vol. 1*, ed. Richard Bauckham, James R, Davila, and Alexander Panayotov (Grand Rapids: Eerdmans, 2013), 277.

enemies who are warring against the Jews as dogs: "[A] besieging and scattering by dogs of enemies [κύνας εἰς διασπασμὸν ἐχθρῶν]". The writer specifies the identity of the enemies in the preceding verse to be "foreigners" (ἀλλοφύλοις), that is, "detestable gentiles" (βδελύγμασιν ἐθνῶν). The context suggests that κύνας likely refers to those soldiers of the Gentiles scattering the Jewish people. In 1 Enoch, forms of κύων occur five times in the context of equating dogs with gentile enemies in Judges.[140]

Such doggish descriptors for outsiders are also found in Philo and Josephus. Aside from identifying the Cynics and their followers as "dogs", Philo also contrasts the Jewish ascetics (Therapeutae) in Alexandria with drunken gentile revellers whom Philo says "strike hard and are raging in the manner of wild dogs [τρόπον κυνῶν ἀτιθάσων] and attack and bite each other [ἐπανιστάμενοι δάκνουσιν ἀλλήλους] and chew off noses, ears, fingers, and some other parts of the body".[141] Regarding the writings of Josephus, in *Ant.* 6.186, Josephus offers Jewish commentary support for the LXX reading of 1 Sam 17:43 in which David's slur (χείρω κυνὸς) is recorded against his gentile opponent, Goliath. In *J.W.* 5.526 (cf. 6.196), Josephus refers to Jewish brigand rebels (οἱ λῃσταὶ) led by Simon bar Giora as "raging dogs" (λυσσῶντες κύνες). Thus, there were some Jewish factions in Josephus's day referred to as dogs in intra-Jewish dialogue. Josephus also uses the term "dog" (*impudentiam canis*) as a derogatory descriptor of the gentile Apion. Hence, the Second Temple Jewish literature reveals that the dehumanizing descriptor "dog(s)" can be used to denote both gentile and Jewish "outsiders", who serve as perceived threats (ideologically, politically, and physically) to the insider communities. What of Paul's repeated rhetorical use of βλέπω?

While the semantic range of βλέπω is wide and is often used in the NT to connote vision or sight in both a physical and metaphorical sense,[142] Paul uses it in his corpus to connote a warning to his insider audiences.[143] This appears to be the sense of Paul's triadic usage of βλέπω in Phil 3:2. This appears to be the sense of Paul's triadic usage in Phil 3:2, but also in other

---

[140] 1 En. 89.42–49.

[141] *Contempl.* 1.40.

[142] So Walter Bauer et al. eds., "βλέπω", in *A Greek-English Lexicon of the New Testament and Other Early Christian Literature*, 3rd ed. (Chicago: University of Chicago Press, 2000), 178–79. Hereafter, "BDAG".

[143] The term βλέπω can connote a warning and the urgent need "to beware" in classical Greek literature. See Henry G. Liddell and Robert Scott, "βλέπω", in *A Greek-English Lexicon*, ed. Henry S. Jones, 9th rev. ed. (Oxford; London; New York: Oxford University Press, 1996), 318. Hereafter, "LSJ". Both LSJ (318) and BDAG (179) take Paul's repeated use of βλέπω in Phil 3:2 to connote this urgent, hazardous warning and rhetorical sense of "to beware".

passages such as 1 Cor 10:12 and Gal 5:15. In these passages, Paul warns the Corinthian insiders to "watch out" (βλεπέτω) against falling in a spiritual sense. He warns the Galatian saints to "beware" of imposter insiders who intend to devour and destroy the inside group. In Gal 5:14–15, Paul joins the law of the neighbour with his warning against infiltrating outsiders when he writes, "For the entire Law has been fulfilled in one word, in this passage: 'You shall love your neighbour as yourself.' But if you all are biting and devouring one another, beware that you should not be consumed by one another". The remedy for such biting and devouring is to "walk by the Spirit" in Gal 5:16, which means to follow the Spirit's lead in acting commensurately with their in-Christ, superordinate identity.

Similar to the imagery of "dangerous dogs" in Phil 3:2, Paul warns against vicious beast-like biting, devouring, and in-fighting among those incognito outsiders trying to infiltrate and destroy the Galatian Christ community(-ies). Paul employs βλέπω in these letters to warn in-Christ insiders against such monstrous, beast-like opponents in both Galatians and Philippians. Given the rhetorical repetition of βλέπω in Phil 3:2, Paul is perhaps more concerned by the threat of these outsider groups to the flourishing of the Philippian saints than he is regarding the opponents implied in Gal 5:15.

Given the brief survey of Paul's usage of outsider designations in the *Corpus Paulinum* above, what can be said of his dehumanizing boundary marker concepts against outsiders in Phil 3:2? First, these terms signify what Trebilco has identified as "high boundary markers" and appear to be among Paul's most strongly "othered" groups in his letters—what Trebilco has labelled Category Three.[144]

Second, while Trebilco sees these strongly othered groups as being the most proximate to the inside groups, such vilification does not necessitate ideological proximity.[145] Paul makes a clear distinction in the worldly/fleshly mindsets of

---

[144] Trebilco, *Outsider Designations*, 4–5, 25.

[145] See Trebilco, *Outsider Designations*, 4–5. Regarding Trebilco's schema, Paul's triadic tempest of terms in 3:2 could be best understood as representing Category Three—the most proximate outsiders to the insider group(s), who pose the greatest threat. Trebilco, *Outsider Designations*, 4–5. However, given the recent pushback by Nanos et al. within the PWJ movement against understandings of Paul's opponents as being Jewish or "Judaizers", much scholarly pause and reflection are needed here. Perhaps, Paul's "proximity" to his opponents is not religious or ideological in nature, but geographic and political. Moreover, Paul's repeated warning and dehumanizing terms in 3:2 could reflect the proximity of the Philippian saints' formerly pagan religious traditions and praxes of which Paul is concerned over the threat of syncretism and a falling away of the saints under the pressures of pagan persecution (Phil 1:14; 1 Thess 2:2). In either case, Trebilco's criterion of "proximity" for Category Three boundary markers does not a priori

the enemy outsiders in Phil 3:2, 18 vis-à-vis the mindsets of in-Christ insiders, which are to reflect the positive characteristics referenced in texts like Phil 4:8. Thus, Paul's highest boundary marker language in Philippians stems not from an ideological proximity but from Paul's perceived threat level of these outsiders in disrupting and destroying the fledgling Christ communities. The examples above show that Paul uses his highest and most vilifying boundary marker terminology toward those posing the greatest perceived threat to the nascent Christ communities he and others founded. By using such vivid language, Paul suggests that these vicious, beastly opponents seek to bite, devour, work evil, and mutilate the Philippian saints.

Third, while Paul is more inclusive regarding certain outsiders elsewhere in his letters, the monstrous, dehumanized portrayal of opponents in Phil 3:2 suggests that there is no eschatological hope of reconciliation for these outsiders. Perhaps the reason for Paul's lack of optimism stems from their apparent rejection and hardening toward Christ and the Christ communities. Just as Paul describes his former identity as an outsider and vehement persecutor of Christ using monstrous, dehumanizing language in 1 Cor 15:8, Paul describes other outsiders who wish to infiltrate, attack, bite, and devour insiders—in monstrous, dehumanized terms. Yet, despite his lack of eschatological optimism toward enemies in Philippians, Paul does not return his opponents' hatred.[146] Paul "rehumanizes" them in Phil 3:18 when he says: "For many are walking, whom I was often telling you [about], and now I tell you even while weeping, these [are] the enemies of the cross of Christ". Paul's use of the adverb πολλάκις here highlights both the diachronic danger these outsiders pose to the Philippian saints as well as Paul's ongoing concern and repeated warnings to the Philippians regarding these outsiders.

Paul does not display *odium humani generis* ("hatred for the human race") in Phil 3:2, as Tacitus quipped regarding the first-century Christ-allegiants.[147] While many examples within Second Temple Jewish literature reveal a vitriolic

---

assume a Jewish or Judaizing identity for Paul opponents in Phil 3:2—albeit Trebilco sees the "dogs" of Phil 3:2 as "former insiders who are now 'othered' by the author and as deviants in some way". Trebilco, *Outsider Designations*, 4, esp. n. 10.

[146] Hellerman writes, "Paul weeps here for the perilous condition of πολλοὶ who claimed to be followers of Jesus but lived as 'enemies of the cross of Christ,' and for the potential threat they posed to the church in Philippi". Hellerman, *Philippians*, 217.

[147] Tacitus, *Ann.* 15.44.

antipathy toward outside enemies,[148] Paul nevertheless remains compassionate and rehumanizes his enemies in Phil 3:18 through his tears over their eschatological demise.

Conclusion: Comparison, Categorization, and Charting a New Path Forward

What can be said of the law of the neighbour and the Jesus tradition in comparison to Paul? The law of the neighbour injunction is against hatred toward neighbouring fellow Jews.[149] This could be an argument for gentile enemies in Phil 3:2 since the law of the neighbour seems to prevent Paul from speaking in such a way to his Jewish people. However, the Jesus tradition reimagines the law of the neighbour in terms of loving all peoples—Jew and gentile alike.[150]

Commands to bless/love enemies are featured in Jesus's Sermon on the Mount/Plain, and Jesus's Great Commandments in Matt 22:36–40 summarize the Torah as love for God and neighbour. Does Paul's harsh warning against outsiders in Phil 3:2 abdicate or stand in contradistinction to the Jesus tradition and the law of the neighbour? *In nuce*, no. The chief difference between Paul and Second Temple Jewish texts, pagan curse tablets, and

---

[148] See e.g., Jub. 22:16, 22; Pss. Sol. 17:21–27; 2 Macc 6:14, 26; 7:9, 14, 17, 19, 31, 35–37; Wis 4:19; Jdt 13:4–19 *et passim.* Don Garlington notes that there was at least some variation in the Second Temple literature regarding Jewish attitudes toward outsiders within Hellenistic Diaspora Judaism (more inclusive) and Palestinian Judaism, which was less inclusive and more marked by a "theology of zeal" toward torah keeping and less keen on accepting outsiders into the Jewish religious community. Such vitriol and disparity in Jewish and gentile relations is unsurprising since many within Palestinian Judaism had witnessed first-hand the double destruction of their homeland by the Syrian and Roman gentiles. Garlington, *Faith, Obedience, and Perseverance: Aspects of Paul's Letter to the Romans* (Eugene, OR: Wipf & Stock, 2009), 67 n. 114.

[149] The immediate, micro context of Lev 19:18 delimits the intra-Jewish boundaries and scope of this command: אֶת־בְּנֵי עַמֶּךָ ("and the sons of your kinsmen") and τοῖς υἱοῖς τοῦ λαοῦ σου ("the sons of your people").

[150] On Jesus's inclusive interpretation of the Mosaic law of the neighbour in Luke 10:25–37, see Lauri Thurén, *Parables Unplugged: Reading the Lukan Parables in Their Rhetorical Context* (Minneapolis: Augsburg Fortress, 2014), 62, 65; and François Bovon, *Luke 2: A Commentary on the Gospel of Luke 9:51–19:27*, ed. Helmut Koester, trans. Donald S. Deer, Hermeneia (Minneapolis: Augsburg Fortress, 2013), 65. No longer is the concept of "neighbour" restricted to ethnic, familial, religious, or socio-economic boundaries. Rather, for Jesus, everyone is a potential "neighbour", and Jesus's followers are beckoned to emulate the example of the Samaritan, in becoming a neighbour to all who may be in need—including those falsely considered outsiders and enemies due to their ethnicity (Luke 10:37).

"magical" spells contemporaneous to Paul that highlight hating hostile outsiders is that Paul never displays hatred or ill wishes toward outsiders in Philippians.[151] Paul does not soften the seemingly inevitable eschatological fate of his enemies, but neither does Paul delight in their destruction.[152] Rather, Paul appropriated Mosaic and Jesus traditions to challenge his Christ communities to adopt the counter-cultural posture of compassionate concern even toward those outsiders treating insider saints with open hostility.

What can be gleaned from Paul's categorization of insiders, outsiders, and "monsters" in the *Corpus Paulinum*? Paul displays a wide swath of terminology and concepts in Philippians and elsewhere in the *Corpus Paulinum* to distinguish between insider and outsider groups. Insider and outsider epithets served both practical and theological purposes. Practically, these descriptors served as useful labels and methods of identification as insiders within the first-century Jesus movement engaged the wider culture.[153] How would a travelling saint locate a proper house-church gathering with which to worship? Fictive kinship terms such as "brother" and "sister" helped insiders locate like-minded Christ-allegiants in a world of competing religio-cultural beliefs and ideologies.

---

[151] Numerous Second Temple Jewish texts highlight antipathy toward gentile and intra-Jewish enemies. Such texts include the story of the martyred Jewish woman and her seven sons in 2 Macc 6:14, 26; 7:9, 14, 17, 19, 31, 35–37 *et passim* and Wis 4:19, which describes the "wicked" outsiders' corpses as being dishonored on earth and shame will follow them in the afterlife. Pagan curse tablets (*defixiones*) and spells against enemies were also pervasive in the ancient world. Over fifteen hundred extant curse tablets— dating back as early as the fourth to fifth centuries BCE—have been identified that curse and condemn enemies of the inscriber or their clients, who seek to dominate and harm these outsiders. See John G. Gager, *Curse Tablets and Binding Spells from the Ancient World* (Oxford; London; New York: Oxford University Press, 1992), 1–5, 21. Regarding magical spells, The *Papyri Graecae Magicae* (*PGM*), a body of magical papyri originating between the second century BCE to fifth century CE from within Greco-Roman Egypt, continues this concept of conquering and dominating enemy outsiders. H. D. Betz, ed., *The Greek Magical Papyri in Translation: Including the Demotic Spells* (Chicago: The University of Chicago Press, 1986), xli. See e.g. the spell in *PGM* 4.2170–77, which highlights the spellcaster's invincibility over enemy attacks and the destruction of outsider enemies. The source Greek text for my translation of *PGM* 4.2170–77 is Karl Preisendanz, ed. and trans., *Papyri Graecae Magicae: Die griechischen Zauberpapyri*, 3 vols. (Leipzig: Teubner, 1928–1941).

[152] Holloway links the fleshly focused enemies of 3:18 as the same group(s) in 3:2. See Holloway, *Philippians*, 179.

[153] Paul Trebilco, *Self-Designations*, xi, 1.

Conversely, dehumanizing language showed them who to avoid. Theologically, dehumanizing, monstrous descriptors served a protective purpose in the preservation of the apostle's teaching[154] and the flourishing growth—physically and spiritually—of the Christ communities to whom Paul ministered and wrote. As Nicolet explains, "He [Paul] tries to use monsters to create or maintain boundaries, but monsters can subsist on the margins, frequently threatening to cross or decompose these boundaries, particularly those around identity".[155] For Paul in Philippians, the unifying, superordinate identity marker denoting the inside group is their being "in Christ", which supersedes all other personal, subordinate identities. Paul often juxtaposes his complex and variegated terminology for in-Christ insiders to highlight the contrast with the outside groups—take the contrast between "the mutilation", "the uncircumcision", and "the [true] circumcision", for example.

While Paul is more hopeful and optimistic regarding the possibility of eschatological reconciliation with God and inclusion into the insider communities for certain neighbouring outsiders, Paul also uses vivid apocalyptic imagery to describe others more violently and harshly. Paul uses dehumanizing, monstrifying concepts for dangerous and potentially deadly outsiders, whom he perceives to threaten the life and flourishing of these fledgling insider Christ communities. Paul gives the example of his former "lifeless" existence as a monstrous ἔκτρωμα in 1 Cor 15:8 to represent outsiders who would seek to harm and destroy Christ's community.[156] These outsiders can be construed as "lifeless" and "monstrous", since for Paul, "living is Christ", and these lifeless, biting outsiders are enemies of Christ's cross.

What are the implications for Pauline studies and charting a new path forward in the discussion? This study has attempted to show that Paul uses βλέπετε in Phil 3:2 as a high rhetorical boundary marker, vividly highlighting outsiders whom Paul perceives to pose a potential threat to the Philippian saints. Why does Paul refer to them specifically as "the dogs", "the evil workers", and "the mutilation?" These monstrous metaphors resonate with Paul's audience in describing outsiders behaving in ways incommensurate to

---

[154] Rom 16:17; Gal 1:6–9.

[155] Nicolet, "Monstrous Bodies", 135.

[156] Paul likely thought of himself as an "abnormal", "grotesque infant" in 1 Cor 15:8 due to his former rebellion against Christ and Christ's church as a violent outsider—murdering and jailing insider saints. See Roy E. Ciampa and Brian S. Rosner, *The First Letter to the Corinthians*, The Pillar New Testament Commentary (Grand Rapids: Eerdmans, 2010), 751. Cf. Gal 1:11–17; Nickelsburg, "An Ἔκτρωμα", 201–02; and Johannes Munck, "*Paulus Tanquam Abortivus* (1 Cor. 15:8)", in *New Testament Essays: Studies in Memory of Thomas Walter Manson 1893-1958, sponsored by Pupils, Colleagues, and Friends*, ed. A. J. B. Higgins (Manchester: Manchester University Press, 1959), 180–93.

Paul's expected norms for the insider Christ communities and, as trespassing border breakers, threaten the unity and flourishing therein.[157] Rather than invite the Philippian saints to "occupy the space of the monstrous" in Philippians,[158] Paul apocalyptically invites and warns his hearers/readers to transcend the "fleshly" and "earthly" realms of such monsters in becoming heavenly citizens. Such usage of βλέπω and Paul's dehumanizing outsider and boundary marker terminology in Phil 3:2 is commensurate with his usage elsewhere in his corpus. In Christ, outsiders have the potential to become insiders, but outsiders, as depicted in Phil 3:2, who remain Christ's enemies and incessantly pose threats to Pauline Christ communities, become "monsters" to be vilified and shunned. What is unique in Philippians, in comparison to the other letters studied above, is Paul's lack of inclusivity and eschatological optimism regarding these outside groups, which would be expected if Philippians really were Paul's warmest, friendliest, and most joy-filled letter as many claim.

Moreover, a focus on Paul's insider, outsider, and boundary marker terminology in Phil 3:2 moves beyond the scholarly entanglement regarding the identities of Paul's opponents and issues of literary integrity. Paul's intent in Phil 3:2 is not to specifically identify these outsiders, as is the case with many contemporary scholarly discussions. Rather, Paul's concern in Philippians is to warn the Philippians saints repeatedly and rhetorically against these potentially threatening and hostile groups by invoking *ekphrastic* and apocalyptic terminology that would resonate with the Philippians saints as high boundary markers denoting outsiders to be avoided.[159] When the text of Philippians is read carefully—taking into consideration Paul's rhetorical construction and delineation of social identities and boundaries regarding insiders and outsiders—issues of literary integrity tend to fall to the wayside, and an artful literary unity, not fragmentation, emerges.[160]

---

[157] Jeremy Punt notes that the space for resistance within Pauline Christ communities was rather limited, since Paul's familial insider language replicates "the reigning sociocultural values..., opportunities for serious counter-cultural and other deviations from socially acceptable practice were limited". Jeremy Punt, "Pauline Brotherhood, Gender and Slavery", *Neot* 47 (2013): 149–69, here 165. Cited in Nicolet, "Monstrous Bodies", 133.

[158] Nicolet, "Monstrous Bodies", 131, 134.

[159] Angela Standhartinger suggests that Paul represents himself as an apocalyptic "seer" and "ideal wise man" in Philippians and that his development of apocalyptic imagery in Philippians 3 is shared by his Philippian audience. Standhartinger, "Apocalyptic Thought", 238–39.

[160] Representative of those arguing against Paul's literary artistry in Philippians is H. A. A. Kennedy, who states regarding Philippians, "The perusal of the Epistle cannot fail to produce the impression of 'artlessness.'" Kennedy, "The Epistle to the Philippians", in *The*

Bibliography

Abram, Christopher. "At Home in the Fens with the Grendelkin". In *Dating Beowulf: Studies in Intimacy*, edited by Daniel C. Reimin and Erica Weaver. Manchester: Manchester University Press, 2020.

Aland, Barbara et al., eds. *Nestle-Aland Novum Testamentum Graece*, 28th ed. Stuttgart: Deutsche Bibelgesellschaft, 2012.

Allred, Tyler. "Philippians 4:2–3: An Alternative View of the Euodia-Syntyche Debate", *Priscilla Papers* 33.4, 2019.

Baker A. Coleman. "Social Identity Theory and Biblical Interpretation". *BTB* 42.3 (2012).

Barr, James. *The Semantics of Biblical Language*. Oxford; London; New York: Oxford University Press, 1961.

Bauer, Walter et al. eds. "βλέπω", in *A Greek-English Lexicon of the New Testament and Other Early Christian Literature*. Chicago: University of Chicago Press, 2000.

Beare, F. W. *The Epistle to the Philippians*. Edinburgh; London: Black, 1973.

Bernier, Jonathan. *Rethinking the Dates of the New Testament: The Evidence for Early Composition*. Grand Rapids: Baker Academic, 2022.

Betz, H. D. Betz, ed. *The Greek Magical Papyri in Translation: Including the Demotic Spells*. Chicago: The University of Chicago Press, 1986.

Black, David A. "The Discourse Structure of Philippians: A Study in Textlinguistics". *NovT* 37.1 (1995).

Blaske, Andreas Blaske. *Beschneidung: Zeugnisse der Bibel und verwandter Texte*.Tübingen: Francke, 1998.

Blois, Isaac D. *Mutual Boasting in Philippians: The Ethical Function of Shared Honor in its Biblical and Greco-Roman Context*. London; New Delhi; New York; Sydney: Bloomsbury, 2020.

Bockmuehl, Markus. *The Epistle to the Philippians*. Grand Rapids: Baker Academic, 2013.

Bovon, François. *Luke 2: A Commentary on the Gospel of Luke 9:51–19:27*, edited by Helmut Koester, translated by Donald S. Deer. Minneapolis: Augsburg Fortress, 2013.

Brunson, Hal. *Lesbos, Narcissus, and Paulos: Homosexual Myth and Christian Truth*. New York; Lincoln; Shanghai: iUniverse, 2006.

Carter, T. L. *Paul and the Power of Sin: Redefining "Beyond the Pale"*. Cambridge; New York: Cambridge University Press, 2004.

Ciampa, Roy E. and Brian S. Rosner. *The First Letter to the Corinthians*, The Pillar New Testament Commentary. Grand Rapids: Eerdmans, 2010.

Cohen, Jeffrey J. ed. "Monster Culture (Seven Theses)". In *Monster Theory: Reading Culture*. Minneapolis: University of Minnesota Press, 1996.

Expositors Greek Testament, 3 vols., repr. ed. (Grand Rapids: Eerdmans, 1976), 3.409. T. E. Pollard also adds regarding Philippians' so-called "artlessness": "its 'artlessness' is due to the fact that ... it consists of a 'stream of consciousness' rather than 'follows a predetermined plan". Pollard, "The Integrity of Philippians", *NTS* 13.1 (1966): 59.

Coutsoumpos, Panayotis and Panagiotis L. Kampouris. *Reading Philemon: Christianity and Slavery in the First-Century Roman Empire.* Eugene, OR: Wipf & Stock, 2022.

Dunn, James D. G. *The Epistle to the Galatians.* Peabody, MA: Hendrickson, 1993.

Ehrensperger, Kathy. "'Join in Imitating Me' (Phil 3:17): Embodying Christ in the Face of 'the Enemies of the Cross'" Paper presented at the Annual Meeting of the Society of New Testament Studies, Pretoria, South Africa, 10 August 2017.

Esler, Philip. "An Outline of Social Identity Theory". In *T&T Clark Handbook to Social Identity in the New Testament,* edited by J. Brian Tucker and Coleman A. Baker. London; New Delhi; New York; Sydney: Bloomsbury, 2016.

Eyl, Jennifer. "'I Myself am [*sic*] an Israelite': Paul, Authenticity, and Authority". *JSNT* 40.2 (2017).

Fee, Gordon D. *Paul's Letter to the Philippians.* Grand Rapids: Eerdmans, 1995.

Franco, Cristiana. "Dogs and Humans in Ancient Greece and Rome: Towards a Definition of Extended Appropriate Interaction". In *Dog's Best Friend?: Rethinking Canid-Human Relations,* edited by John Sorenson and Atsuko Matsuoka. Montreal; Kingston, ON: McGill-Queen's University Press, 2019.

Fujimura, Makoto *Culture Care: Reconnecting with Beauty for Our Common Life.* Downers Grove, IL: InterVarsity Press, 2017.

Gager, John G. *Curse Tablets and Binding Spells from the Ancient World.* Oxford; London; New York: Oxford University Press, 1992.

Garland, David E. "The Composition and Literary Unity of Philippians: Some Neglected Factors", *NovT* 27.1 (1985).

Garlington, Don. *Faith, Obedience, and Perseverance: Aspects of Paul's Letter to the Romans.* Eugene, OR: Wipf & Stock, 2009.

Geoffrion, Timothy C. *The Rhetorical Purpose and the Political and Military Character of Philippians: A Call to Stand Firm.* Lewiston, NY: Mellen, 1993.

Gieniusz, Andrzej. "As a Miscarriage': The Meaning and Function of the Metaphor in 1 Cor 15:1–11 in Light of Num 12:12 (LXX)". *The Biblical Annals* 3 (2013).

Halberstam, Judith. *Skin Shows: Gothic Horror and the Technology of Monsters.* Durham, NC: Duke University Press, 1995.

Hayward, C. T. R. "The Aramaic Song of the Lamb (The Dialogue between David and Goliath)". In *Old Testament Pseudepigrapha: More Noncanonical Scriptures, Vol. 1,* edited by Richard Bauckham, James R, Davila, and Alexander Panayotov. Grand Rapids: Eerdmans, 2013.

Hellerman, Joseph H. *Philippians, Exegetical Guide to the Greek New Testament.* Nashville: Broadman & Holman, 2015.

Hollander, H. W. and G. E. van der Hout. "The Apostle Paul Calling Himself an Abortion: 1 Corinthians 15:8 within the Context of 1 Cor 15:8–10". *NovT* 38.3 (1996).

Holloway, Paul A. *Philippians.* Minneapolis: Augsburg Fortress, 2017.

Inselmann, Anke. "Zum Affekt der Freude im Philipperbrief: Unter Berücksichtigung pragmatischer und psychologischer Zugänge". In *Der*

Philipperbrief des Paulus in der hellenistisch-römischen Welt, edited by Jörg Frey and Benjamin Schliesser. Mohr Siebeck, 2015.

Jewett, Robert. *Romans*. Minneapolis: Augsburg Fortress, 2007.

Joshel, Sandra R. and Sheila Murnaghan, eds. *Women and Slaves in Greco-Roman Culture: Differential Equations*. London; New York: Routledge, 1998.

Kennedy, H. A. A. "The Epistle to the Philippians", in *The Expositors Greek Testament*. Grand Rapids: Eerdmans, 1976.

Keown, Mark J. *Philippians*, Evangelical Exegetical Commentary, 2 vols. Bellingham, WA: Lexham, 2017.

Kitchell Jr., Kenneth F. *Animals in the Ancient World from A to Z*. London; New York: Routledge, 2014.

Koskenniemi, Heikki. *Studien zur Idee und Phraseologie des griechischen Briefes bis 400 n. Chr.* Helsinki: Suomalainen Tiedeakatemia, 1956.

Krentz, Edgar M. "Military Language and Metaphors in Philippians". In *Origins and Methods: Toward a New Understanding of Judaism and Christianity: Essays in Honour of John C. Hurd*, edited by Bradley H. McLean. Sheffield: Sheffield Academic, 1993.

Lamb, Gregory E. Lamb, review of *Mutual Boasting in Philippians: The Ethical Function of Shared Honor in its [sic] Biblical and Greco-Roman Context*, by Isaac D. Blois, *RBL* 24 (2022).

Lamb, Gregory E. "Sinfully Stereotyped: Jesus's Desire to Correct Ancient Physiognomic Assumptions in the Gospel according to Luke". *WW* 37.2 (2017).

Liddell, Henry G. and Robert Scott. "βλέπω". In *A Greek-English Lexicon*, edited by Henry S. Jones, 9th rev. ed. Oxford; London; New York: Oxford University Press, 1996.

Lührmann, Dieter. *Galatians: A Continental Commentary*, translated by O. C. Dean, Jr. Minneapolis: Augsburg Fortress, 1992.

Malherbe, Abraham J. *The Letters to the Thessalonians: A New Translation with Introduction and Commentary*. Garden City, NY; New York: Doubleday, 2000.

Marchal, Joseph A. *Philippians: Historical Problems, Hierarchical Visions, Historical Anxieties*. London; New Delhi; New York; Sydney: Bloomsbury, 2017.

Marchal, Joseph A. Marchal, ed. "Slaves as Wo/men and Unmen: Reflecting Upon Euodia, Syntyche, and Epaphroditus in Philippi". In *The People Beside Paul: The Christian Assembly and History from Below*. Atlanta: SBL Press, 2015.

Martin, Ralph P. *Carmen Christi: Philippians ii. 5–11 in Recent Interpretation and in the Setting of Early Christian Worship*. Cambridge; New York: Cambridge University Press, 1967.

Martyn, J. Louis. *Galatians: A New Translation with Introduction and Commentary*. New Haven: Yale University Press, 1997.

Marzouk, Safwat. *Egypt as a Monster in the Book of Ezekiel*. Tübingen: Mohr Siebeck, 2015.

Moore, Thomas. *Philippians: An Exegetical Guide for Preaching and Teaching*. Grand Rapids: Kregel, 2019.

Mueller, Dierk. "Military Images in Paul's Letter to the Philippians", (PhD diss., University of Pretoria, 2013).

Nanos, Mark D. "Paul's Reversal of Jews Calling Gentiles 'Dogs' (Philippians 3:2): 1600 Years of an Ideological Tale Wagging an Exegetical Dog?" *BibInt* 17.4 (2009).

Nanos, Mark D. *Reading Corinthians and Philippians within Judaism: Collected Essays of Mark D. Nanos.* Eugene, OR: Cascade, 2017.

Nebreda, Sergio Rosell. "Echoes of Paul's Philippians in Polycarp: Texts that Create Identity". In *T&T Clark Handbook to Social Identity in the New Testament,* edited by J. Brian Tucker and Coleman A. Baker. London; New Delhi; New York; Sydney: Bloomsbury, 2016.

Nickelsburg, George W.E. "An Ἔκτρωμα", 201–02; and Johannes Munck, "*Paulus Tanquam Abortivus* (1 Cor. 15:8)". In *New Testament Essays: Studies in Memory of Thomas Walter Manson 1893-1958, sponsored by Pupils, Colleagues, and Friends,* edited by A. J. B. Higgins. Manchester: Manchester University Press, 1959.

Nickelsburg, George W. E. "An Ἔκτρωμα, Though Appointed from the Womb: Paul's Apostolic Self-Description in 1 Corinthians 15 and Galatians 1". *HTR* 79.1–3 (1986).

Nicolet, Valérie. "Monstrous Bodies in Paul's Letter to the Galatians". In *Bodies on the Verge: Queering Pauline Epistles,* edited by Joseph A. Marchal. Atlanta: SBL Press, 2019.

Osiek, Carolyn. *Philippians, Philemon,* Abingdon New Testament Commentaries. Nashville; New York: Abingdon, 2000.

Park, Eung Chun. *Either Jew or Gentile: Paul's Unfolding Theology of Inclusivity.* Louisville: Westminster John Knox, 2003.

Pollard, T. E. "The Integrity of Philippians". *NTS* 13.1 (1966).

Porter, Christopher. "Which Paul? Whose Judaism? A Socio-Cognitive Approach to Paul within Judaism". In *Paul within Judaism,* edited by Michael F. Bird et al., WUNT 1, Reihe 507. Tübingen: Mohr Siebeck, 2023.

Preisendanz, Karl, ed. and trans. *Papyri Graecae Magicae: Die griechischen Zauberpapyri,* 3 vols. Leipzig: Teubner, 1928–1941.

Punt, Jeremy. "Paul and the Others: Insiders, Outsiders, and Animosity". In *Animosity, the Bible, and Us: Some European, North American, and South African Perspectives,* edited by John T. Fitzgerald, Fika J. van Rensburg, and Herrie F. van Rooy, Global Perspectives on Biblical Scholarship 12. Atlanta: SBL Press, 2009.

Punt, Jeremy. "Pauline Brotherhood, Gender and Slavery". *Neot* 47 (2013).

Reumann, John. *Philippians.* New Haven: Yale University Press, 2008.

Schenk, Wolfgang. *Die Philipperbriefe des Paulus: Kommentar.* Stuttgart: Kohlhammer, 1984.

Schlueter, Carol J. *Filling Up the Measure: Polemical Hyperbole in 1 Thessalonians 2:14–16.* Sheffield: Sheffield Academic Press, 1994.

Schwaller, Tyler M. "'A Slave to All': The Queerness of Paul's Slave Form". In *Bodies on the Verge: Queering Pauline Epistles,* edited by Joseph A. Marchal. Atlanta: SBL Press, 2019.

Smith, David Livingstone. *On Inhumanity: Dehumanization and How to Resist It.* Oxford; London; New York: Oxford University Press, 2020.

Sourvinou-Inwood, Christiane, "Myth as History: The Previous Owners of the Delphic Oracle". In *Interpretations of Greek Mythology*, edited by Jan Bremmer, Routledge Revivals. London; New York: Routledge, 2014.

Standhartinger, Angela. "Apocalyptic Thought in Philippians". In *The Jewish Apocalyptic Tradition and the Shaping of New Testament Thought*, edited by Benjamin E. Reynolds and Loren T. Stuckenbruck. Minneapolis: Augsburg Fortress, 2017.

Stewart, Alistair C. "Euodia, Syntyche and the Role of *Syzygos*: Phil 4:2–3", *ZNW* 109.2, 2018.

Stowers, Stanley K. *Letter Writing in Greco-Roman Antiquity*, edited by Wayne A. Meeks, Library of Early Christianity 5. Philadelphia: Westminster, 1986.

Tajfel, Henri, ed. *Differentiation between Social Groups: Studies in the Social Psychology of Intergroup Relations.* European Monographs in Social Psychology. London: Academic Press, 1978.

Tajfel, Henri et al. "Social Categorization and Intergroup Behaviour". *European Journal of Social Psychology* 1.2 (1971).

Thiessen, Matthew. "Gentiles as Impure Animals in the Writings of Early Christ Followers". In *Perceiving the Other in Ancient Judaism and Early Christianity*, edited by Michel Bar-Asher Siegal, Wolfgang Grünstäudl, and Matthew Thiessen. Tübingen: Mohr Siebeck, 2017.

Thurén, Lauri. *Parables Unplugged: Reading the Lukan Parables in Their Rhetorical Context.* Minneapolis: Augsburg Fortress, 2014.

Trebilco, Paul. *Outsider Designations and Boundary Construction in the New Testament: Early Christian Communities and the Formation of Group Identity.* Cambridge; New York: Cambridge University Press, 2017.

Trebilco, Paul. *Self-Designations and Group Identity in the New Testament.* Cambridge; New York: Cambridge University Press, 2012.

Vuković, Sonja and Mladen Jovičić. "Dog Burials from the Cemeteries of the Roman City of *Viminacium* (Moesia Superior, Kostolac, Serbia)". In *Proceedings of the 22nd International Congress of Roman Frontier Studies, Ruse, Bulgaria, September 2012*, edited by Lyudmil Ferdinandov Vagalinski and Nicolay Sharankov. Bulletin of the National Archaeological Institute 42. Sofia: National Archaeological Institute with Museum at the Bulgarian Academy of Sciences, 2015.

Webb, Ruth. *Ekphrasis, Imagination and Persuasion in Ancient Rhetorical Theory and Practice.* Burlington, VT; Farnham, Surrey, UK: Ashgate, 2009.

White, L. Michael. "Morality between Two Worlds: A Paradigm of Friendship in Philippians". In *Greeks, Romans, and Christians: Essays in Honor of Abraham J. Malherbe*, edited by David L. Balch, Everett Ferguson, and Wayne A. Meeks. Minneapolis: Augsburg Fortress, 1990.

Witherington III, Ben. *Friendship and Finances in Philippi.* Valley Forge, PA: Trinity International, 1994.

Chapter 3

Manufacturing the Monstrous (Heretic): The Constructed Judgement of Nestorius

Allan E.C. Wright

University of Alberta

Abstract

Within monster studies, the insider/outsider dichotomy becomes an important classification. The "insiders" are perceived as "the good guys," whereas the "outsiders" are labelled as devious, corrupt, and destructive. The constructed classification lines of what is deemed Orthodoxy and Heresy are akin to this division. The separation between Orthodoxy and Heretics are also artificial lines of constructed classifications established through discourse and ritual performances. The ramifications for artificial social classification lines have a dramatic effect on the surrounding society. One is deemed "correct," while the opposing outlook is seen as deviancy (the monstrous). This leads to one specific group being designated as the authority and representative for a tradition, while the other is used as a warning against decent who is then designated to the realm of the "monstrous." To side with them, is to side with a monster, according to public discourse. Overall, this suggest certain classifications of the monstrous, heresy, and social deviancy are primarily a socio-political phenomenon, in order to construct a clear insider/outsider dichotomy. This article argues that the Council of Ephesus was not an occasion to rectify theological differences, but was employed to establish political power, authority, and to display any opposition as monstrous. In this case, the figure of Nestorius becomes the "monstrous" through the designation of heresy. Nestorius became an outside (monstrous) threat to the perceived unity of a social system.

Keywords: Monster Theory, Insider/Outsider Dichotomy, Council of Emphasis, Nestorius, Cyril

* * *

Introduction

Ever since Jeffery Jerome Cohen wrote his influential theses on the concept of monsters,[1] the insider/outsider dichotomy has become an important classification for the "monstrous". In general, the "insiders" are labelled "the good guys", whereas the "outsiders" are labelled as devious, corrupt, and destructive. The constructed classification lines of what is deemed Orthodoxy and Heresy are akin to this division. The separation between Orthodoxy and Heretics are also artificial lines of constructed classifications established through discourse and ritual performances.[2] This article argues that the Council of Ephesus was not an occasion to rectify theological differences but was employed to establish political power and authority and to display any opposition as monstrous. In this case, after losing public support, the figure of Nestorius becomes the "monstrous" through the designation of heresy.

The classification lines that labelled Nestorius a heretic represent an example of an artificial classification line created by employing discourse and ingenuity. The actors who construct the classification lines of "orthodoxy" and "heresy" utilize various methods of human ingenuity to drive their discourses in an effort to obtain their intentions and objectives. The ramifications of artificial social classification lines have a dramatic effect on the surrounding society. One is deemed "correct", while the opposing outlook is labelled as deviancy (the monstrous). Defining "orthodoxy" and "heresy" is tricky and dependent. Within the fourth century, when Christianity became the Roman state religion, Christian ideals were utilized to formulate many Roman laws. The Christian legitimization led to more social authority for the bishops.

Additionally, disputed discourses regarding the "nature" of Christ became public affairs. Kevin W. Kaatz states, "Endless bickering came after the Council of Nicea, which was to decide the issue once and for all".[3] The result of these divisions was the official Catholic Church being deemed orthodox, and whoever did not succumb to their line of thought was labelled heretics, outsiders, and even monstrous. As Alister McGrath states:

> The binary opposition "heresy-orthodox" began to emerge as a way of excluding certain groups and individuals from the Christian Church. *Hairesis* now meant a school of thought that developed ideas that were

---

[1] Jeffrey Jerome Cohen, ed., *Monster Theory: Reading Culture* (Minneapolis: University of Minnesota Press, 1996).

[2] It should be noted that the constructed lines of classification can be fluid. Meaning, who was considered the "monster" can change throughout time and location.

[3] Kaatz, 142.

subversive of the Christian faith, which was to be opposed to *orthodoxia*—an authentic and normative version of the Christian faith.[4]

The purpose of this article is to suggest that the division between Orthodoxy and Heretics, using the example of the Nestorians,[5] are artificial lines of constructed classifications established through discourse and ritual performances within the Council of Ephesus to establish political power and authority, as opposed to actual theological disagreements. This leads to one specific group being designated as the authority and representative for a tradition, while the other is used as a warning against descent. The deviant, or even seditious, figure is then designated to the realm of the "monstrous". To side with them is to side with a monster, according to public discourse. Overall, this suggests certain classifications of the monstrous, heresy, and social deviancy are primarily socio-political phenomena in order to construct a clear insider/outsider dichotomy.

To begin, I will provide a brief historical background of the people of Nestorius and Cyril of Alexandria.[6] For Nestorius, I will discuss his becoming the patriarch of Constantinople, his ambition to be a "heresy hunter", the perceived notion that people saw him as arrogant, and the fact that he caused civil unrest in Constantinople. For Cyril, I will discuss his rise to Alexandria's patriarch and the violence within Alexandria against the Jewish population and "pagans" during his reign. Next, I will examine the main theological points of contention between Nestorius and Cyril. The main points of contention are their divergent Christologies and the title *Theotokos* being applied to Mary. Then, I will examine whether Nestorius and Cyril's contention points were just a matter of terminology. An article by George Zito argues that heretics employ "insider" language but for divergent "goals". In a sense, this argument suggests that the perceived monsters embrace their titles and deviancy. I will argue, however, that Nestorius' actual teachings did not deviate from loosely defined orthodox teachings.

Instead, the hostilities between Nestorius and Cyril appear to be more personal. I will examine the political hostilities and the power struggles between Cyril and Nestorius and, by extension, the Alexandrian school, which was affiliated with Rome, and the Antiochian school, which was associated more with Constantinople. Afterwards, I will examine the various synods within the Council of Ephesus and their specific ramifications. I will then

---

[4] Alister McGrath, *Heresy: A History of Defending the Truth* (New York: HarperOne, 2009), 39.

[5] Just to be clear when I use the term Nestorians, I am speaking about Nestorius' and his contemporaries, not what later became known as Nestorianism.

[6] I acknowledge there were other "players" involved, but I will focus on Nestorius and Cyril of Alexandra specifically because there where the main role players.

explore how the Council of Ephesus was utilized to display and establish power and authority. For theoretical and methodological purposes, I will examine David Kertzer's book Ritual, Politics, and Power and how ritual can act as a type of social illustration for a specific group to establish legitimate power and authority while monstering "outsiders" or others. Also, I will examine the public discourse on the importance of the city of Ephesus as the designated location for the Council. Finally, I will argue that through the ritual showcase of Ephesus and Cyril's persuasive discourse on labelling Nestorius a monstrous threat to the political community and a threat to Christianity's unity itself; the artificial lines of "orthodox" classifications were socially constructed to establish legitimate political power and authority. The ramification of this classification is that Nestorius is classified as a monster by the inside orthodox community. He is now labelled a heretic, deviant, and even someone monstrous within the history of orthodox movements.

Historical Background

The details concerning Nestorius' early life are limited. The only facets that are known entail Nestorius being born in Germanicia, "a city in Syria at the foot of Mount Taurus",[7] and that he "entered a monastery near Antioch out of which he was often called upon to preach in the city's cathedral church".[8] He was a persuasive and influential speaker, which helped him gain notoriety as a popular preacher.[9] According to Socrates Scholasticus, Nestorius was "distinguished for his excellent voice and fluency of speech; qualifications which they judged important for the instruction of the people".[10] Due to his eloquence as a speaker, his reputation grew beyond his Antiochene locality.[11]

In December 427 C.E., Sisinnius I, the Patriarch of Constantinople, passed away.[12] Intense bickering arose between various clerical factions within Constantinople, leading Emperor Theodosius II to search "outside" for a successor.[13] On April 10, 428 CE, Theodosius II appointed Nestorius as the new patriarch of Constantinople. With Constantinople proliferating politically, its

---

[7] Mar Aprem, *The Council of Ephesus of 431* (Kerala, India: Mar Narsai Press, 1978), 28.

[8] Samuel Hugh Moffett, *A History of Christianity in Asia. Vol..1.* (New York: Orbis Books, 1998), 173.

[9] Ibid.

[10] Socrates Scholasticus, Ecclesiastical History. 7.29.

[11] Aprem, 29.

[12] Mark Dickens, "Nestorius and the 'Dual Nature of Christ,'" in *Popular Controversies in World History* (Entry 2.08A), 5.

[13] Norman Russell, *Cyril of Alexandra* (London & New York: Routledge, 2000), 31. I purposely employ the term "outside" here. This is an important point because Nestorius was already deemed and seen as an "outsider" when he was first selected to be patriarch.

patriarch's position was considered extremely significant within the realm of Christendom as it possessed tremendous authority and influence.[14] Nestorius' appointment, however, was not without contestation. Samuel Hugh Moffett notes, "His opponents later sneeringly suggested that only his beautiful voice and fluent phrases could account for the unexpected promotion of this fairly obscure priest to the ecclesiastical throne of Eastern Rome".[15]

At Nestorius' consecration as the patriarch of Constantinople, he famously stated in his inaugural sermon: "Give me, O Emperor, the earth purged from heretics, and I will give you heaven in return. Assist me in destroying heretics, and I will assist you in vanquishing the Persians".[16] With these words, Nestorius began his campaign against the Arians. To begin his quest, he closed the Arians' only chapel within Constantinople.[17] As a result, the Arians set the chapel on fire, which spread to the adjacent neighbourhoods.[18] Socrates notes the ramifications, "A tumult accordingly arose on account of this throughout the city".[19] In other words, civil unrest resulted from Nestorius' actions. Nestorius' heretic hunting did not end with the Arians as "he also persecuted the Novations, Quartodecimans, and the Macedonians".[20] Some might observe the irony here. Nestorius began his career seeking to seek out and destroy social deviants (monstrous), only for him to become the social monster.

Not content on heresy (monster) hunting, Nestorius "continually disturbed the public tranquillity"[21] due to his religious fervor, political inexperience, and gullibility. Mark Dickens states that

> Nestorius proceeded to attack immorality in public entertainment, to bring the city's monks under his ecclesiastical jurisdiction, to restrict the involvement of aristocratic women in ecclesiastical affairs, and to challenge the role of the Augusta (Empress) Pulcheria, the powerful sister of Theodosius II. In so doing, he alienated the general population, the monks, the aristocracy and the Empress.[22]

The notion that an "outsider" (again, another term for the monstrous) of Constantinople was responsible for this social unrest was highly contentious. Instead of familiarizing himself with Constantinople's culture and customs or

---

[14] Moffett, 172. Here, Moffett also outlines the "insider" hostilities towards Nestorius.
[15] Moffett, 172-173.
[16] Russell, 31.
[17] Moffett, 173.
[18] See Socrates, 7.29. and Aprem, 29.
[19] Socrates, 7.29.
[20] Aprem, 29-30. See also Socrates, 7.29.
[21] Socrates, 7.29.
[22] Dickens, 5

utilizing Socrates' proverbial phrase, "before he had tasted the water of the city",[23] Nestorius began implanting his proclivities. Overall, despite being labelled as an eloquent and enthralling speaker, Nestorius' actions within Constantinople were considered socially disruptive and divisive.

Cyril of Alexandria was born at Theodosiou in Lower Egypt in 378 C.E.[24] Cyril appears to provoke extreme sentiments from scholars. Some label him "a great fifth-century thinker",[25] while others accuse him of being "an unscrupulous political operator ... out to achieve maximum power for the Alexandrian see by whatever possible means".[26] Norman Russell mentions, "The first secure date we have for Cyril was 403 when he accompanied his uncle to the Synod of the Oak, the council that deposed John Chrysostom".[27] Cyril's uncle, Theophilus, was Alexandra's patriarch until his death on October 15, 412 CE. For three days after Theophilus' death, Cyril was involved in a tumultuous contest with Archdeacon Timothy for the patriarchy.[28] Despite Timothy's military support, Cyril's faction ultimately won "the throne of St. Mark".[29]

Even though the actual characteristics of Cyril of Alexandra remain in dispute among scholars,[30] his reign as the patriarch of Alexandria was as tumultuous as Nestorius' rule in Constantinople. Cyril's first action as patriarch "was to eject the Novatianists and seize their churches and other property".[31] Also, he opened hostilities with the Neoplantionists[32] , and tensions with the Jewish population of Alexandria were running high. After some civil quarrels,[33] Cyril "seized the synagogues in the name of the Church [and the] Jews were driven out of their homes and their property plundered by [Cyril's] mob".[34]

It is important to note another tragedy that occurred in Alexandria during Cyril's reign. In March 415 CE, the famous and beloved philosopher Hypatia was killed by a Christian horde. Led by a cleric named Peter, the Christian

---

[23] Socrates, 7.29.

[24] Russell, 4.

[25] Frances M. Young, *From Nicaea to Chalcedon: A Guide to the Literature and its Background* (London: SCM Press, 1983), 240.

[26] Young, 241.

[27] Young, 6.

[28] Young, 242.

[29] Russell, 6. According to apostolic tradition, the apostle Mark is perceived to be the first patriarch of Alexandria.

[30] See Aprem, 25 and Young, 240.

[31] Russell, 7.

[32] Aprem, 22.

[33] See Socrates, 7.13-14. and Russell, 7.

[34] Russell, 7.

mob attacked Hypatia on her way home. Socrates provides the disturbing details of her death:

> Some of them, therefore, hurried away by a fierce and bigoted zeal whose ringleader was a reader named Peter, waylaid her returning home, and dragging her from her carriage, they took her to the church called *Cæsareum*, where they completely stripped her, and then murdered her with tiles. After tearing her body in pieces, they took her mangled limbs to a place called Cinaron, and there burnt them.[35]

Russell suggests that "Hypatia's body had indeed been treated like the cult images of the pagan temples, which had been broken up and burned as dwelling places of the demons".[36] The Christian flock treated Hypatia's body as a type of ritual iconoclasm. After Hypatia's death, the Christian mob proclaimed Cyril "the new Theophilus" as he had eradicated the last seen remnants of idolatry in Alexandria.[37] In this particular instance, Cyril has already deemed political opponents to be monstrous. Mar Aprem notes, however, "The murder of 'Hypatia' is a great crime for which Cyril is still held responsible, though it is a fact that it was not Cyril, but one of his clergy, a reader named Peter, who murdered [her]".[38] Therefore, one can see the changing discourse through the history of who is indeed the monster. This can be considered a controversial topic, but it is impossible to know for sure if Cyril was ignorant of Peter's attack on Hypatia or if he was the insidious force guiding Peter to perform this horrendous and malicious act.

Theological contentions

There are two main theological contentions between Nestorius and Cyril. Namely, the terminologies employed referring to various Christologies and the title Theotokos applies to Mary. Regarding the former, there are four contentious terms: *Ousia, Physis, Prosopon,* and *Hypostasis*. One problem with these terms is that they are not static. Their meaning continually changes throughout various cultures and timeframes, leading to confusion and misunderstandings. As Russell states: "The key words *ousia, physis, hypostasis* and *prosopon* were still in the process of becoming technical terms and are used by both protagonists in a fluid, not to say confusing, manner".[39]

---

[35] Socrates, 7.15.
[36] Russell, 9.
[37] Ibid.
[38] Aprem, 23
[39] Russell, 40.

The first contentious term, *ousia*, is usually translated as "being", "substance", or "essence". Russell claims that "in Aristotelian usage, it could also mean the universal, the genus or the substratum".[40] However, even Aristotle's view of *ousia* is a topic that scholars cannot agree on. Eugene Ryan dismisses the claim that there are variations of Aristotle's usage of the term. He states, "There are difficulties and inconsistencies in Aristotle's account of form and *ousia*, but the paradoxical doctrine of pure form as formulated by his commentators is not, I think, one of them".[41] Ryan believes that for Aristotle, *ousia* is some pure form. Additionally, Michael Loux claims that "Aristotle construed the term as neutral between opposing Ontologies".[42] The term *physis* is typically translated as face, mask, or role. It also has various meanings that could be seen as similar to *ousia*. Still, as Russell notes, "it also means nature as manifested in the physical world".[43]

The third contentious term, *Hypotasis*, can be translated as foundation or "actual reality as opposed to appearance".[44] Finally, *prosopon* is usually translated as representation, guise, the individual self, or a tangible representation of the abstract *ousia*.[45] Basil of Caesarea (circa 379 CE), however, had a profound influence on how *hypostasis* and *prosopon* became viewed within the Orthodox Church. Lucian Turcescu summarizes Basil's effect on these terms nicely:

> One can say that in his earlier writings, Basil was not overtly concerned with the meanings of the terms *prosopon* and *hypostasis*; for the faith. Yet, as he became increasingly involved in the doctrinal fights against various heretics, especially after being appointed a bishop, Basil felt responsible for the cultivation and preservation of the Orthodox faith. In his early years, he used *prosopon* with the sense of "face", "mouth", "character in a play", or even "person" in the largest sense as opposed to "thing". Later, he became aware that *prosopon* was a term compromised by Sabellius when the latter used it with the meaning of "mask" devoid of any subsistence in regard to the Father, Son and Holy Spirit. So, when using *prosopon*, Basil asked for its qualification to be "perfect" or "existing in a true subsistence". Nevertheless, despite these qualifications, he strongly discouraged the use of *prosopon* as a technical term to refer to the divine persons. Concerning *hypostasis*,

---

[40] Ibid.

[41] Eugene E. Ryan, "Pure Form in Aristotle", in *Phronesis* 18.3 (1973): 209-224, 224

[42] Michael Loux, "Ousia: A Prolegomenon to Metaphysics Z and H", in *History of Philosophy Quarterly* 1.3 (July, 1984: 241-265), 241.

[43] Russell, 40.

[44] Ibid.

[45] Ibid.

a development in its use can also be noted. In CEun, it could mean "substance" (synonymous with ousia), "subsistence", "substratum", or even "person". Later, Basil began to distinguish it from "substance", so much so as to force the interpretation in this direction of the Nicene anathema that condemned those who would discriminate between *hypostasis* and *ousia*. A little later (ca. 375-6), besides the Nicaeanum, the confession of three persons and one substance in God became a touchstone of orthodoxy to him.[46]

Despite scholars' attempts at the etymology of these terms, one can witness the murky and unclear status, leading to ambiguity and confusion.

Nestorius proclaimed that the tangible manifestation of Jesus was one *prosopon*, but underlining the *prosopon* is the two *ousiai*, namely the divine and the human.[47] Nestorius appears to have neglected the term *hypotasis*, but as Frances M. Young notes, Nestorius appears to equate *hypotasis* with *ousia*.[48] Nestorius' theological influence was through the Antiochene School, which placed "equal emphasis on the Godhead and the manhood"[49] of Jesus. Wilhelm Baum and Dietmar W. Winkler suggest that "the fundamental Antiochene concern is soteriological: salvation is attainable for humanity only by Christ's taking on a perfect human nature ... it is necessary to emphasize its distinction from the incomprehensible Godhead".[50] Cyril, on the other hand, was employing his Alexandrian allegorical training. The Alexandrian school focused more on the divine aspects of Jesus. As Moffett notes, "For only a divine Christ could save sinners".[51] Cyril utilized *physics* as an equivalent to *hypostasis*, and means a tangible reality.[52] Thus, "Cyril can speak indifferently of a single incarnate *physis* or a single incarnate *hypostasis* of God the Word".[53]

The second theological contention between Nestorius and Cyril was the title *Theotokos* being applied to Mary. This particular theological contention instigated the hostilities between Nestorius and Cyril. Near the end of the summer in 428 CE, Nestorius was asked to resolve a theological dispute: should Mary be labelled *Theotokos*, meaning she gave birth to God, or

---

[46] Lucian Turcescu, "Prosōpon and Hypostasis in Basil of Caesarea's 'Against Eunomius' and the Epistles", in *Vigiliae Christianae* 51.4 (Nov., 1997): 374-395, 394-395.

[47] Young, 236.

[48] Ibid.

[49] Young, 237.

[50] Wilhelm Baum and Dietmar W. Winkler, *The Church of the East: A concise history* (London & New York: RoutledgeCurzon, 2000), 23.

[51] Moffett, 171.

[52] Russell, 40.

[53] Ibid.

Anthropotokos, meaning she who gave birth to man.[54] Nestorius stated that neither label was incorrect, but the title *Christotkos* would be preferred because "it was closer to the language of the New Testament".[55] This title would have been controversial and contentious in Constantinople since Mary was perceived as a city's defender. Thus, Nestorius could be viewed as attacking the defending local "goddess". Although, it appears Nestorius was attempting to reach some form of compromise. Young states, "Both titles were acceptable with certain reservations, but it would be better to avoid difficulties by using *Christotokos*".[56]

In November, however, a sermon by an Antiochian priest named Anastasius denounced the term *Theotokos*: "Let no one call Mary *Theotokos*, for Mary was only a human being, and it is impossible that God should be born of a human being".[57] Socrates states that this sermon "created a great sensation and troubled many both of the clergy and the laity".[58] In response, the bishop of Cyzicus, Proclus,[59] "preached an ecstatic sermon on the Mother of God".[60] The crowds greeted Proclus' sermon ecstatically, which displeased Nestorius. Nestorius's response stated, "That God passed through from the Virgin Christotokos, I am taught by the divine Scriptures, but that God was born from her, and I have not been taught anywhere. Those who call Mary *Theotokos* are heretics".

It should be noted that the source of this particular statement by Nestorius is from his adversaries. It is essential to realize that this is a dubious source and should be viewed with suspicion. If Nestorius had indeed uttered these statements, they would have caused massive shock within the populace. Cyril reacted by circulating his first letter against Nestorius, arguing the applicability of the title *Theotokos*.[61] He also sends a message directly to Nestorius with a similar argument.[62]

It is evident through examination that the various terminologies employed by Nestorius and Cyril are murky, unclear, and confusing. It would be easy to

---

[54] Russell, 33.

[55] Ibid.

[56] Young, 235.

[57] Socrates, 7.32.

[58] Ibid.

[59] It should be noted that Proclus "had been the strongest of the local candidates passed over for the Constantinopolitan throne". Russell, 33.

[60] Ibid.

[61] See Cyril of Alexandria, *FIVE-BOOK CONTRADICTION OF THE BLASPHEMIES OF NESTORIUS* OR THE FIVE TOMES OF S. CYRIL.

[62] See Cyril of Alexandria, "Second Letter to Nestorius", in *Select Letters*, ed. Lionel R. Wickham (Oxford: The Clarendon Press, 1983).

understand if one were to dismiss these disagreements as trivial or minuscule. However, it is important to realize that some would have had strong convictions regarding these terminologies since they would have been taught by their perspective "school" what is considered orthodox. Indeed, both Nestorius and Cyril would have considered and even privileged their position as "orthodox".[63] For example,[64] Cyril protested to Pope Celestine I about Nestorius's language, and Celestine's response was for Cyril to investigate further.[65] Cyril responded by writing letters to Nestorius, and his convictions about his terminology are specified within these letters. Cyril wrote twelve anathemas, which "sought to impose the terminology of Alexandrian theology upon Nestorius".[66] Here, one can already witness Cyril attempting to gain a massive political advantage by arguing that Nestorius should adopt Cyril's, and by extension, the Alexandrian schools, insider language. This point is vital as language is a major component of who obtains "insider" status. Nestorius believed that Cyril was targeting him unjustly: "Why have you set aside these utterances and anathematized mine? *For I have said nothing different*".[67] With these perceived theological contentions, the battle lines were set for a possible immense schism within Christianity.

In his article "Toward a Sociology of Heresy",[68] George V. Zito provides an interesting theory regarding semiotics. He states that "the social nature of heresy may best be examined by employing the methods of discursive analysis".[69] By a discursive analysis, Zito is merely saying that heresy can be examined as a "semiotic or linguistic phenomenon, upsetting an institutionalized way of speaking, or at least threatening to do so".[70] This manipulation of language, however, must be employed by an authoritative group or person.[71] Zito warns that heresy must not be confused with apostasy. Apostasy "involves losing one's allegiance to the language of the parent group. In apostasy, one moves from the in-group to the out-group and may be ostracized

---

[63] Moffett, 171.

[64] See Cyril of Alexandria, "Third Letter to Nestorius", in *Select Letters*, ed. Lionel R. Wickham (Oxford: The Clarendon Press, 1983).

[65] Michael C. Thomsett, *Heresy in the Roman Catholic Church: A History* (Jefferson, North Carolina & London: McFarland & Company, Inc., Publishers, 2011), 51.

[66] Baum and Winkler, 24.

[67] Nestorius, *Nestorius and his Teaching: A Fresh Examination of the Evidence* (ed. J.F. Bethune-Baker., Cambridge: University Press, 1908), 165. Added emphasis.

[68] George V. Zito, "Toward a Sociology of Heresy", in *Sociological Analysis* 44.2 (Summer 1983): 123-130.

[69] Zito, 123.

[70] Zito, 124.

[71] Zito, 125.

as a consequence".[72] Thus, the exiled member now becomes socially monstrous. Heresy, however, is not scepticism or non-belief. It is also not a "term used to refer to a non-Christian belief system".[73] Instead, perceived heretics employ "the *same language* as the parent group, retains its values, but attempts to order its discourse to some other end".[74] The "heretics" always have to appeal to similar, or identical, values and language as its parent group to be viewed as a credible movement.[75] Overall, Zito argues that heretics employ "insider" language but for divergent "goals". Or, as Lester R. Kurtz states, "Heretics are within the circle, or the institution; consequently, they are close enough to be threatening but distant enough to be considered in error ... the heretic is a deviant insider".[76] An "insider" deviant can be considered even more monstrous and troublesome for the general social order than an "outsider". Alister McGrath notes, "From an orthodox perspective, the divergence creates incoherence and instability within the *doxa* as a whole".[77]

Zito's methodology is intriguing. The largest schism in Church history, the Protestant Reformation, utilized "insider" language and values by appealing to the sacrality of Biblical scripture for divergent ideas, theologies, and sentiments. But can Zito's method be applied to Nestorius' language, leading him to be considered a heretic? This topic is still being argued within academia.

Within their articles "Christological and Soteriological Themes In The Third Letter of St. Cyril of Alexandria to Nestorius"[78] and "Fifth Century Christology Between Soteriological Perspective and Metaphysical Concerns: Notes On The Nestorian Controversy",[79] Kelly Anna Tsoi and Doru Costache argue that Nestorius' language, and theological ideas, were indeed considered heretical at the time. Tsoi states that "the essence of Cyril's Christological teaching is subtle, yet powerful ... It is Cyril's Christ who is the *Theanthropos* and epitomizes true humanity".[80] Additionally, Costache states that "Cyril managed to articulate

---

[72] Ibid.

[73] McGrath, 83.

[74] Zito, 125. Original emphasis.

[75] Zito, 126.

[76] Lester R. Kurtz, "The Politics of Heresy", in *American Journal of Sociology* 88.6 (May, 1983): 1085-1115, 1087.

[77] McGrath, 83.

[78] Kelly Anna Tsoi, "Christological and Soteriological Themes in The Third Letter of St. Cyril of Alexandria to Nestorius", in *Phronema* 22 (2007): 67-80.

[79] Doru Costache, "Fifth Century Christology Between Soteriological Perspective and Metaphysical Concerns: Notes On The Nestorian Controversy", in *Phronema* 21 (2006): 47-59.

[80] Tsoi, 76.

the traditional existential perspective of the Church in a daring and admirable synthesis".[81]

The problem with these two analyses is that they are apologetic towards Cyril. Their articles read similar to Catholic Church doctrine and describe why their Church fathers were "correct" in historical conflicts. Moreover, Tsoi's article raises all sorts of underlying problems dealing with the ambiguous and problematic notions of religious "essences" and "true humanity". By employing the terms "essences" and "true humanity", Tsoi's endeavour pursues universal epistemologies. This method promotes a monolithic classification system which universalizes complex taxonomies of social networks. Jonathan Z. Smith notes this universalization "eschews the postulation of a unique *differentium* in favour of a large set of characteristics, any one of which would be necessary, but not sufficient, to classify a given entity as an instance of religion".[82]

Conversely, I stand in the growing camp of scholars[83] who think Nestorius was not classified as a heretic based purely on theological grounds. Moffett states:

> There is a subtle distinction between "two natures" (Dyophysitism, which is what Nestorius and the school of Antioch taught) and "two persons", which is how Alexandria interpreted the phrase as if Nestorius were teaching "dyhypostatism". By insisting that one person (hypostasis) can have but one nature (physis), Alexandria sought to make the teaching of Nestorius heretical.[84]

---

[81] Costache, 57.

[82] Jonathan Z. Smith, "A Matter of Class: Taxonomies of Religion", in *Relating Religion: Essays in the Study of Religion* (Chicago & London: University of Chicago Press, 2004), 160-178, 166. Also see Jonathan Z. Smith, "Fences and Neighbors: Some Contours of Early Judaism", in *Imagining Religion: From Babylon to Jonestown* (Chicago & London: The University of Chicago Press, 1982): 1-18. In this article, Smith describes how a monolithic classification, in this case he utilized circumcision, for early Judaism is insufficient. He states, "Students of religion need to abandon the notion of 'essence,' of a unique differentium for early Judaism as well as the socially impossible correlative of a community constituted by a systematic set of beliefs. The cartography of a community appears far messier. We need to map the variety of Judaisms, each of which appears as a shifting cluster of characteristics which vary over time ... religious studies must set about an analogous dismantling of the old theological and imperialistic impulses toward totalization, unification, and integration. The labour at achieving the goal of a polythetic classification of Judaisms, rather than a monothetic definition of early Judaism, is but a preliminary step toward this end". (18)

[83] See Dickens, Young, Russell, and Grillmeier.

[84] Moffett, 176.

However, the problem is that Nestorius did not deny Jesus' divinity or unity as he was charged.[85] He was attempting to distinguish Jesus' divinity from his humanity.[86] Regarding the title of *Theotokos* being applied to Mary, Nestorius did not vehemently object to the title. He was more concerned with the theological implications of the term.[87] Aloys Grillmeier states,

> If Nestorius and Cyril could have been compelled to discuss their differences calmly and to define their terms with precision under the supervision of a strict and impartial arbiter who could have kept them under control until they had explained themselves clearly, there is little doubt that they would have found themselves in substantial agreement theologically.[88]

Additionally, Socrates thought that the theological charges brought against Nestorius were without merit:

> Having myself perused the writings of Nestorius, I have found him an unlearned man and shall candidly express the conviction of my own mind concerning him: and as in entire freedom from personal antipathies, I have already alluded to his faults, I shall in like manner be unbiased by the criminations of his adversaries, to derogate from his merits. I cannot then concede that he was either a follower of Paul of Samosata or of Photinus, or that he denied the Divinity of Christ: but he seemed scared at the term *Theotokos*, as though it were some terrible phantom. The fact is, the causeless alarm he manifested on this subject just exposed his extreme ignorance: for being a man of natural fluency as a speaker, he was considered well educated, but in reality, he was disgracefully illiterate.[89]

It appears that terminology confusion and theological contentions were definitely part of the hostilities between Nestorius and Cyril. Still, the main point of contention, the root or foundation, of their conflict runs deeper. As Moffett states: "*Added* to this *political* enmity was the long-standing theological rivalry between the school of Antioch and the school of Alexandria".[90]

---

[85] See Nestorius, *The Bazaar of Heracleides*. Book 1, Part 1 &2 for a clear indication of Nestoius' thoughts regarding the nature of Jesus which is well beyond the semiotic scope of this paper. Also see Aloys Grillmeier, *Christ in Christian Traditions: From the Apostolic Age to Chalcedon (451)*, trans. J.S. Bowden (London: A.R. Mowbray & Co., 1965), 363-388 & 406-412 for a detailed analysis.

[86] Moffett, 176.

[87] Young, 235.

[88] Grillmeier, 371.

[89] Socrates, 7.32.

[90] Moffett, 174. *Emphasis added.*

Political Hostilities

The political tensions between Nestorius and Cyril, and by extension, Antioch and Alexandria, were anxious and bitter. Moffett states, "Up to the end of the fourth century, Alexandria had been the greatest patriarchate in the world next to Rome. But the Second Ecumenical Council (Constantinople, 381) had declared that Rome and Constantinople [through Canon 3] were equal. However, Rome, of course, had the precedence of antiquity".[91] This rearrangement particularly irritated "the patriarchs of Alexandria, who looked back to the evangelist Mark as their apostolic founder and had called themselves 'popes' since the patriarchate of Heracles (232-248)".[92] In other words, the perceived apostolic succession in political terms would deem Alexandria "ahead" of Constantinople due to Mark's professed apostolic significance over Andrew. Additionally, as a result of the realignment, the patriarch of Alexandria, Cyril, had been politically relegated below Constantinople. As the previous examination of Cyril's historical background stated, he was indeed a figure seeking as much social power and authority as possible. Cyril would have been dismayed at his political demotion. As Baum and Winkler note:

> As patriarch of Alexandria, Cyril, like his predecessor Theophilus, took little pleasure in the fact that the second ecumenical Council (381) had placed the church of Constantinople, and the "new Rome" in second position ahead of Alexandria. Earlier, at the Council of Nicaea (325), the patriarchate order had been established in Rome, Alexandria, and Antioch. Since then, arguments over pre-eminence in the east of the empire have been a smouldering source of conflict and have contributed greatly to the controversy.[93]

Nestorius also moved to emphasize his authority and the pre-eminence of the patriarch of Constantinople. At one point, Nestorius questioned Pope Celestine regarding his excommunication of the Pelagians, "evidently with the intention of proceeding to a formal review of their case".[94] Celestine only answered back, "After several more letters from Nestorius [had] already reached Rome and the struggle [was] already at its height".[95] Nestorius' bravado on questioning an ultimate decision by the Pope is highly significant. It can be perceived as commendable due to his challenge against Roman authority, as the Roman Pope had almost infallible authority. However, his so-

---

[91] Moffett, 173.
[92] Dickens, 3.
[93] Baum & Winkler, 23.
[94] Russell, 36.
[95] Grillmeier, 392.

called defiance can also be viewed as naïve, pompous, and questionable, especially from the perspective of social power struggles. As Young notes, "Nestorius tended to act in haste, and that he was over-sure of his position can hardly be doubted".[96] Also, his letter response to Cyril was "deeply hostile, and the whole affair turned on personal animosity; really he and Cyril were not far apart, and where they differed, Cyril was confused or wrong".[97]

When peoples' power and authority are questioned, they tend to appeal to higher authorities to retain or regain their social control.[98] In Cyril's case, he appealed to a perceived transcendent authority (this could be considered the ultimate authority) by engaging in theological debates. He also appealed to a terrestrial authority in Pope Celestine I. Concerned with Constantinople's rising power, Pope Celestine ultimately sided with Cyril. Obviously, Celestine's opinion and conclusion were driven by socio-political issues, not theologies. Russell notes: "Nestorius's interest in the Pelagians' case ensured that Rome would wish to be involved".[99] By contrast, Emperor Theodosius II favoured Nestorius.[100] It is unclear precisely why Theodosius preferred Nestorius. Still, I am inclined to think that it was because Nestorius was the patriarch of the highest see in the Eastern Roman Empire.

Through Nestorius' swift actions against the urban monasteries in Constantinople, he gained a potent adversary, namely Augusta Pulcheria, the Emperor's sister. Russell notes that "Pulcheria was no ordinary Byzantine princess. Although technically a nun, she lived the life of a consecrated virgin in the imperial palace, devoting herself to prayer and good works ... Her combined status as Augusta and professed virgin gave her a unique role in ecclesiastical affairs".[101] Nestorius ordered the urban monks to "confine themselves to the liturgical routine of their monasteries and not engage in urban ministries".[102] One of these Monks was Hypatius, who was Pulcheria's spiritual advisor.[103] Also, Nestorius removed a portrait of Pulcheria from the cathedral of Constantinople and refused her communion on Easter.[104] Pulcheria, being accustomed to partaking in communion, was outraged. She indicated to Nestorius that she should be allowed to participate in

---

[96] Young, 234.

[97] Young, 232.

[98] See Craig Martin, *A Critical Introduction to the Study of Religion* (Sheffield: Equinox, 2012), 117-144.

[99] Russell, 37.

[100] Moffett, 174 and Aprem, 31.

[101] Russell, 32.

[102] Ibid.

[103] Ibid.

[104] Ibid.

communion because she was a consecrated virgin who was akin to the Mother of God.[105] Shocked that a woman might challenge his authority and equate herself to God's mother, Nestorius replied, "That she had given birth to Satan".[106] Nestorius outlines his version of events,

> You have further with you against me a contentious woman, a princess, a young maiden, a virgin, who fought against me because I was not willing to be persuaded by her demand that I should compare a woman corrupted of men to the bride of Christ. This I have done because I had pity on her soul and that I might not be the chief celebrant of the sacrifice among those whom she had unrighteously chosen. Of her I have spoken only to mention [her], for she was my friend; and therefore I keep silence about and hide everything else about her little self, seeing that [she was but] a young maiden; and for that reason she fought against me.[107]

The ramification of their tensions was that "when Nestorius began to preach against the title *Theotokos*, the response was led by people close to Pulcheria".[108] The foundation of hostilities was now complete, and the battle lines were now drawn. On the one hand, there was Cyril, Pope Celestine, and Pulcheria. By extension, the school of Alexandria, Rome, and certain clergy, especially monastic monks, within Constantinople. On the other hand, there was Nestorius and (loosely) Theodosius. By extension, the Antiochene school and certain sections of Constantinople were also involved.

The tensions within Christianity due to this controversy grew and began to become paramount. Emperor Theodosius was faced with a genuine possibility that a massive schism could occur if he did not react. Thus, "as tempers mounted, a Third Ecumenical Council was summoned to meet in Ephesus in 431 to make peace among the warring patriarchs".[109]

The Council of Ephesus

The Council of Ephesus, held in June 431 CE, is muddy and difficult to comprehend. Moffett claims that the Council "was the most violent and least equitable of all the great councils. It is an embarrassment and blot on the history of the church".[110] All of the proceedings, synods, and ramifications are well beyond the scope of this paper, but I will note the "highlights". Nestorius

---

[105] Ibid.
[106] Ibid.
[107] Nestorius, *The Bazaar of Heracleides*. Book 1. Part 3.
[108] Russell, 33.
[109] Moffett, 174.
[110] Ibid.

was the first to arrive at Ephesus with a military escort and sixteen bishops. Russell notes that Nestorius was "met with a hostile reception from Memnon, the bishop of Ephesus, who with his forty Asian bishops was solidly pro-Cyril".[111] Afterwards, Cyril arrived with fifty of his bishops. Cyril called the first synod under some controversies since John of Antioch, who was coming to defend Nestorius, was late.[112] Due to other circumstances, Theodosius could not attend, but the Pope's commission still recognized this synod.[113] In protest, Nestorius refused to partake.

Cyril and Nestorius' letters were read,[114] and the bishops debated their validity in accordance with Nicea: "Whatever corresponded with Nicaea was to be accepted, and whatever differed was to be rejected".[115] The pro-Cyril bishops unsurprisingly favoured Cyril. The favouritism resulted in the council voting to excommunicate Nestorius. The decree of the Council against Nestorius reads:

> As, in addition to other things, the impious Nestorius has not obeyed our citation and did not receive the holy bishops who were sent by us to him, we were compelled to examine his ungodly doctrines. We discovered that he had held and published impious doctrines in his letters and treatises, as well as in discourses that he delivered in this city and that have been testified to. Compelled thereto by the canons and by the letter of our most holy father and fellow-servant Celestine, the Roman bishop, we have come, with many tears, to this sorrowful sentence against him, namely, that our Lord Jesus Christ, whom he has blasphemed, decrees by the holy Synod that Nestorius be excluded from the episcopal dignity, and all priestly communion.[116]

Baum and Winkler state, "The judgement was handed down in the absence of the accused and without his testimony".[117] Nestorius vents his frustration within the Bazaar of Heracleides Book II, Part I:

> Cyril then is the persecutor and the accuser, while I am persecuted; but it was the Council which heard and judged my words and the emperor who assembled [it]. If then he was on the bench of judges, what indeed shall I say of the bench of judges? He was the whole tribunal, for everything which he said they all said together, and without doubt, it is

---

[111] Russell, 46.

[112] See Aprem 62-63.

[113] Grillmeier, 413.

[114] See Council of Ephesus, Session I.

[115] Grillmeier, 414.

[116] Council of Ephesus, Session I.

[117] Baum & Winkler, 24.

certain that he in person took the place of a tribunal for them. For if all the judges had been assembled and the accusers had risen in their place and the accused also likewise, all of them would equally have had freedom of speech, instead of his being in everything both accuser and emperor and judge. He did all things with authority, after excluding from authority him who had been charged by the emperor, and he exalted himself; and he assembled all those whom he wanted, both those who were far off and those who were near, and he constituted himself the tribunal. And I was summoned by Cyril, who had assembled the Council, even by Cyril who was the chief thereof. Who was the judge? Cyril. And who was the accuser? Cyril. Who was bishop of Rome? Cyril. Cyril was everything. Cyril was the bishop of Alexandria and took the place of the holy and saintly bishop of Rome, Celestinus.[118]

When John of Antioch finally arrived, he was understandably livid that the first Council did not wait for his arrival. Immediately, he "proceeded to hold his own council attended by the dissident bishops".[119] The result of this council "declared the result illegal and [held] a countercouncil that excommunicated Cyril".[120]

Confused at the puzzling and conflicting reports from the Council, Theodosius sent an imperial official to bring the warring sides together and straighten out their differences. The sides, however, refused to cooperate, resulting in Cyril, Memon, and Nestorius being arrested.[121] However, Cyril quickly bribed his way back into power, whereas Nestorius "accepted the verdict with only a quiet protest at its injustice".[122] The imperial inquiry proved inconclusive but still resulted in the Formulary of Reunion of 433 to restore peace within Christendom.[123] To establish peace within his empire, Theodosius had to succumb to the pressures of Cyril and Rome. Aprem states that "Cyril's willingness to accept the Christology [within the Formulary of Reunion] as long as Nestorius was condemned, confirms ... that he was more led by personal antagonism than by theological conviction".[124] After the Council, Nestorius was already in a monastery in Antioch. Some scholars argue that he wanted to return to a life of peace and solitude and asked Theodosius to return.[125] Others argue that the Emperor had told him to withdraw from the public eye. Regardless, Nestorius, who is now excommunicated, was labelled a

---

[118] Nestorius, *Bazaar of Heracleides*. Book II, Part I.
[119] Russell, 50.
[120] Moffett, 174.
[121] Russell, 51.
[122] Moffet, 175.
[123] Russell, 51.
[124] Aprem, 100.
[125] See Russell, 37.

heretic. Boundary demarcations were realigned, and Nestorius and his theologies (ideologies) were now deemed monstrous.

Manufacturing the Heretical "Monster"

Through the ritual showcase of the Council of Ephesus and Cyril's persuasive discourse labelling Nestorius a political threat or a threat to Christianity's unity, the artificial lines of "orthodox" classification were socially constructed to establish legitimate political power and authority. The ramification of this classification is Nestorius being labelled a heretic and a deviant. As McGrath notes, "Heresy is not an observable or empirical reality but a socially constructed entity ... What makes a heresy is not so much its ideas as the way it is characterized and categorized by others".[126] The same reasoning can be applied to the monstrous. Regarding human "monsters", the category and classification are not neutral but a social construction built by socio-political rivals.

It is clear that the Council of Ephesus was a confusing and dubious affair that ultimately led to Nestorius being labelled a "heretic". The Council of Ephesus was utilized by Cyril, Pope Celestine, and Pulcheria as a method to display and establish power and authority through the means of a "showcase" ritual.[127] Rituals can be employed by political leaders "to assert their right to rule... [by seeking] to bolster their authority ... [and] to create political realities for the people around them".[128] David I. Kertzer argues,

> If the assumption of political office is ritually marked, so are attempts to divest an officeholder of his authority. Having been previously ritually joined to the office, the individual must also be separated from their authority by further ritual ... This ritual must fuse strong emotions— often associated with the notion that the power holder has sinned against the community—with the idea that the individual who a moment ago could legitimately exercise power over them can do so no longer.[129]

Nestorius would have to undergo a type of ritual to be disposed of and negatively characterized. The Council of Ephesus provided a ritualistic opportunity for Cyril, Pope Celestine, Pulcheria, and others to excommunicate Nestorius. As Kertzer suggests, "an organization's political position is often

---

[126] McGrath, 82.

[127] For clarification, in this instance, I do not refer to ritual as repetitive actions with a known or preconditioned outcome. Conversely, "ritual is an analytical category that helps us deal with the chaos of human experience and put it into a coherent framework". See David I. Kertzer, *Ritual, Politics, and Power* (New Haven & London: Yale University Press, 1988), 8.

[128] Kertzer, 1.

[129] Kertzer, 28.

communicated more effectively, and more credibly, through ritual than through simply written platforms or oral addresses".[130] First, Cyril and Celestine attempted to undermine Nestorius' power and authority through their letters. Nestorius failed to submit to their pressure. Therefore, there was a need for a ritual to dispose of him *formally*. When standard methods fail, "the solution lies in the performance of extraordinary rituals that symbolically and materially undo the discredited".[131] Overall, ritual can create "an emotional state that makes the message uncontestable because it is framed in such a way as to be seen as inherent in the way things are. It presents a picture of the world that is so emotionally compelling that it is beyond debate".[132]

The location of the Council in Ephesus is also crucial. The goddess Artemis had been worshipped in Ephesus since the eleventh century BCE.[133] Ephesus was the centre of the Artemis cult, and located just outside the city was the "great temple of Artemis ... one of the seven wonders of the ancient world".[134] Also, Ephesus was a city "hostile to Constantinople and already a centre of devotion to the Virgin".[135] Maxwell E. Johnson states that "prayers, hymns, and other texts illustrate that such devotion ... was becoming rather widespread".

Additionally, a group of women, known as the Collyridians, "who worshipped Mary as a 'goddess,'... and had a female priesthood".[136] There are even references to a "Virgin's festival" being celebrated.[137] The political implications are clear. The city of Ephesus had a long history of goddess veneration and highly revered Mary as *Theotokos*. Nestorius was stepping into hostile territory. The location of Ephesus for this particular ecumenical Council is anything but neutral ground.

The Council of Ephesus was "assembled in the cathedral of Ephesus, the Great Church of St. Mary the *Theotokos*".[138] I have already mentioned why the city of Ephesus was vital for Cyril's agenda. Still, the notion of holding the Council within the perceived sacred location of the Virgin cannot be understated. As Jonathan Z. Smith notes, "When one enters a temple [or Great Church], one enters marked-off space in which, at least in principle, nothing

---

[130] Kertzer, 31

[131] Bruce Lincoln, *Discourse and the Construction of Society: Comparative Studies of Myth, Ritual, and Classification* (New York & Oxford: Oxford University Press, 1989), 101.

[132] Kertzer, 101.

[133] C.L. Brinks, "'Great is Artemis of Ephesus': Acts 19:23-41 in Light of Goddess Worship in Ephesus", in *Catholic Biblical Quarterly* 71.4 (Oct 2009): 776-794, 783.

[134] Brinks, 781.

[135] Russell, 38.

[136] Johnson, 68.

[137] Johnson, 69.

[138] Russell, 48.

is accidental; everything, at least potentially, is of significance".[139] In other words, since the Council of Ephesus gathered in an area deemed "sacred", the resulting discourse and ramifications have an aura of transcendent authority. By assembling within the Great Church of St. Mary, the Council attempts to authorize their results as divinely ordained. Through the ritual of the Council of Ephesus, Cyril and the anti-Nestorian bishops projected "the secular socio-political order in which they live onto a cosmological plane".[140] Therefore, despite Nestorius' and others' protests, the result of an assembly within a "sacred" location is difficult to reverse since the results are perceived as deriving from the cosmos and the divine. By rendering their councils' results sacred due to the use of ritual, they also legitimized their power and authority.[141] As Kertzer notes, "Ritual not only structures our perceptions and suggests certain interpretations of our experience, but *it does so in a setting that makes these perceptions and interpretations particularly salient and compelling*".[142] By utilizing the "sacred" location of the Council, Cyril and company were able to strip Nestorius' power while retaining ritually, and perhaps even gaining their power and authority.

In addition to the ritual performance at the Council of Ephesus, Cyril's discourse[143] effectively labelled Nestorius as a political threat and a threat to Christian unity. In other words, a social deviant becomes equated with perceived monstrous ideologies in order to break social ties and structures. Through Cyril's perceived authority on Biblical exegesis, he was able to coerce others, utilizing the discourse of hermeneutics, into supposing that his interpretation of the disputed terminology was correct. As I mentioned earlier, the theological language was substantial. Attached to this terminology are people's sentiments. Sentiments can be a significant driving force for societal change or reconfiguration. Bruce Lincoln states that "ultimately, that which either holds society together or takes it apart is sentiment, and the chief instrument with which such sentiment may be aroused, manipulated, and

---

[139] Smith, *Imagining Religion*, 54.

[140] Kertzer, 37.

[141] Kertzer, 38.

[142] Kertzer, 86. *Emphasis added.*

[143] Before beginning, it is essential to include a reference to how I am utilizing the term "discourse". Tim Murphy states, "The term 'discourse' in discourse theory is used in two different ways, ... On the one hand, discourse may simply refer to language ('discourse' in the more common sense of the term); on the other hand, the meaning of the term may be extended to designate not just language systems but any unified, coded or systematic practice of signification. See Tim Murphy, "Discourse", in *Guide to the Study of Religion*, eds. Willi Braun and Russell T. McCutcheon (London & New York: Continuum, 2000): 396-408, 397-398.

rendered dormant is discourse".[144] Evoking these sentiments can occur by implying that a divine force guides his interpretations of "sacred" theologies.[145] Cyril capitalized on "specific human preferences with transcendent status by misrepresenting them as revealed truths, primordial traditions, divine commandments and so forth".[146] By appealing to the transcendent, Cyril cloaks and shields himself and his interpretations from popular critique and debate due to its perceived nature as "sacred". By suggesting that Nestorius' terminology was "unorthodoxy", Cyril's discursive method successfully portrayed Nestorius as a subversive "other" or monstrous. McGrath notes, "Orthodoxy is indeed a 'discursive institution,' concerned with 'naming' the other, the outsider, and potential threats".[147] Moreover, "heresy is a socially embodied notion, designating communities of discourse as much as ideas".[148]

The terms "orthodoxy" and "heresy" are not static. They gain their credibility through specific social designations such as rituals and discourse. The result is legitimizing social power and adversely labelling others who fall outside the normalized defined scope. McGrath notes, "Heresy is not an empirical, but an evaluative, notion. At one level, it is a constructed notion, in that it is the outcome of a judgement or evaluation of a set of ideas by a community".[149] Therefore, it is not a natural reality or even discernible but a socially constructed designation.[150] To reiterate, the division between what is classified as "Orthodoxy" and "Heresy" (Right and Wrong, Standard and Monstrous) is an artificial line constructed and established through discourse and ritual performances to establish political power and authority.

Conclusion

In conclusion, the dichotomy of "insiders/outsiders" is vital for socio-monster theory. It enables us to comprehend the constructed classification lines of what is deemed Orthodoxy (standard) and Heresy (monstrous). It is employed to establish socio-political power and authority. Any person or group who displays any opposing stance are designated monstrous. For this essay, Nestorius became an outside (monstrous) threat to the perceived unity of a social system. The "monstrous" becomes tangible and is put on a human face to display to the public the repercussions of social deviancy or possible

---

[144] Lincoln, *Discourse*, 11.

[145] See Cyril's second and third letter to Nestorius

[146] Bruce Lincoln, "Culture", in *Guide to the Study of Religion*, Eds. Willi Braun and Russell T. McCutcheon (London & New York: Continuum, 2000), 416.

[147] McGrath, 84.

[148] McGrath, 34.

[149] McGrath, 33.

[150] McGrath, 84.

sedition. But why are people who are "within" the same social body intent on labelling others within pejorative markers over matters of superficial and trivial differences? Jonathan Z. Smith provides an intriguing answer. Smith argues that societies or cultures are involved in an evolving process that makes a difference but, at the same time, relativizes those differences.[151] He states, "One of our fundamental social projects appears to be our collective capacity to think of and to think away the differences we create".

Regarding language, "real" differences can be negotiated with ease. One can learn various languages and overcome constructed differences through a cognitive process. Therefore, it is not the "remote 'other' being perceived as problematic and dangerous. It is the proximate 'other,' the near neighbour, who is most troublesome".[152] In other words, the problem is not with people who are not like us but with people who are too much like us or claim to be.

Smith argues that "the issue of problematic similarity or identity seems to be particularly prevalent in religious discourse and imagination".[153] This examination explains why there appears to be more discourses and rhetoric directed against perceived monstrous heretics, such as Nestorius, within an "insider" group than against the far-removed "outsiders". Especially when people are engaging in a struggle for power and authority under their broader community's social umbrella. As Smith suggests, "Relations are discovered and reconstituted through projects of differentiation".[154] Cohen offers a similar explanation to Smith. In Cohen's fourth monster thesis, he argues that "The Monster Dwells at the Gates of Difference". He states,

> The monster is difference made flesh, come to dwell among us... The monster threatens to destroy not just individual members of a society but the very cultural apparatus through which individual is constituted and allowed... Political or ideological difference is as much a catalyst to monstrous representation on a micro level as cultural alterity in the macrocosm. A political figure suddenly out of favour is transformed like an unwilling participant in a science experiment by the appointed historians of the replacement regime.[155]

---

[151] Jonathan Z. Smith, "Differential Equations: On Constructing the Other", in *Relating Religion: Essays in the Study of Religion* (Chicago & London: University of Chicago Press, 2004): 230-250, 242.

[152] Ibid., 245.

[153] Ibid.

[154] Ibid., 246.

[155] Cohen, 7, 8, & 12.

Bibliography

Primary

Cyril of Alexandria. *FIVE-BOOK CONTRADICTION OF THE BLASPHEMIES OF NESTORIUS OR THE FIVE TOMES OF S. CYRIL.*

Nestorius. *Nestorius and his Teaching: A Fresh Examination of the Evidence.* Ed. J.F. Bethune-Baker. Cambridge: University Press, 1908.

Pearse, Roger. Trans. Nestorius. *The Bazaar of Heracleides.* Book 1. Part 1, 2, and 3. Ipswich, UK, 2006.

Percival, Henry. Trans. Council of Ephesus. *Nicene and Post-Nicene Fathers,* Second Series, Vol. 14. Edited by Philip Schaff and Henry Wace. Buffalo, NY: Christian Literature Publishing Co., 1900.

Wickham, Lionel R. Ed. Cyril of Alexandria. *Select Letters.* Oxford: The Clarendon Press, 1983.

Zenos, AC Trans. Socrates Scholasticus. Ecclesiastical History. Book 7. *Nicene and Post-Nicene Fathers,* Second Series, Vol. 2. Edited by Philip Schaff and Henry Wace. Buffalo, NY: Christian Literature Publishing Co., 1890.

Secondary

Aprem, Mar. *The Council of Ephesus of 431.* Kerala, India: Mar Narsai Press, 1978.

Baum, Wilhelm and Dietmar W. Winkler. *The Church of the East: A concise history.* London & New York: Routledge, Curzon, 2000.

Brinks, C.L. "'Great is Artemis of Ephesus': Acts 19:23-41 in Light of Goddess Worship in Ephesus", Pages 776-794 in *Catholic Biblical Quarterly* 71.4, Oct 2009.

Costache, Doru. "Fifth Century Christology Between Soteriological Perspective and Metaphysical Concerns: Notes On The Nestorian Controversy", Pages 47-59 in *Phronema* 21, 2006.

Dickens, Mark. "Nestorius and the 'Dual Nature of Christ,'" in *Popular Controversies in World History.* (Entry 2.08A).

Grillmeier, Aloys. *Christ in Christian Traditions: From the Apostolic Age to Chalcedon (451).* Trans. J.S. Bowden. London: A.R. Mowbray & Co., 1965.

Johnson, Maxwell E. "Sub Tuum Praesidium: The Theotokos in Christian Life and Worship Before Ephesus", Pages 52-75 in *Pro Ecclesia* 17.1 Wint, 2008.

Kaatz, Kevin W. *Early Controversies and the Growth of Christianity.* Santa Barbara, Denver, & Oxford: Praeger, 2012.

Kertzer, David I. *Ritual, Politics, and Power.* New Haven & London: Yale University Press, 1988.

Kurtz, Lester R. "The Politics of Heresy", Pages 1085-1115 in *American Journal of Sociology* 88.6 May 1983.

Lincoln, Bruce. "Culture", in *Guide to the Study of Religion.* Eds. Willi Braun and Russell T. McCutcheon. London & New York: Continuum, 2000.

Lincoln, Bruce. *Discourse and the Construction of Society: Comparative Studies of Myth, Ritual, and Classification.* New York & Oxford: Oxford University Press, 1989.

Loux, Michael. "Ousia: A Prolegomenon to Metaphysics Z and H", Pages 241-265 in *History of Philosophy Quarterly* 1.3 Jul. 1984.

Martin, Craig. *A Critical Introduction to The Study Of Religion.* Sheffield: Equinox, 2012.

McGrath, Alister. *Heresy: A History of Defending the Truth.* New York: HarperOne, 2009.

Moffett, Samuel Hugh. *A History of Christianity in Asia.* Vol..1. New York: Orbis Books, 1998.

Murphy, Tim. "Discourse", in *Guide to the Study of Religion.* Eds. Willi Braun and T. McCutcheon. London & New York: Continuum, 2000.

Russell, Norman. *Cyril of Alexandra.* London & New York: Routledge, 2000.

Ryan, Eugene E. "Pure Form in Aristotle", Pages 209-224 in *Phronesis* 18.3, 1973.

Smith, Jonathan Z. *Imagining Religion: From Babylon to Jonestown.* Chicago & London: The University of Chicago Press, 1982.

Smith, Jonathan Z. *Relating Religion: Essays in the Study of Religion.* Chicago & London: University of Chicago Press, 2004.

Thomsett, Michael C. *Heresy in the Roman Catholic Church: A History.* Jefferson, North Carolina & London: McFarland & Company, Inc., Publishers, 2011.

Tsoi, Kelly Anna. "Christological and Soteriological Themes In The Third Letter of St. Cyril of Alexandria to Nestorius", Pages 67-80 in *Phronema* 22, 2007.

Turcescu, Lucian. "Prosōpon and Hypostasis in Basil of Caesarea's Against Eunomius' and the Epistles", Pages 374-395 in *Vigiliae Christianae* 51.4 Nov., 1997.

Young, Frances M. *From Nicaea to Chalcedon: A Guide to the Literature and its Background.* London: SCM Press, 1983.

Zito, George V. "Toward a Sociology of Heresy", Pages 123-130 in *Sociological Analysis* 44.2 Summer, 1983.

Chapter 4

Strange News: Monstrous Births and Popular Prints in Reformation England

Helena L. Martin

Yale University

Now the earth brought forth monsters and ugly shapes, strange, and full of terror… and sin being the cause of all.

Strange News of a Prodigious Monster (1613)[1]

Abstract

In 1613, the Reverend W. Leigh testified to a "monstrous birth" in his parish. A twelve-page pamphlet explains the religious and political significance of the birth of these conjoined twins. As printing technology improved in the early modern period, printed materials like this pamphlet became increasingly popular. Along with news, oddities, and ballads, stories of "monstrous births" were sold as information and entertainment. This chapter retrieves ephemeral sources about "monstrous births" in 16th century England as primary texts for theological inquiry. These "monstrous birth" stories proliferated in the turmoil of the early English Reformation. In them, the monstrous human body was a vehicle for divine communication with the masses. Ephemeral sources, such

---

A version of this chapter was originally presented as part of the *New Directions in the Study of Religion, Monsters, and the Monstrous Seminar* at the American Academy of Religion Annual Meeting in November 2021. I am grateful to Gabrielle Thomas and the anonymous reader for their helpful comments and suggestions on earlier drafts of this chapter.

[1] *Strange Newes of a Prodigious Monſter, Borne in the Towneſhip of Adlington in the Pariſh of Standiſh in the Countie of Lancaſter, the 17 Day of Aprill Last, 1613. Testified by the Reuerend Diuine Mr. W. Leigh, Bachelor of Diuinitie, and Preacher of Gods Word at Standiſh Aforeſaid,* 1613, Printed by I.P. for S.M., 1613, 1–2, Early English Books Online, https://www.proquest.com/books/strange-newes-prodigious-monster-borne-townesh ip/docview/2240897751/se-2. The original pamphlet has no marked pagination. I have imposed my own page numbers for clarity, with page 1 being the first page of the body of the text. In quotes from Middle English sources, I have preserved capitalization but modernized spelling. Citations in footnotes and the bibliography maintain the original spelling.

as pamphlets, interrogated the non-normative body as text and interpreted it for readers who were hungry for a deeper understanding of the turbulence of their time. The bodies of these "monsters" acted as canvases onto which authors painted their social and theological angst. What was God trying to tell society by sending messages coded into the bodies of these infants? In historical theology, works of genius by well-educated men have been studied most often. These offer an incomplete story, insofar as they are not usually trying to preserve information about the interests of the masses. As a precursor to modern journalism, pamphlets and broadsides reveal some of the complexity in the religious imagination of the time. Using disability and monster theories, I examine several sources as case studies in which monstrosity variously reveals, transgresses, and upholds boundaries—theological and social—in reformation England.

Keywords: "Monstrous Births," 16th century England, Monster Theory, Disability Studies

***

Introduction

In April 1613, the Reverend W. Leigh testifies to a "monstrous birth" in his parish. He recounts that twins have been born to a woman in Adlington, England, just northwest of Manchester. A depiction of their bodies covers most of the front page of the pamphlet. The girls are drawn naked, back-to-back, and they appear to be conjoined at the back of the head, neck, and shoulders. In a widely distributed twelve-page pamphlet, the anonymous writer recounts the Rev. Leigh's story and then explains the significance of the birth of these children. Their bodies, which the author finds unquestionably grotesque, are proof of God's anger. The author writes, "The most impious of all could not but confess that [the birth] was a notable example of Gods (sic) fearful wrath".[2] The pamphlet goes on to explain how sin has distorted creation, then interprets political events in Ireland, Spain, and Rome—all spurred by a single anomalous birth in the English countryside. Throughout, the author instructs the people of England to repent. After all, clearly, God sent this "monster" to embody "the ugliness of sin".[3]

Such "monstrous birth" stories in early modern England were built on the belief that the uncommonly embodied human could be a medium for divine

---

[2] *Strange Newes of a Prodigious Monfter*, 7.
[3] *Strange Newes of a Prodigious Monfter*, 3.

communication.[4] This belief is common across many cultures and times, especially in Christianity. Rosemarie Garland-Thomson writes that "cultural intolerance of anomaly is one of the most pervasive themes in Western thought".[5] From Aristotle's dislike for anomalies to Kant's aesthetic theory, which centres around uniformity, things (and people) that transgress against the norm invite dismissal and even suspicion. In much of Christian history, this has been particularly true of human bodies. As Meghan Henning summarizes, "Deformed, disabled, or effeminate bodies were frequently but not exclusively associated with damnation and sin".[6] A natural consequence is that uncommon, undesirable embodiment might be understood as divine punishment—of the individual, their family, or their community.[7] Given this premise, disability and illness cannot exist as mere facts; they demand explanation. The idea that uncommon embodiment bears messages from the divine was taken up in "monstrous birth" literature. The Adlington twins could not be a mere product of circumstance; their surprising birth must have a greater meaning, discernable to those privy to God's anger and desires.

Amidst the tumult of the English Reformation, popular prints like broadsides and pamphlets offered moral guidance to their readers about shifting societal boundaries. Properly contextualized, these ephemeral texts offer a window into popular understandings of those boundaries. During the mid-seventeenth century, for example, beheadings were the common punishment for traitors during the civil wars. "Thus instances of monstrous deformation of the head were particularly resonant in this period, with beings that were headless, bore the wrong number of eyes and ears, or exhibited other unnaturally shaped heads being interpreted as signs that England was politically monstrous".[8] Also, then, close readings of the "monstrous birth" stories that proliferated in

---

[4] The phrase "uncommonly embodied people" comes from Rosemarie Garland-Thomson, *Staring: How We Look* (Oxford: Oxford University Press, 2009).

[5] Rosemarie Garland-Thomson, *Extraordinary Bodies: Figuring Physical Disability in American Culture and Literature* (New York: Columbia University Press, 1997), 33.

[6] Meghan Henning, *Hell Hath No Fury: Gender, Disability, and the Invention of Damned Bodies in Early Christian Literature* (New Haven: Yale University Press, 2021), 36.

[7] The unconscious link between depravity and uncommon embodiment persists even today. Susan Schweik has catalogued legal cases regarding so-called "ugly laws" into the twenty-first century. These laws try to hide disabled and other uncommonly embodied people from public view simply because their bodies are considered unseemly. See: Susan M. Schweik, *The Ugly Laws: Disability in Public* (New York: New York University Press, 2009), 284–85.

[8] Surekha Davies, "The Unlucky, the Bad and the Ugly: Categories of Monstrosity from the Renaissance to the Enlightenment", in *The Ashgate Research Companion to Monsters and the Monstrous*, ed. Asa Simon Mittman and Peter J. Dendle, Ashgate Research Companion (Farnham, UK: Ashgate, 2012), 56.

Reformation England lay bare the ways some people made sense of the anxieties of the time. The bodies of these infants, categorized as "monsters", became channels through which people could express social and religious angsts.

Monsters challenge the boundaries created by a society.[9] Zakiya Hanafi writes, "In the jumbled limbs and motley order of its body, the monster threatens to destabilize all order, to break down all hierarchies".[10] How appropriate is the figure of the monster, then, to make sense of a time like the Reformation, when order and hierarchies are shifting and even crumbling. In these pamphlets, the uncommonly embodied infants, styled as monsters, transgress the barriers between natural and supernatural, between biological and theological. In his seminal essay in *Monster Theory: Reading Culture*, Jeffrey Cohen proposes understanding cultures through an examination of their monsters. The monster is "an embodiment of a certain cultural moment".[11] By "reading" monsters, he argues, we gain a unique perspective into the cultures that produced them. Furthering that thought, Andrew Sharpe explains that the figure of the monster is "a vehicle for the expression of cultural anxiety about boundaries: national, religious, sexual and human".[12] As expressions of anxiety, the popular prints' authors are not reliably narrating eyewitness accounts but interpreting and making sense of the stories they have heard. According to pamphlet authors, the "monstrous births" demand attention because of the messages the infants bear for English society. I argue that the pamphlets themselves should demand *our* attention to read behind the words for the anxieties of the cultures that produced them.

I adopt the term "monstrous birth" with a great deal of trepidation and offer the following caveats. Historically and today, uncommonly embodied people are marginalized in a multitude of ways.[13] Given that reality, scholarship applying monster theory to so-called "human monsters" has a responsibility to deploy language carefully. This responsibility is not merely to avoid problematic or potentially offensive words but, more importantly, to centre the humanity of the person in question. "Monstrous birth" is a term that refers not simply to *any* anomalous birth or disabled infant but to the birth of an infant whose

---

[9] The figure of the monster as a "harbinger of category crisis" is one of Jeffrey Cohen's "seven theses" toward understanding a culture through its monsters. Jeffrey Jerome Cohen, "Monster Culture (Seven Theses)", in *Monster Theory: Reading Culture* (Minneapolis: University of Minnesota Press, 1996), 6.

[10] Zakiya Hanafi, *The Monster in the Machine: Magic, Medicine, and the Marvelous in the Time of the Scientific Revolution* (Durham: Duke University Press, 2000), 2–3.

[11] Cohen, "Monster Culture", 4.

[12] Andrew N. Sharpe, "England's Legal Monsters", *Law, Culture and the Humanities* 5 (2009): 110, https://doi.org/10.1177/1743872108096865.

[13] This statement includes, but is not limited to, people who consider themselves disabled.

body was subsequently displayed and theorized as monstrous. Truly, the "monster" is not the human in question but the meaning constructed from their body as text. Using a disability studies framework, I use language wherever possible to highlight the humanity of the infants being written about in the pamphlets. For example, when discussing the children themselves, I use their names and pronouns, call them "infants" instead of monsters, and generally write about them as people rather than things. The language of monstrosity is helpful when applied to a phenomenon (e.g. the spectacle surrounding an anomalous birth) or fictional figure (e.g. a vampire) but dehumanizing when applied directly to people.

Using monster theory, I show how popular print sources offer valuable information about how ordinary people experienced the turmoil of the English Reformation. England's broadsides, pamphlets, and chapbooks about "monstrous births" should be treated as important primary texts for theological and historical inquiry. The ephemeral texts trying to make sense of "monstrous births" convey complex information about some attitudes of the time about the body, providence, and God's relationship with creation. The twentieth-century interest in "history from below" has since been expanded to interest in history from the outside, from above, and from the margins and subaltern.[14] In an era of social turmoil like the English Reformation, how did ordinary people make sense of the changes raging around them? As a precursor to the modern tabloid—and even, in some sense, to modern journalism—popular prints can offer insight.

I here employ monster theory in a close reading of two texts. Both are reports of "monstrous births" from Reformation England that make theological claims based on the bodies of uncommonly embodied infants. The first, *The true Discripcion of a Childe with Ruffes borne* (*Child with Ruffs*, 1566), is aimed at a broad audience. The author of this pamphlet "reads" the body of this infant for theological and moral conclusions about a hotly debated social topic of the time. The second case, *Strange newes of a prodigious Monster* (*Strange News*, 1613), speaks to a more educated audience. I read it in context to understand the theological discourse to which it tries to contribute. Using monster theory to examine these popular sources can add depth and complexity to our understanding of this time.

The Setting for "Monstrous Birth" Literature

To analyze the rhetoric in my two case studies, I begin with some background on the landscape of literature from which these pamphlets emerged. In the

---

14 Robert Darnton, "'What Is the History of Books?' Revisited", Modern Intellectual History 4, no. 3 (2007): 496, https://doi.org/doi:10.1017/S1479244307001370.

Middle Ages, ownership of books had been reserved for the elite. Books were expensive because they were labour- and material-intensive prior to the printing press. As printing technology improved in the fifteenth and sixteenth centuries, not only books but other printed materials became increasingly accessible and ubiquitous. Simultaneously and due to a multitude of factors, literacy rates grew significantly, particularly in England and the Netherlands.[15] With these technological and educational advancements as a backdrop, printed stories of "monstrous births" were sold alongside news, oddities, and ballads as information and entertainment. One may assume that readers of these popular prints must have been uneducated, the *hoi polloi* clamouring to the newsstand for the latest tabloid distraction. However, this assumption ignores the porosity of social strata and, more significantly, the complexities of people's engagement with media.[16]

Rather than seeing these prints as antithetical to elite publications like books, with mutually exclusive readerships, historians now understand popular prints to cut across social strata.[17] This was especially true as literacy rates rose sharply in England beginning in the sixteenth century, reaching around fifty per cent by the end of the seventeenth.[18] Since popular prints were relatively affordable and included imagery like woodblock prints, many of them were accessible to a larger portion of the population than might be expected.[19] However, the physical realities of these prints present a challenge for historiography. Namely, by their nature, they were not built to last. Single sheets and short pamphlets were relatively fragile, and more importantly, they were regarded as disposable. Thus, the survival rate of popular ephemeral printings is low compared with the survival rate of popular books. There is no guarantee that the surviving materials accurately represent the popularity of the pamphlets at the time. For sixteenth-century broadside ballads, for example, Tessa Watt estimates around 3 million copies that were proliferated, of around 3,000 different titles, with today only 300 extant examples.[20] A broadside *may* have survived because its popularity demanded many copies, or it may have been rather obscure but piqued the interest of the collector who preserved

---

[15] Tyrel C. Eskelson, "States, Institutions, and Literacy Rates in Early-Modern Western Europe", *Journal of Education and Learning* 10.2 (2021): 110.

[16] A.W. Bates, *Emblematic Monsters: Unnatural Conceptions and Deformed Births in Early Modern Europe*, Clio Medica 77, The Wellcome Series in the History of Medicine (New York: Rodopi, 2005), 43.

[17] Tessa Watt, *Cheap Print and Popular Piety 1550-1640*, Cambridge Studies in Early Modern British History (New York: Cambridge University Press, 1991), 265.

[18] Eskelson, "Literacy Rates", 118.

[19] Watt, *Cheap Print*, 265. Emphasis added.

[20] Watt, 141.

it.[21] The low survival rate of these thousands of pamphlets, chapbooks, and broadsides needs to inform any conclusions drawn from these materials.

Even with that caveat, the early decades of the English Reformation saw an increasing popularity of monster rhetoric in popular literature like pamphlets and broadsides. In fact, "English monstrous births were perceived to be more plentiful in the 1550s and 1560s than they had been at any time earlier in the century".[22] Prior to 1550 within England, monstrous births were reported almost exclusively outside the United Kingdom. The sudden rise in these incidents (or, more likely, the sudden rise in noticing and reporting them) is likely due to the political turmoil at the time. The middle of the sixteenth century was characterized by the unrest that followed the 1534 Act of Supremacy: the act that made Henry VIII the Supreme Head of the Church of England and effectively severed the Church of England's ties to the Pope and the Church of Rome. Then, with the quick succession of three sovereigns in just eleven years, the church and country swung wildly from Protestant inclinations to Catholic ones—and back.[23]

Amidst the unrest, pamphlet authors interpreted "monstrous births" to offer insight into divine displeasure in one or the other of these changes. The surge in reports of these human monsters in England at the time showed, as Kathryn Brammall puts it, "that God had uttered a message intended specifically for the English, as opposed to the rest of Christendom".[24] In the face of disorder, pamphlet writers were capitalizing on the public's desire for insight. Clergy, in particular, made use of the monstrous to persuade their congregations and readers as a warning to abandon sin.[25] After all, if the infants' bodies constituted divine communication, then they demanded broad attention. What did God think of the wild theological and social swings that people were

---

[21] The scope of this inquiry does not permit a full incorporation of book studies' potential insight into this topic. One may see a connection, for example, between the pamphlets' disposable "bodies" and those of the children described in them. On the physical realities of printing at the time, see: Darnton, "'What Is the History of Books?' Revisited".

[22] Kathryn M. Brammall, "Monstrous Metamorphosis: Nature, Morality, and the Rhetoric of Monstrosity in Tudor England", *The Sixteenth Century Journal* 27.1 (Spring 1996): 8.

[23] Edward VI (1547–1553), Mary I (1553–1558), and Elizabeth I (1558–1603). I reluctantly adopt the terms "Protestant" and "Catholic" to distinguish between groups in the English Reformation. Although these terms were assigned later and are anachronistic, they are nevertheless a useful shorthand in this context.

[24] Brammall, "Monstrous Metamorphosis", 10.

[25] Davies notes that it is unclear whether the clergy truly believed the portents about which they wrote or were merely using them as convenient tools to manipulate their flocks. See: Davies, "The Unlucky, the Bad and the Ugly", 62.

witnessing? The answer could be found in a "correct" reading of the signs. This is physiognomy made manifest on a social level; the bodies of these infants conveyed information about God's will for an entire society's moral behaviour.

The correct interpretation of the appearance of a monstrous birth was, therefore, of profound importance. Brammall explains:

> God, having covenanted with Noah to preserve mankind after the Flood, preferred to reform rather than to destroy his misguided subjects. It was, therefore, imperative that his warnings, particularly those announced in England, be correctly interpreted. A great many authors of both learned and popular works took up the challenge.[26]

Figure 4.1. "The true descripcion of a Childe with Ruffes borne" (1566)
With permission of the British Library.

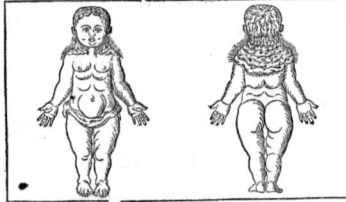

In the prints I examine below, the infants' bodies did not offer divine correction for *individual* sin. This is somewhat surprising. Usually, Julie Crawford explains, monstrous births would be "interpreted as the result of the

---

[26] Brammall, "Monstrous Metamorphosis", 12.

parents', particularly the mothers', sins".[27] However, in these examples, the births offer condemnation for entire communities or even nations.[28] Blame on the parents was peripheral. After all, "Daily observation would have shown that adulterers, fornicators, heretics and blasphemers did not give birth to monsters".[29] Therefore, the exhortations below addressed their *readers*, not the child or their parents. Through the infant's body, God delivered a discernible message for the whole society.

Case: Morality in a Child with Ruffs

To best examine the rhetoric of the "monstrous births" in this context, I offer two close readings as case studies. In the first, I turn to *The true Discripcion of a Childe with Ruffes borne* (*Child with Ruffs*, 1566).[30] This single-page print explains that Helene Jermin has given birth to a girl named Christina. The title stretches large across the top of the page, with an eye-catching woodcut print of Christina's body underneath. On the left is the image of her from the front: lying in a neutral position, her legs parallel, her hands open at her sides. Her eyes are open, and she is naked but for a piece of cloth draped under her belly to cover her groin. Her legs and belly display gentle rolls of fat. The remarkable thing about the image is the layers of skin folds extending from under her jawline to the edges of her shoulders. They have little lines extending off them, almost like a halo. Next to that image, on the right, appears the same depiction of Christina but from the back. Here, the skin folds begin at the base of her skull and cascade down her neck. The folds end draped across her back like, according to the broadside's author, a neckerchief.

According to the broadside, Christina's uncommon embodiment is not a mere curiosity at which readers can marvel. Two paragraphs of explanation extend beneath these images, telling the story of Christina's birth and describing her body—and its likeness to a popular fashion of the time: the ruff. Throughout this report, the broadside uses tender words to describe Christina: "the face

---

[27] Julie Crawford, *Marvelous Protestantism: Monstrous Births in Post-Reformation England* (Baltimore: Johns Hopkins University Press, 2005), 94. Such will be the case with the second case study below.

[28] Elizabeth Grosz, "Intolerable Ambiguity: Freaks as/at the Limit", in *The Monster Theory Reader*, ed. Jeffrey Andrew Weinstock (Minneapolis: University of Minnesota Press, 2020), 275.

[29] Bates, *Emblematic Monsters*, 50.

[30] H. B., *The True Discripfion of a Childe with Ruffes Borne in the Parifh of Michelham in the Cou[n]Tie of Surrey in the Yeere of Our Lord MDLXvi*, August 10, 1566, Imprinted at London by John Illde and Richarde Johnes, August 10, 1566, Early English Books Online, https://www.proquest.com/books/true-discripcion-childe-with-ruffes-borne-parish/d ocview/2240916267/se-2.

comely", "cheerful countenance", and "well apportioned in due form".[31] These words contrast with the stark prints of her naked body that lie above the description. In this pamphlet, Christina's body no longer belongs to her or her family; her monstrosity overrides any right to privacy and demands that she be available for public consumption.

Below the paragraphs, there is "An admonition unto the reader". In verse form, the admonition summarizes the meaning of Christina's birth. Crawford suggests that "the rhyming and scanning verse might have helped the less literate to follow the text".[32] The fifteen verses act as a warning and exhortation to all readers, an explanation of the omen that Christina's birth brings. The author, named only as H.B., describes Christina's body again, perfectly formed but for the many rolls of extra flesh growing around her neck, "much like unto the Ruffs that many do use to wear about their necks".[33] The final line beseeches: "God grant us grace how ever we go, for to repent with speed".[34]

This invective against the frilly ruffs worn on women's dresses is not unique to *Child with Ruffs*. Indeed, concern about women's fashion extended to the highest levels of church authority. A few years before Christina was born, the Church of England published an authorized Second Book of Homilies (1562–63), written primarily by Bishop John Jewel. These homilies, on the whole, take up practical questions, such as drunkenness, idleness, and almsgiving. The sermons in books like these were designed to be read to a congregation repeatedly as necessary. To settle the social and religious turmoil, Acts of Uniformity were passed to legally enforce attendance at worship and compliance with the Book of Common Prayer's order for worship.[35] So, when reading from books like this Second Book of Homilies, ministers could be sure their preaching, too, would be orthodox as long as they read aloud from these authorized books. Every person in the land would be sure to hear accurate and uniform church teaching on these important practical topics.

In this Second Book of Homilies, Jewel offers a sermon entitled "Homily Against Excess of Apparel". This homily, as its title promises, condemns the

---

[31] H. B.

[32] Bates, *Emblematic Monsters*, 43.

[33] H. B., *Childe with Ruffes*.

[34] H. B.

[35] The Acts of Uniformity standardized worship, administration of sacraments, and prayer in the Church of England. The first, "An Acte for the Uniformitie of Common Prayoure and Dyvyne Service in the Churche, and the Administration of the Sacramentes", was passed in 1558. The second, "An Act for the Uniformity of Publique Prayers and Administracion of Sacramentes & other Rites & Ceremonies and for establishing the Form of making ordaining and consecrating Bishops Priests and Deacons in the Church of England", was passed in 1662.

prideful fashions of the mid-sixteenth century and urges the listener to repent of this excess. Jewel writes of the dangers of pride for people who enjoyed dressing in overly elegant clothing. Those who "delight in gorgeous apparel are commonly puffed up with pride".[36] This fashion, for Jewel, proves not only the pride of the individual but also that of the country as a whole. In a delightful turn of phrase, he censures those who "hang their revenues about their necks, ruffling in their ruffs".[37] He does not directly refer to monstrosity herein, but other clerics and broadsides did employ that language when discussing sartorial excess.

Regarding so-called "fashion monsters", Surekha Davies writes that monstrosity need not be limited to an inborn characteristic; monstrosity "could be a(n im)moral choice".[38] Pride, Jewel urges in his Second Book of Homilies, is a sin to be avoided at all costs; pride puts the self in the place of God and, therefore, violates natural order. Jewel's widely distributed sermon makes it clear that ruffs and other overtly elegant clothing are dangers to avoid.

As *Child with Ruffs* is a microcosm of a larger conversation about secular fashion, so too is that conversation about secular fashion a microcosm of an ecclesiastical battle. In this case, that battlefield was: what should ministers wear when leading worship? This was no small question as the country and its church wrestled with its identity and how alike the Church of England should be to the Church in Rome. Would priests be required to wear Roman-style vestments, or were those a symbol of the institution the Church of England was rejecting? During this vestarian controversy, as it was called, Elizabeth I attempted to regulate secular apparel alongside religious apparel. Julie Crawford reports that in the 1560s, "Elizabeth published no fewer than seven proclamations on secular apparel, indicating that her concerns with 'decency and order' extended to all forms of dress".[39] Private fashion was a secular battlefield on which religious proclivities could be defended. At the highest levels, then, ruffs were not just a religious concern but a political one—a concern that would be taught to every English citizen (now legally required to attend worship) from the pulpits on Sunday mornings, thanks to resources like Jewel's book of homilies.

As a matching exhortation, *Child with Ruffs* enters this dispute just a few years after Jewel's homily was published for wide distribution and in the midst

---

[36] John Jewel, "Book 2, Homily 6: Homily Against Excess of Apparel", in Renaissance Electronic Texts 1.1, ed. Ian Lancashire, Short-Title Catalogue 13675, 1994, http://www.anglicanlibrary.org/homilies/bk2hom06.htm.

[37] Jewel.

[38] Davies, "The Unlucky, the Bad and the Ugly", 70.

[39] Crawford, *Marvelous Protestantism*, 36.

of Elizabeth's many proclamations. Christina Anne Furtado argues that *Child with Ruffs* was the first in "a trend in cheap print of censuring the fashion of ruffs as being 'monstrous' and 'deformed'"—a trend which continued through the late eighteenth century.[40] The broadside's influential admonition explains that Christina's body is a vehicle for God's condemnation of the decadent fashion of wearing ruffs. Several couplets from the admonition read:

Our filthy lives in Pigs are showed, our Pride this Child doth bear:
Our rags and Ruffs that are so lewd, behold her flesh and hear…

Pray we the Lord our hearts to turn, whilst we have time and space:
Lest that our souls in hell do burn, for voiding of his grace.

And ye O England whose womankind, in ruffs do walk too oft:
Persuade them still to bear in mind, this Child with ruffs so soft.[41]

H.B. understands the "monstrous birth" to be a portent, with the infant's body acting as a vehicle for divine pedagogy. They write that the child bears "*our Pride*"—this places the blame for Christina's ruffs squarely on the shoulders of the whole society, not just her parents, as might be expected.

The author exhorts the reader to "behold her flesh" since it is a means of God's communication. Garland-Thomson writes that the social act of *staring* is physiological, of course, but also pedagogical. "Stares are urgent efforts to make the unknown known, to render legible something that seems at first glance incomprehensible".[42] In this case, the natural urge to stare to tame the anomaly of Christina's body combines with the Christian cultural belief that uncommon embodiment is a sign of divine punishment. All this results in a broadside that exhorts the very deed of staring as (the start of) a moral act. The "monster" depicted on the page catches the audience's eye to share a divine message. Throughout the poem, the author moves from God to Christina to the reader; Christina's body is a mediating force between God and humanity.

It is worth noting that the author could have used Christina's body to endorse the fashion of ruffs rather than indict it.[43] For someone writing in support of the opposite opinion, the same child could conceivably be understood to be a

---

[40] Christina Anne Furtado, *Bloody, Strange, and Unnatural Women: Advertising on Early Modern English Title Pages, 1565-1640* (Ann Arbor: ProQuest Dissertations Publishing, 2014), 25, https://www.proquest.com/eebo/docview/1504639716/79BCAA50B6B24007 PQ/4?accountid=15172.

[41] H. B., *Childe with Ruffes*. I am indebted to Shana Maloney decoding one of these lines of Middle English print for me.

[42] Garland-Thomson, *Staring*, 15.

[43] Consider, for example, the cases of conjoined twins in India being honored as gifts from the divine when their bodies look like multi-limbed gods from Hinduism.

message from God *approving* the fashion of ruffs. After all, God created her with her natural "ruffs". However, rather than introducing new information into a cultural system, monsters act as mirrors for the hopes and anxieties that already exist within that culture.[44] In these snappy, singable verses, the admonition echoes a thoroughly orthodox Church of England suspicion of excess.

Figure 4.2. "Strange Newes of a prodigious Monster" (1613) STC 15428 Bd.w. STC 20863.5, image 017255, used with permission of the Folger Shakespeare Library

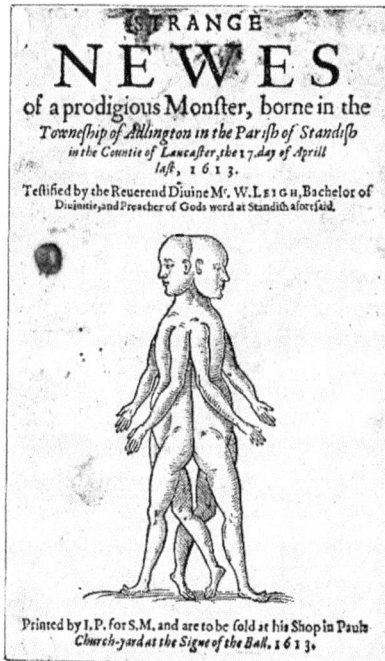

H.B.'s negative interpretation derives from the supposition that a body like Christina's must be a problem. This assumption reflects the origins of the word "monster" in the French verb *monere*, "to warn". *Monere* emphasizes God's wrath, while the Latin origin of the word *monstrare* emphasizes the showing forth of God's glory.[45] Christina is not simply "showing forth" a message from God. Instead, her body offers a warning because its differences are, to its interpreters, obviously negative. As uncommonly embodied as she was, Christina's body could not exist neutrally—or naturally; she bore a message from God, and individuals in her society needed to take heed.

---

[44] Timothy K. Beal, *Religion and Its Monsters* (New York: Routledge, 2002), 4.
[45] Sharpe, "Legal Monsters", 110.

Case: Theology in the Bodies of Conjoined Twins

My second case study is a close reading of *Strange newes of a prodigious Monster* (*Strange News*, 1613). This pamphlet offers an example of more intricate theological reasoning than that of *Child with Ruffs*. *Strange News* explains God's meaning conveyed in the birth of conjoined twins. As was often the case, *Strange News* treats its twins, unnamed and born in Adlington, as a single entity, referring to them only as "the monster".

But despite the author's clear condemnation of the girls' embodied forms, their depiction is not particularly disturbing. The woodcut print is a simple line drawing of the girls, whose bodies seem to be perfectly formed, except that their heads, necks, and shoulders are conjoined at the back. The image is somewhat clinical; like Christina, the Adlington twins are depicted naked, presumably so readers can fully appreciate their monstrosity. The image also seems to derive more from imagination than from accurate depiction.[46] After all, the girls were only three days old when they died, but the proportions of the figures in the image (e.g. length of limbs, body fat distribution, facial proportions) are those of an adult. Moreover, the girls are depicted standing on the ground, their legs evoking movement as if they are trying to walk in opposite directions. Their arms reach gently forward, their faces placid.

The chapbook reports that, at first, the public could not believe verbal reports of the girls' bodies. And because this "monster" was so important for the public to understand properly, the twins were later exhumed. The pamphlet reports five hundred people in attendance at the event, all of whom can attest to the "wonder and admiration" they felt at seeing their little bodies.[47] Indeed, this author goes to great lengths to prove to the reader that this account, though it seems wonderous, is true. The outside cover indicates that the "strange news" inside has been "testified by the Reverend Divine Mr. W. Leigh, Bachelor of Divinity, and Preacher of Gods (sic) word". For further veracity, the author includes details of the approximate date, the town, parish, and county, and the mention of many gentlemen and commoners who were present at the birth. "Not only did these lend credibility to the account, but they were also integral to the cultural meaning of the monster as a prodigy".[48]

---

[46] The question of whether the twins—or any of these reported monstrous births—actually existed is somewhat beside the point. "Most monsters exist by dint of being repeatedly described in words rather than by being sighted in the flesh" (Hanafi, *Monster in the Machine*, 6). The monster exists, whether or not the infants did, because of the accounts that shaped them into meaning.

[47] *Strange Newes of a Prodigious Monſter*, 9.

[48] Lorraine Daston and Katharine Park, *Wonders and the Order of Nature, 1150-1750* (New York: Zone Books, 1998), 182.

In order to know who was being warned, the readers needed to know where and when the warning appeared. The depiction of the girls takes up more than half the front cover, calling out for the attention of anyone who sees it.

In contrast to *Child with Ruffs*, *Strange News* seems to be intended for a more educated audience. The anonymous author expends no fewer than 2,500 words on the case, and the second sentence alone spans 164 words. In part, it reads: "The earth itself innocent of [humankind's] crime was accursed for his fate... and brought forth thorns, briars, and stinking weeds, where before it was full of pleasure, and delight, and so had continued, if man had continued in his first creation".[49] The "thorns and briars" pair evokes the biblical prophet, Isaiah. There, God speaks of the "pleasant vineyard" of the earth—and the wrath God promises against that vineyard when its beauty is marred: "If it gives me thorns and briers, I will march to battle against it. I will burn it up" (Isa. 27:4). *Strange News* is filled with such references for the educated: uncited biblical allusions, Latin sentences, and unexplained references to Roman gods. This is no singable ballad for the barely literate.

Still, *Strange News* is a work that helps blur perceived boundaries between "popular" and "elite" literature. On the one hand, this pamphlet uses the above references that indicate it expects a more educated audience. Sandra Clark notes that some pamphlets could have broad appeal, especially news and comics. *Child with Ruffs* is in this category, with its single page, the centrality and simplicity of Christina's depicted body, and its message conveyed in a simple rhyme. But other popular prints, like *Strange News*, were more sophisticated. These seem to "presuppose an audience capable of recognizing parody, burlesque... who appreciated, even if they could not necessarily understand, quotations in Latin and French".[50] Still, even the most sophisticated of these prints were accessible to the literate public. Tessa Watt writes that many people "would no doubt have picked up the news pamphlets as we do a paper: in addition to, rather than as a substitute for, more substantial reading matter".[51] Most likely, then, people from all backgrounds would have consumed all varieties of popular prints.

In the case of *Strange News*, the text luxuriates in its own sophistication. At one point, the author employs a sentence in Latin in their argument: "*Spuria vitulamina non agent radices altas*".[52] The sentence immediately following translates the line for the reader whose Latin is rusty: "Bastard slips shall

---

[49] *Strange Newes of a Prodigious Monfter*, 1.
[50] Sandra Clark, *The Elizabethan Pamphleteers: Popular Moralistic Pamphlets 1580-1640* (East Brunswick, N.J.: Fairleigh Dickinson Universty Press, 1985), 21.
[51] Watt, *Cheap Print*, 265.
[52] *Strange Newes of a Prodigious Monfter*, 7.

never take deep root". (This explains the author's theory that the birth likely proves, in addition to God's wrath, adultery or fornication on the part of the parents.) Why include the Latin if the author will immediately translate it? Presumably, the interpolation of Latin lends authority, or at least erudition, to the pamphlet. The reader does not need to understand Latin to be impressed by the pamphlet's use of it. The Latin line is also featured in the play *Edward IV*, which was popular in the early 1600s.[53] Such allusions—along with references to global political events, long sentences, and biblical allusions— may have cultivated a feeling of exclusivity for those who understood. And even for those who did not, the author perhaps hopes they will appreciate the sophistication and afford the pamphlet greater authority.

This pamphlet delves deeper into its analysis of the birth because of its comparative length (twelve pages) and the underlying education it assumes of its readers. The tract begins with a lengthy explanation of the results of original sin. It says, "So deep hath Man's iniquity descended, that it hath brought misshapen forms and devices out of hell".[54] That is, humanity's original sin not only caused our *souls* to be in peril; it destroyed the natural order of creation. Thus, we have only ourselves to blame for the presence of monsters in our midst. Natural forces, too, rebel against us. Air brings choking fumes and infectious clouds, while water destroys crops. Earth remains barren, and fire shows God's displeasure with us. Because of the fall of humanity, the pamphlet begs readers to understand creation is a dangerous place. "All that is above us, and all that is under our feet, have conspired to work our overthrow or to cause our amendment".[55] The writer sees deformity and destruction on all sides.

Therefore, the monsters are clear evidence of humanity's fallenness: if humanity had abided by God's rules in the Garden of Eden, creation would be orderly and blissful. And now, monsters prove that society has fallen even farther from God's good graces. The writer shows the particular problem of monstrosity as national rather than universal, insisting that no other country has had so many "monstrous births" with such grave meanings.[56] According to the author, England's sin problem is causing its monster problem.

The tract goes on to show how the correct interpretations of monsters in the recent past have been beneficial. The treatise expects that the readers should know about these other examples; it does not appear to be recounting them for the first time but rather reminding readers of information they already

---

[53] Thomas Heywood, *The First and Second Parts of King Edward IV*, ed. Barron Field (London: The Shakespeare Society, 1842). Act IV, Scene II.

[54] *Strange Newes of a Prodigious Monfter*, 3.

[55] *Strange Newes of a Prodigious Monfter*, 10.

[56] *Strange Newes of a Prodigious Monfter*, 3.

know. It reminds the reader, for example, that in 1588, "the Sea cast forth a horrid Monster of a strange shape and bigness" on the coast of Cornwall.[57] The Cornwall monster was God's warning to England that the Spanish Armada was planning a surprise invasion on those shores. This example—along with the others later given in the pamphlet—demonstrates for the reader the value of a sign rightly understood. It impresses upon them the urgency of these signs God is sending.

Not until the fifth page of twelve does the tract even mention the Adlington twins as "this Monster, we are now to write of".[58] Then, on the sixth page, the tract finally addresses the birth in its title. The author describes the conjoined twins thus:

> There was a child born of a strange and wonderful shape, with four legs four Arms, two bellies, proportionably joined to one back, one head two faces, like double faced Janus, the one before, the other behind, four eyes, and two noses.[59]

Interestingly, the Adlington twins' remarkable bodies are not read here in the same way as that of Christina Jermin's. That is, their bodies act as a general warning, but the specifics of their bodies are not addressed in *Strange News*. It seems that the perceived horror at the twins' bodies is so self-evidently a warning that the author hardly needs to mention them again.

It is perhaps no accident, though, that the omen catching the attention of this pamphlet was a set of conjoined twins. Interpretations of conjoined twins may have been the most commonly reported "monstrous births" in this period. They accounted "for a little over a third of the 249 printed and publicized accounts of human deformed births identified by A.W. Bates for the period 1500-1700".[60] The Adlington twins have two heads and two torsos, yet something about their identity is singular and shared. Elizabeth Grosz writes that conjoined twins raise the question of "a continuum of identities, ranging from the so-called normal, individuated singular object to a nonindividuated, collectivized multiple subject".[61] As the one holy, catholic, and apostolic church seemed to be splitting into Catholic and Protestant, Christians like this tract's author were distraught. Could two (opposing) Christian identities coexist,

---

[57] *Strange Newes of a Prodigious Monfter*, 3.

[58] *Strange Newes of a Prodigious Monfter*, 5.

[59] *Strange Newes of a Prodigious Monfter*, 6. Note that the child's "wonderful" shape is not a compliment but a comment on the wonder it evokes in the observer.

[60] Harriet Lyon, "The Fisherton Monster: Science, Providence, and Politics in Early Restoration England", *The Historical Journal* 60, no. 2 (2017): 336, https://doi.org/10.10 17/S0018246X16000212.

[61] Grosz, "Intolerable Ambiguity", 283.

especially within one country? The conjoined twins are simultaneously two and one. A conjoined twin "monster" "is the image of the kingdom and also of Christianity divided into two religious communities".[62] The pamphlet does not say this explicitly—as mentioned above, the portion about the twins themselves is relatively sparse—but conjoined twins make for a particularly useful object of consideration in this context.

Bates writes that after 1600, "monsters were no longer used as moralizing emblems in the popular literature", but this pamphlet appears to be an exception.[63] Instead, the whole treatise builds to the conclusion that, despite humanity's depravity, there is still hope in Jesus: "There is yet a means to be made for reconciliation, the firstborn of the great King of heaven and earth, goes between his father and us as a mediator to work our peace and atonement".[64] This pamphlet need not debase itself with the details of excessive rolls of skin; its purpose is to exhort the reader to repent of sin—both original and personal. It is a more subtle conclusion for an educated crowd.

Conclusion

Monsters tend to infringe upon the boundaries created by a society. In early modern culture, monsters broke down barriers between natural and supernatural, between biological and theological. The ephemeral texts that tried to make sense of "monstrous births" convey complex information about some attitudes of the time about the body, providence, and God's relationship with creation. Monsters draw attention because they give language to questions within a culture; they make invisible angst visible. The two "monstrous births" I have examined here allowed an *expression* of messy boundaries in a *time* of messy boundaries. As we have seen, further dichotomies such as elite vs popular and education vs entertainment also break down under the weight of "monstrous birth" rhetoric. These monsters may help readers loosen their grip on these polarizations, thereby creating a more nuanced understanding of history.

Chapbooks, pamphlets, and broadsides are often relegated to specialist inquiry, much like disability studies or monster theory. But they offer a perspective on ethics and theology that can enrich the insights we have gleaned

---

[62] Michel Foucault, *Abnormal: Lectures at the Collège de France 1974-1975*, ed. Valerio Marchetti and Antonella Salomoni, trans. Graham Burchell (London: Verso, 2003), 66.

[63] Bates, *Emblematic Monsters*, 52. Bates says the only accounts that remained after the seventeenth century were formulaic and did not include in-depth moralizing. In contrast to her conclusion, the opening sentence of *Strange News* exhibits sweeping moralization: "Man at the first losing of his Innocence, lost also his place, and contracted a heavy curse both to himself, and to his posterity" (p. 1).

[64] *Strange Newes of a Prodigious Monfter*, 11.

from theological tomes and the proclamations of sovereigns. Polarization "underestimates the ability of the culture to absorb new beliefs while retaining old ones, to forge hybrid forms, to accommodate contradictions and ambiguities".[65] When writing about a tempestuous historical period like the English Reformation, feeding into the narrative of polarization can be tempting. The forces of Protestantism indeed stood in opposition to those of what would later come to be called Roman Catholicism. However, individuals, institutions, and theologies are more complex. Dichotomies such as Protestant vs. Catholic or elite vs. common are oversimplifications that obfuscate the complexity of history.

The last time H.B. heard about the baby with her ruffs, Christina was ten weeks and four days old and "not unlikely to live long".[66] Her uncommon embodiment would not affect her health and longevity. Aside from the message her body carried for H.B. or their readers, Christina was just a little girl, born to farmers Helene and John Jermin in the summer of 1566. I wonder if the folds of skin on her neck, shoulders, and back remained as she grew, if the other children teased her for them. I wonder if she loved to read or to skip stones, if she had any siblings. Did she go to school? Did her "cheerful countenance" lift to hear the priest's voice bounce off the stone walls of the small church in her village? Once the sensationalism of her existence wore thin, I hope that her time as a "monster" faded and that she lived a thoroughly human life.

Society would do well to be mindful of how we construct difference into monstrosity. Humanity is more wonder-full and more complicated than the boxes we use to categorize each other. In the end, our monsters reveal little about them and a great deal about us.

Bibliography

Bates, A.W. *Emblematic Monsters: Unnatural Conceptions and Deformed Births in Early Modern Europe*. Clio Medica 77. The Wellcome Series in the History of Medicine. New York: Rodopi, 2005.

Beal, Timothy K. *Religion and Its Monsters*. New York: Routledge, 2002.

Brammall, Kathryn M. "Monstrous Metamorphosis: Nature, Morality, and the Rhetoric of Monstrosity in Tudor England". *The Sixteenth Century Journal* 27, no. 1: 3–21, 1996.

Clark, Sandra. *The Elizabethan Pamphleteers: Popular Moralistic Pamphlets 1580-1640*. East Brunswick, N.J.: Fairleigh Dickinson University Press, 1985.

Cohen, Jeffrey Jerome. "Monster Culture (Seven Theses)". In *Monster Theory: Reading Culture*, 3–25. Minneapolis: University of Minnesota Press, 1996.

---

[65] Watt, *Cheap Print*, 126.
[66] H. B., *Childe with Ruffes*.

Crawford, Julie. *Marvellous Protestantism: Monstrous Births in Post-Reformation England.* Baltimore: Johns Hopkins University Press, 2005.

Darnton, Robert. "'What Is the History of Books?' Revisited". *Modern Intellectual History* 4, no. 3 (2007): 495–508. https://doi.org/doi:10.1017/S147924430700 1370.

Daston, Lorraine, and Katharine Park. *Wonders and the Order of Nature, 1150-1750.* New York: Zone Books, 1998.

Davies, Surekha. "The Unlucky, the Bad and the Ugly: Categories of Monstrosity from the Renaissance to the Enlightenment". In *The Ashgate Research Companion to Monsters and the Monstrous*, edited by Asa Simon Mittman and Peter J. Dendle, 49–76. Ashgate Research Companion. Farnham, UK: Ashgate, 2012.

Eskelson, Tyrel C. "States, Institutions, and Literacy Rates in Early-Modern Western Europe". *Journal of Education and Learning* 10, no. 2 (2021): 109–23.

Foucault, Michel. *Abnormal: Lectures at the Collège de France 1974-1975.* Edited by Valerio Marchetti and Antonella Salomoni. Translated by Graham Burchell. London: Verso, 2003.

Furtado, Christina Anne. *Bloody, Strange, and Unnatural Women: Advertising on Early Modern English Title Pages, 1565-1640.* Ann Arbor: ProQuest Dissertations Publishing, 2014. https://www.proquest.com/eebo/docview/1504639716/79BCAA50B6B24007PQ/4?accountid=15172.

Garland-Thomson, Rosemarie. *Extraordinary Bodies: Figuring Physical Disability in American Culture and Literature.* New York: Columbia University Press, 1997.

———. *Staring: How We Look.* Oxford: Oxford University Press, 2009.

Grosz, Elizabeth. "Intolerable Ambiguity: Freaks as/at the Limit". In *The Monster Theory Reader*, edited by Jeffrey Andrew Weinstock, 272–85. Minneapolis: University of Minnesota Press, 2020.

H. B. *The True Discripfion of a Childe with Ruffes Borne in the Parifh of Michelham in the Cou[n]Tie of Surrey in the Yeere of Our Lord MDLXvi.* August 10, 1566. Imprinted in London by John Illde and Richarde Johnes. Early English Books Online. https://www.proquest.com/books/true-discripcion-childe-with-ruffes-borne-parish/docview/2240916267/se-2.

Hanafi, Zakiya. *The Monster in the Machine: Magic, Medicine, and the Marvelous in the Time of the Scientific Revolution.* Durham: Duke University Press, 2000.

Henning, Meghan. *Hell Hath No Fury: Gender, Disability, and the Invention of Damned Bodies in Early Christian Literature.* New Haven: Yale University Press, 2021.

Heywood, Thomas. *The First and Second Parts of King Edward IV.* Edited by Barron Field. London: The Shakespeare Society, 1842.

Jewel, John. "Book 2, Homily 6: Homily Against Excess of Apparel". In *Renaissance Electronic Texts 1.1*, edited by Ian Lancashire. Short-Title Catalogue 13675, 1994. http://www.anglicanlibrary.org/homilies/bk2hom06.htm.

Lyon, Harriet. "The Fisherton Monster: Science, Providence, and Politics in Early Restoration England". *The Historical Journal* 60, no. 2 (2017): 333–62. https://doi.org/10.1017/S0018246X16000212.

Schweik, Susan M. *The Ugly Laws: Disability in Public.* New York: New York University Press, 2009.

Sharpe, Andrew N. "England's Legal Monsters". *Law, Culture and the Humanities* 5 (2009): 100–130. https://doi.org/10.1177/1743872108096865.

Strange Newes of a Prodigious Monfter, Borne in the Townefhip of Adlington in the Parifh of Standifh in the Countie of Lancafter, the 17 Day of Aprill Last, 1613. Testified by the Reuerend Diuine Mr W. Leigh, Bachelor of Diuinitie, and Preacher of God's Word at Standifh Aforefaid. 1613. Printed by I.P. for S.M. Early English Books Online. https://www.proquest.com/book s/strange-newes-prodigious-monster-borne-towneship/docview/224 0897751/se-2.

Watt, Tessa. *Cheap Print and Popular Piety 1550-1640.* Cambridge Studies in Early Modern British History. New York: Cambridge University Press, 1991.

Chapter 5

The Serpent Dancer: Multiple Identities and Competing Rituals in Noh Play *Dōjōji*

Dunja Jelesijevic
Northern Arizona University

Abstract

The fifteenth-century play Dōjōji is one the best-known in Noh, a genre of medieval Japanese performance art. A tortured serpent demon, once a young girl enamored with and rejected by a Buddhist monk, returns to the site of the tragic outcome of her misguided infatuation – Dōjōji temple – amidst the preparations for dedication of the temple bell. Posing as a beautiful shirabyōshi dancer, she tricks the attending monks into allowing her near the bell, symbol of her attachment. She performs her dance, only to reveal her true form and is eventually driven away by the monks` prayer, disappearing into the river, with the final outcome of the priests` exorcist intervention unclear. The following essay analyzes Noh Dōjōji and its complex relationship with its source materials, a number of folk tales and Buddhist picture scrolls treating a traditional narrative known as the Kiyohime legend. Through examining the transformation of the original Kiyohime legend the essay places particular emphasis on how the play complicates the issues of gender and gender dynamics in the context of religion, ritual, and performance, thereby subverting the expected outcomes by nixing those already embedded within the legend.

The play transforms the Kiyohime legend in several significant ways. It recasts the original protagonist, a lustful widow, as a naive young girl; it replaces the carnal desire with an innocent infatuation prompted by a cruel joke played on the girl by the monk and her father; finally, and most importantly, contrary to the tradition which had already granted the protagonist's salvation, the play ignores this, and brings the demonic serpent back to the stage centuries later. Why does Noh create a more empathetic figure of its female protagonist and then proceeds to summarily deny her salvation? In what kind of dialogue with the tradition is Dōjōji, and what are the implications of this dialogue? What is the significance of the serpent's disguise as a woman, and the woman's appearance on the stage as a shirabyōshi? The answers to these questions, I suggest, lie in how the character of the play's protagonist is gradually constructed over time through meticulous layering of distinct but related identities, how these identities are contested and interrogated, and the ways in which these identities function together in the narrative as well as on the stage.

Uniting the religio-ritual frameworks of Buddhist and non-Buddhist traditions by navigating interaction between Buddhist concepts and non-Buddhist mythologies in a dialectical process, Dōjōji problematizes the efficacy of the salvific efforts ostensibly at the basis of the tradition, and offers up an alternative rooted in and born out of this interaction. Finally, the performative nature of the genre allows it to maximize the narrative potential of the Kiyohime legend, transforming it from a seemingly straightforward cautionary tale about the danger of carnal lust for Buddhist monks, into a complex and layered piece about suffering and salvation, transgressing boundaries, and overlapping religious frameworks. By circumventing the Buddhist androcentric perspective, Noh redirects the focus to the female instead, providing different or additional venues of interpretation.

Keywords: Dōjōji, Japanese Buddhism, Kiyohime Legend, Serpent Demon

* * *

Introduction

The play *Dōjōji*, a tale of a woman-turned-serpent demon who is doomed to reenact the murder of the travelling mountain ascetic who snubbed her, is one the best-known in Noh, a genre of medieval Japanese performance art. Through examining the complex relationship between the play and its source material, this essay analyzes *Dōjōji* and the ways in which it relates to its sources by looking at the character of the play's *shite*, the protagonist in Noh, as a culmination of the gradual process of meticulous layering of distinct but related identities over time and across genres. Utilizing the central symbol of the women-serpent, the play complicates issues of gender and gender dynamics in the context of religion, ritual, and performance, thereby subverting the expected outcomes by nixing those already embedded within the tradition.

Namely, unlike its narrative predecessors, *Dōjōji* ends neither in the triumph of the Buddhist enlightenment nor the ultimate punishment for the transgression of excessive desire and attachment. Rather, it concludes in an ambiguous, open-ended non-resolution, following two competing ritual acts where the serpent-woman emerges both as a ritualist and an object of ritual, respectively. In what kind of dialogue with the tradition is *Dōjōji*, and what are the ritual implications of this dialogue? What is the significance of the serpent's disguise as a woman and the woman's appearance on the stage as a *shirabyōshi*? The answer to these questions lies in the character of the *shite* and layers of her identities and the ways these identities function together in the narrative as well as on the stage.

My work on this essay follows in the footsteps of the trailblazing scholarship on women in Buddhism and Shinto, as well as women and premodern Japanese performance, by scholars such as Wakita Haruko, "Women in Medieval Japan" *Nihon Chūsei Joseishi No Kenkyū* (2006), and "Origins and Development of Female Performance Arts" *Josei Geinō No Genryū* (2001), Barbara Ruch-edited volume "Engendering Faith" (2002), Wakita-, Ueno Chizuko-, and Anne Bouchy-edited volume "Gender and Japanese History" (1999). In terms of women in Buddhism more broadly, I relied, among others, on the seminal studies by Diana Paul, "Women in Buddhism" (1985) investigating issues of women and enlightenment in Mahayana Buddhism, and Liz Wilson's "Charming Cadavers" (1996), focusing on the utilization of (visualizations of) disfigured and decaying female bodies in Theravada Buddhist practice, as a way for men to achieve enlightenment. For scholarship on women and gender in medieval *setsuwa* and other literary genres, I found helpful studies such as Tonomura Hitomi's "Black Hair and Red Trousers" (1994), Raechel Dumas' Historicizing Japan's Abject Femininity (2013), and Rajyashree Pandey's "Perfumed Sleeves and Tangled Hair" (2016). Finally, for Dōjōji-related narratives in particular, I found indispensable Virgina Skord's meticulous analysis of the narrative and visual dimension of *Dōjōji engi emaki* (1997), Susan Blakeley Klein's analysis of Noh renditions of the Dōjōji tale, in which she combines Freudian/Lacanian psychoanalysis with feminist theories to explore the misogynist acts of exclusion of women from enlightenment through symbolic representations (1995), and Monika Dix' work, inspired by Klein in her research, on gender and the body in serpent-centered medieval narratives (2009). In this essay, I want to combine the above-mentioned feminist approaches to Buddhist and Shinto studies with Jeffrey Jerome Cohen's monster theory, specifically placed in the premodern Japanese context of the interplay of religious traditions and gender dynamics underlying the construction of religious authority, in order to explore how the monstrous feminine is utilized as a symbolic expression of cultural anxieties as they relate to religion and religious authority in medieval Japan.

Dōjōji tradition and *Dōjōji* play combine two prominent religious motifs regarding the feminine serpent for Japan. One draws on non-Buddhist traditions, that of serpent deities as Chthonic goddesses, and the other concerns the Lotus Sutra and the possibility of enlightenment for women (and its ambiguity thereof). Addressing the conceptualizations of the monstrous feminine in Buddhism, Wilson speaks of the depiction of monstrous women who embody desire, the voracious cannibalistic ogresses and demons,[1] whereas Rebecca Copeland posits that Japanese myths and succeeding narratives have assessed the female body with mystery, anxiety, and yearning, and inscribed women inviting desire and fear with the mysterious and the uncontrollable. She further contends that "threatened by the potential of female strength to disrupt the patriarchal social order,... [mythmakers] rescripted female potency and consigned it to positions of abjection and debility".[2] Calling back to Karen Blecker's ground-breaking work on shamanism in Japan (1975), Copeland describes how Buddhism slowly went on to usurp female religious/ritual power by reframing it in terms of danger and pollution and had the Buddhist ascetic supplant the oracular and placative qualities of shamanic female practitioners. In this way, Noh presents a peculiar ritual model which is, moreover, rendered possible only and precisely due to the traditional Japanese religious, mythic, and performative contexts of the female sex, women's ritual authority, and both Buddhist and non-Buddhist contextualization of the figure of the serpent. Thus, uniting the religio-ritual frameworks of Buddhist and non-Buddhist traditions by navigating interaction between Buddhist concepts and non-Buddhist mythologies, *Dōjōji* problematizes the efficacy of the salvific efforts ostensibly at the basis of the tradition and provides a ritual alternative to the existing regimens.

Origins of *Dōjōji*: The Kiyohime Legend and Its Rebirths

Noh, as we know it today, was developed in the fourteenth century by Kan'ami and Zeami, a father-and-son pair of actors and playwrights. The theatre form was developed from a complex set of early ritual practices and folk performance traditions associated with them. These, in turn, were incubated in the context of Buddhist ideology and practice, introduced from the continent seven centuries earlier, and continuously embraced and developed by the upper echelons of Japanese society. In their storylines, Noh plays incorporate well-known narratives from Japanese and Chinese classics, folk tales, or historical events, often providing a "sequel" to the original story.

At first glance, *Dōjōji*, a fifteenth-century play of uncertain authorship,[3] appears as a tale of damning and dangerous attachment to earthly passions.

---

[1] Wilson, Liz, Charming Cadavers: Horrific Figurations of the Feminine in Indian Buddhist Hagiographic Literature Chicago, IL; London: University of Chicago Press, 1996.

[2] Rebecca Copeland "Mythical Bad Girls: The Corpse, the Crone, and the Snake", in Bad Girls of Japan, edited by Miller, Laura and Jan Bardsley (New York: Palgrave Macmillan, 200), 18-20

[3] In the most recent book-length study on the life and work of Kanze Kojiro Nobumitsu, Beng Choo Lim notes that, although having long been attributed to Nobumitsu (after an early history of association with Zeami and Kanami), *Dōjōji* is currently classified as

The play opens with preparations for the bell-dedication ceremony at Dōjōji temple, where no bell has been in place for centuries. In a mysterious tone, the abbot cautions servants in attendance to make sure no woman approaches the bell "for certain reasons [best known to him]" (*mata saru shisai aru aida*).[4] However, a *shirabyōshi*[5] dancer appears and manages to persuade the servants to allow her in under the pretence of having come to perform a dedication dance of her own. Midway through her enticing dance, she suddenly leaps into the bell, which then falls to the ground, blazing hot. Having learned what happened, the abbot is now compelled to shed some light on his initial warning. Long ago, he tells the servants, an innkeeper's young daughter became infatuated with a travelling ascetic who would take lodging at her father's inn when on regular pilgrimages to the Kumano shrine. On one of these occasions, the girl became quite insistent on having the acetic take her as his bride, so in an effort to dodge her advances, he promised to come back for her but took an alternative route on his return instead. Realizing she had been deceived by the ascetic, the girl transformed herself into a furious snake and gave chase. Eventually, she caught up with him at Dōjōji temple, and having found him hiding under the temple bell, she coiled herself around it, whereupon the bell was engulfed in flames, burning the unfortunate man to death. As the abbot concludes his story, the woman reappears from under the bell, now revealed as a serpent demon. The monks' ritual eventually drives her away, and she disappears into the river, with the final outcome of the abbot's exorcist intervention unclear.[6]

As can be seen even from this brief synopsis, the play weaves a number of enduring religious symbols into a complex interplay, outlining a peculiar ritual juxtaposition, with the *shite* acting first as a female performer-ritualist dancing for the bell dedication and then as the object of ritual exorcism following her transformation into a serpent-demon. In order to untangle both this tapestry of symbols and the ritual structure they create, a closer look at the play's source material is needed.

"author unknown". Lim, however, surmises that, given inconsistencies in the language, and 'fragmented narrative,' the play is likely to have been edited multiple times, with Nobumitsu likely being one of its editors. Beng Choo Lim, *Another Stage: Kanze Nobumitsu and the Late Muromachi Noh Theater.* (Ithaca, NY: Cornell Univ East Asia Program, 2012), 71

[4] *Dōjōji.* Sanari, *Yōyoku taikan*, p. 1792

[5] Type of medieval female performers, particularly known for performing their songs and dances dressed as men.

[6] In this essay I relied on versions of *Dōjōji* from Sanari Kentaro's *Yōyoku taikan* and Ito Masayoshi's *Yōyokushū*

Dōjōji's core narrative is based on the so-called Anchin/Kiyohime tradition, a series of tales with pronounced religious associations.[7] The Kiyohime story has been retold and refashioned over time in a number of narrative, performative, and visual media. The earliest recorded sources for the Kiyohime legend come from *setsuwa* collections, the eleventh-century *Dai nihon hokekyō genki* (Miraculous Tales of the *Lotus Sutra* from Japan; abbrev. *Hokke genki*), and the twelfth-century *Konjaku monogatari shū* (Tales of Times Now Past).[8] A somewhat later account, also in the *setsuwa* fashion, appears in the fourteenth-century Buddhist chronicle *Genkō shakushō* (Buddhist Writings of the *Genko* Era). The story was further popularized to wider audiences as the subject of *etoki* performances utilizing painted scrolls based on the tradition, the earliest of which was *Dōjōji engi emaki*, which served as a basis for the subsequent Noh renderings.[9] The Kiyohime legend was eventually transposed to the Noh stage in two different plays, an earlier version, *Kanemaki*, and *Dōjōji*.[10] Each of these renderings presents over time more or less subtle shifts in the emphasis and the objective of the tale, the narrative structure, and properties of the protagonists, slightly but increasingly complicating both the religious and the gender-related agendas of these varied "texts". Playing off and building on each other, the different variants, each drawing on their own unique generic properties, contributed to the process of the narrative and performative development that resulted in Noh *Dōjōji*

---

[7] This tradition is most often referred to as the Anchin/Kiyohime legend (see *Nihon kokugo daijiten, Nihon jinmei daijiten*). Anchin is the personal name of the monk, although the only source that cites his name as such is *Genkō Shakushō*; in other versions of the legend, including the play *Dōjōji*, the monk remains unnamed. The girl's moniker, *Kiyohime*, likely originates in *Dōjōji engi emaki*, where she is cast as the daughter-in-law of a local man named Kiyotsugu, although she is explicitly named as such only in the Jōruri, the early modern puppet theater tradition. In the remainder of this chapter, I will refer to the tradition as Kiyohime, both for the sake of convenience, but also because I feel that this choice highlights my own focus on the protagonist.

[8] Collections of folk tales cast as Buddhist anecdotes for the purpose of proselytizing.

[9] Etoki, meaning "picture explaining", is a practice related to Buddhist preaching and proselytizing by storytelling, with the aid of a painted scroll. The scroll is typically a visual representation of a Buddhist-themed narrative. In the case of specific temples, the practice would frequently be related to narrating the origins of the locale where the "explaining" is taking place, and the painted scroll would depict the founding legend of the temple. Ikumi Kaminishi, *Explaining Pictures: Buddhist Propaganda and Etoki Storytelling in Japan* (Honolulu: University of Hawaii Press, 2006), 5.

[10] The two plays are today considered as separate pieces, with *Kanemaki* being recently re-introduced into the regular repertory, but considering that much of the text of the two plays is identical or nearly identical, scholars such as Beng Choo Lim, and Susan Blakeley Klein have suggested that *Dōjōji* is a later revision of *Kanemaki* rather than a different play. Klein: 1995; Lim: 2012.

The literary incarnations of the Kiyohime legend grew out of the folk tradition and collective imagination woven into a Buddhist framework. The basic plot of both *setsuwa* and *emaki* versions follows a very similar three-part outline:

1) A young monk is on a pilgrimage to the Kumano shrine; at the place where he breaks his journey, he unwittingly entices a young woman (a widow) living there; in an effort to escape the woman's advances, he leaves with a false promise to come back for her.

2) Realizing that she has been duped, the woman catches up to the monk at Dōjōji temple; transformed into a serpent, she kills the monk by burning him under the temple bell.

3) Both the woman and the monk appear to one of the elder Dōjōji monks in a dream-like apparition, requesting that the Lotus Sutra be copied for their salvation; some days after the copying has been performed, they reappear to express their gratitude, each having been born into a separate Buddhist celestial realm.

The denouement of the shared plot thus reflects the fact that *setsuwa* and *emaki* authors were concerned with situating their narrative within the Lotus Sutra discourse of salvation and Buddhist enlightenment. Indeed, *Hokke genki* was devised specifically with the aim of propagating the Lotus Sutra faith. In contrast, the *Engi emaki* was produced for *etoki* performances, primarily with the intention to contribute to the temple's prosperity, and the Kiyohime legend was chosen as fitting that purpose. However, while the two clearly share key elements (a handsome young monk, a young woman/widow, a fearsome serpent, concealment under the bell, the Lotus Sutra memorial service), the subsequent version intervenes in the core narrative with how it combines and re-combines these elements, how it introduces or omits them. A closer look at these interventions conveys the intricacies of the mythmaking process that resulted in the Noh *Dōjōji*, and the shift in ritual and salvific concerns guiding the play.

When it comes to the characterization of the two protagonists, the distinctions between the *setsuwa* and *emaki* sources are subtle and restricted to seemingly minor details. Still, they are revealing when considering the choices later used by the Noh playwright. Below is a parallel comparison of the characterization of the two protagonists. The following citation is from *Hokke genki*:

> *Futari no shamon ari. Hitori wa toshi wakaku shite sono katachi tansei nari. Hitori wa toshioitari. Tomo ni kumano ni mairi, muro no gun ni itarite, ji no hotori no ie ni yadori shinu. Sono ie no aruji wa yamome nari.*

Two wandering monks were together on a pilgrimage to Kumano. One young and handsome, the other old. Arriving at the district of Muro, they stayed the night at the roadside inn. The inn was run by a widow.[11]

Konjaku and *Genkō* differ only in detail. The monk's name, Anchin, appears only in *Genkō*. In *Genkō*, the monk is from Kurama, while in others, without specifying, he is just a monk going on a pilgrimage to Kumano, accompanied by another elderly monk. In all sources, the monk is described as being young and good-looking, having a beautiful face, etc., whereas the woman is only described as a "widow". Considering that the story is told in a Buddhist framework that typically focuses on women being temptresses and drawing men away from the Path with their erotic allure, it is curious that the woman's appearance or attractiveness is not mentioned, while all sources insist on the monk being exceptionally attractive. The *setsuwa* stories (particularly in *Konjaku*) are highly erotically charged and profess a clear didactic objective to warn (men) against the dangers of (female) lust, desire, and attachment.

By the time the story is translated into the *Dōjōji engi emaki*, the monk has changed his place of origin and lost his travelling companion but retained his good looks. At the same time, the young woman has acquired a family (she is the daughter-in-law of a respectable household) rather than just living with a few servants, as was the case in the *setsuwa* versions:

> *Ōshū yori mime yoki sō no jōe kitaru ga kumano sankei suru arikeri. Kii no kuni Muro no gun manago to iu tokoro ni yado ari. Kono teishu, kiyotsugu no shoji to mōsu hito no yome nite, shitagau mono kazu arikeri.*

> From the province of Ōshū, a good-looking man wearing a monk's robe went on a pilgrimage to Kumano. In the district of Muro, province of Kii, he spent the night at a place called Manago. The master of the household, by the name of Kiyotsugu no Shōji, had a (widowed) daughter-in-law and many servants.[12]

This brings a sharper focus on the two who wouldn't be lovers, but it also recontextualizes the woman. She is still a widow but also a daughter, and not a lone woman in a solitary roadside inn, who almost evokes the image of a female demoness lurking in the dark and leading unsuspecting men astray to be consummated and consumed. She is fully socially integrated despite having lost her husband and is clearly a valued member of the household. This

---

[11] Inoue Mitsusada and Shosuke Osone eds., *Ōjōden, Hokke Genki* (Nihon Shisō Taikei 7. Tōkyō: Iwanami Shoten, 49), 217. All translations in this chapter are mine.

[12] Tosa Mitsumochi and Shigemi Komatsu, *Kuwanomidera Engi. Dōjōji Engi* (Zoku Nihon Emaki Taisei 13. Tōkyō: Chūō Kōronsha, 57), 63.

set-up diminishes the lust/desire-centred narrative and hints at something else which will come to full fruition in the play.

In Noh, the young woman is even younger and becomes the innocent daughter of the master of the household:

> Waki: *mukashi kono tokoro ni manago no shōji to iu mono ari. Kano mono ichi nin no sokujo wo motsu. Mata sono koro oku yori kumano he toshi mōde suru yamabushi no arishi ga, shōji ga moto wo shukubō to sadame, itsumo kano tokoro ni kitarinu.*

> Waki: Long ago, in this area, there was a man known as Shōji of Manago. He had an only daughter. At the time, there was a yamabushi who would go on pilgrimage to Kumano every year, and after he stayed at Shōji's place on one occasion, he kept coming back ever since. [13]

The yamabushi is young and, presumably, attractive, like the corresponding characters in the *setsuwa* and *engi*. The Noh libretto does not dwell on his physical appearance. Still, since the lore is well-established by the time the story is put on stage, that characteristic is an assumption that audiences would have brought to a performance. However, not emphasizing the yamabushi's physical attributes and highlighting, instead, a familiar, friendly figure who had been a part of the young woman's life for years provides a new perspective on the established storyline where her gruesome revenge is motivated by sheer lust and anger. The young woman's affection is wholly innocent, and the visits are justified and sanctioned by homosocial bonds (namely, the friendship between the monk and the father).

Examining this narrative shift in *Dōjōji engi emaki* and the way it is treated visually, Virginia Skord Waters notes that positioning the protagonists in the paintings in a certain way and providing additional conventional visual clues, the elements otherwise absent from the written text come to the fore and refigure the familiar narrative, adding to it a new layer of meaning:

> [...] the illustrations of the meeting and interaction reflect contemporaneous conventions of presenting a lyric idyll of two lovers, with the effect of rendering the monk far more perfidious. Rather than a last resort of extreme desperation, his promise to return becomes a premeditated evasion following a casual dalliance. His fate, then, is as much a consequence of the woman's justifiable anger at his deception as of her frustrated sexual desire. This readjustment in culpability has important ramifications for the Dōjōji narrative of the Engi, for

---

[13] *Dōjōji*, Sanari ed., *Yōyoku taikan*, (1799). The waki's monologue narrating the events is identical to *Kanemaki*.

audience reception of the remainder of the tale will be significantly affected by rendering the woman as a far more sympathetic character.[14]

The young woman's sense of betrayal is, therefore, all the more understandable in *Dōjōji*, where the backstory establishes that the two had met long before. At the same time, she was an innocent child and when her father would continuously tease her about surely becoming the yamabushi's bride one day, to which the yamabushi jokingly acquiesced. The girl kept waiting, but once the young man realized she had taken the prospect seriously, he lied his way out of the situation, leaving her in grief at what she understood to be a broken promise. Once we look at the story from the perspective of the young woman's experience, it is clear that in the Noh play, the woman's motivation and the resultant demonic transformation significantly diverge from the *setsuwa* tradition.

Hokke genki, *Konjaku*, and *Genkō* all present a frightening depiction of the woman's anger made manifest as she dies of anguish and emerges from her bedchamber in the form of a giant serpent. *Engi* and *Dōjōji* change this part of the narrative, as they present the transformation in real-time and have it take place at the Hidaka riverbank, where the moment of metamorphosis is no longer concealed. This choice on the part of the storytellers is, undoubtedly, due in part to the fact that being visual and performative genres, *etoki* and Noh can capitalize on the striking imagery depicting the moment of transformation. This is particularly true for Noh, where the moment of transformation can be exploited to the maximum, both in the sense of the theatricality of the performance as well as the meaning and significance of this transformation within the ritual context of Noh.

Therefore, by circumventing the *setsuwa*'s Buddhist androcentric perspective, the *Engi* and the Noh redirect focus to the female instead, providing different or additional venues of interpretation. These need not exclude the already existing interpretations. Still, from both a literary and a religious point of view, they provide a more nuanced reading of the narrative, as well as the performative and religio-ritual structure. Pointing out the significance of the interplay of versions of the story, Waters notes:

> [...] The requirements of the setsuwa genre allow relatively little interpretive play to setsuwa versions of the Dōjōji legend [...] Recast into the format of an illustrated scroll (*emaki*), however, the Dōjōji legend emerges as an independent work in its own right, with a new dynamism and fascinating ambivalence.[15]

---

[14] Virginia Skord Waters "Sex, Lies, and the Illustrated Scroll: The Dojoji Engi Emaki", in *Monumenta Nipponica* 52.1 (1997), 66.

[15] Waters, "Illustrated Scroll", 60.

The transformative power of the generic switch extends especially to the theatre, expanding further the potentiality of "dynamism" and "ambivalence", considering the performative implications of the Noh text (or layers of "texts"). Noh and *etoki* are both performance arts and, as such, possess a religio-ritual dimension different from that of a narrative text such as *setsuwa*. The Noh play is able to benefit from polyvalence in its dramatic expression, which is verbal, graphic, corporeal, and musical. The "theatricality" of the genre allows it to maximize the narrative potential of the Kiyohime legend, transforming it from a seemingly straightforward cautionary tale about carnal lust into a complex and layered piece about suffering and salvation, transgressing boundaries, overlapping religious frameworks and contested religious/ritual authority.

The Noh *Dōjōji*, clearly builds on the legend in several significant ways. The most striking innovation, however, lies not in what is added or changed but rather in the complete omission of one major part of the Kiyohime tale. From the narrative standpoint, *Dōjōji* is a sequel of sorts, and the original story is integrated within in the form of a rumour. A curious element of this "sequel" is that the woman who is ostensibly saved in all versions of the Kiyohime legend now returns. This idea of the return of a well-known character from literature or folklore to the stage is typical in Noh. However, what is interesting about *Dōjōji* is that the tradition had already determined the successful outcome for the protagonist's salvation. In contrast, the play ignores this, thereby turning the entire project of the narrative and performative tradition on its head. To help understand this point better, we need to look at the network of religious meanings and interpretations of the serpent and the dancer, which eventually converge in the play.

Religious Implications of the Serpent Motif

As a religious symbol, the serpent is an ambiguous entity prominent in both the Buddhist tradition and non-Buddhist mythology. Medieval Japanese epistemology assumes a significant position in the Buddhist/Shinto discourse.[16] Discursive development of the serpent motif in the folkloric tradition, myth, Buddhist reinterpretation of the folklore (such as *setsuwa*), and Buddhist literature establishes the serpent as a powerful locus for negotiating aspects of the interacting religious traditions. The malleability of the serpent and its varied, sometimes contradictory qualities allow for it to be the perfect metaphor for this interaction. Discussing the symbolism of the serpent in Japanese

---

[16] One of the most prominent examples would be a hybrid *shinbutsu* cult of Benzaiten and Ugajin; for a detailed discussion of the development of this cult refer to Faure, *Protectors and Predators*, 163-295.

religion and myth, Michael Kelsey suggests that "we can find in these stories the first conflict between Buddhism and Shinto, and then, as the relationships between the two settle down, a creative Buddhist use of those ancient Shinto deities that appeared as reptiles".[17]

The serpent starts as a potent mythical creature, is slowly coopted within the Buddhist episteme, and becomes a protector of the Buddhist law. The process culminates in a "mythos-Buddist" hybrid, and finally, the serpent is the bringer of salvation.[18] Kelsey cautions that, while a general hostility to mortals characterizes the mythical snake, it should not be considered an "evil" deity, "since the reptilian form is only one of the manifestations of the water or thunder deity, a complex creature with both desirable and undesirable personality traits".[19] Nomura Shin'ichi recalls the existence of an old tradition of revering serpents, both in Japan and on the continent. In early Chthonic traditions, the serpent did not have a negative connotation *per se*. Still, it maintained a close relationship with the life of the community and was believed to bring prosperity and good luck.[20]

The *Kiyohime* tradition clearly draws on beliefs in the darker and more violent aspects of the serpent. It also associates these aspects with the feminine and, as such, fits within a rich tradition of *setsuwa* and folk beliefs associating female sexuality and snakes.[21] The *setsuwa* tradition is also responsible for drawing out and framing the mythical serpent (with all its religious, sexual, and other ambivalences) within the Buddhist context, with which *Hokke genki* is particularly credited.[22] This is undoubtedly due to the strong associations between the salvation of serpents and the Lotus Sutra. After all, one of the best-known chapters from the Sutra, and often referenced in Japanese classical literature, is the Devadatta chapter (*Daibadattahon*), which contains the story

---

[17] Michael Kelsey "Salvation of the Snake, the Snake of Salvation: Buddhist-Shinto Conflict and Resolution", in *Japanese Journal of Religious Studies* 8.1/2 (1981), 83.

[18] Ibid., 84.

[19] Ibid., 85.

[20] Nomura Shinichi "Higashi shina kai: hebisei no genshō", in *Keiō gijuku daigaku geibun gakkai*. Geibun kenkyū 77 (1990), 1-5

[21] Folk tradition and beliefs both in Japan and on the continent treated the serpent as the representations of fertility, water, and chtonic forces, and associated those representations with the feminine. This tendency continued when the folk traditions were couched in the Buddhist framework to help proselytize in the form of the setsuwa. As a result, the serpent retained strong association with female sex and female sexuality well into the medieval period and beyond. Shin'ichi 1990: 1-5; Li 2009; Dumas 2013: 270-2; Naito 2014: 95-105.

[22] Dykstra, Yoshiko K "Miraculous Tales of the Lotus Sutra. The Dainihonkoku Hokkegenki", in *Monumenta Nipponica* 32.2 (1977), 1-9.

of the enlightenment of the Naga king's daughter (*Ryūnyo Jōbutsu*).[23] In this famous Buddhist tale, hearing Mañjuśrī tell the story of how the eight-year-old daughter of the Naga King achieved enlightenment in an instant with the help of the Lotus Sutra, Śāriputra challenges the report, as women, being subject to "five obstructions" (inability to become Brahma, Shakra, Mara (a devil king), Chakravartin (a wheel-turning king), and *Buddha*) cannot achieve enlightenment. Mañjuśrī explains how the girl transformed into a man and swiftly perfected bodhisattva practices, transported herself to a spot beneath a bodhi tree and achieved enlightenment.

However, even with this in mind, serpents as such are not necessarily slated to be enlightened given that they are part of the bestial realm – one of the three "lower courses" of rebirth – and this can be inferred even from Lotus Sutra itself; namely, the Naga King's daughter reaches enlightenment only after being transformed into a (human) man, which can be interpreted that she achieved enlightenment *despite* being both a woman and a naga/snake, something Bernard Faure termed "inclusive exclusion".[24] In the sutra, women's inability to achieve enlightenment was ideologically rooted in the doctrine of the "five obstructions" (*goshō/itsutsu no sawari*) corresponding to the five categories of existence they were not able to attain. In Japan, however, this concept acquired an additional dimension. As Yoshida Kazuhiko explains, "The five obstructions came to mean all the transgressions, passions, wrongdoing, or (negative) karma that are inherent to women in particular". [25] This "semantic drift",[26] as Monika Dix puts it, transformed the idea of a barrier preventing women from achieving categories of being external to them to the idea of an insurmountable obstacle due to a characteristic inherent in them.

Moreover, an additional sixth meaning of *sawari*, "menstruation", was added, also reflecting the association with women's intrinsic nature and the concept of female pollution.[27] This notion is particularly significant in theorizing women's (in)ability to become enlightened. In the case of the *Dōjōji* woman, enlightenment seems, at first glance at least, to be precisely what is at stake as

---

[23] Nagas (or Nāgas) are mythical half-human, half-serpentine creatures, present in the traditions of South and Southeast Asia, and incorporated into the Hindu, Buddhist, and Jain mythology.

[24] Bernard Faure, *The Power of Denial: Buddhism, Purity, and Gender* (Buddhisms. Princeton, N.J: Princeton University Press, 2003), 1.

[25] Yoshida Kazuhiko "The Enlightenment of the Dragon King's Daughter in The Lotus Sutra", in *Engendering Faith: Women and Buddhism in Premodern Japan*, edited by Barbara Ruch (Michigan Monograph Series in Japanese Studies, no. 43. Ann Arbor, Mich: Center for Japanese Studies, University of Michigan, 2002), 310

[26] Bryan S Turner and Zheng Yangwen, eds., *The Body in Asia* (Berghahn Books, 2009), 49.

[27] Yoshida, "Enlightenment", 310.

she is doubly condemned, being both ideologically marked as lacking and ritually marked as impure.

In sum, the serpent is, on the one hand, a figure belonging to pan-Asian mythology and Japanese kami worship tradition, and on the other, a prominent figure in Buddhism and a significant part of the *shinbutsu* (Shinto/Buddhist) hybrid cults. The perceived role of the snake, however, changes and transforms as a result of interaction between traditions, especially in the context of Shinto/Buddhist combinatory processes. It is this quality of the serpent that makes it both malleable and resistant enough to endure the generic transformations of the Kiyohime tradition. As the story was reshaped from one telling to the next, the serpent protagonist could draw on a large repository of symbolic, narrative, and religious content attached to her serpentine character to follow up on, respond to, or completely reverse the expectations of the tradition. In the case of Noh, the serpent maiden returns to what the tradition determined to be the site of her transgression and her salvation, having shed parts of the tradition like old skin, interrogating and reevaluating a conclusion that had already been made. Those precise qualities of the snake, the ambiguity and malleability, the simultaneous potential for great good and great evil, are what made it fit for manifestation on the Noh stage in this particular character. The serpent's shape emerges in the play as the vestige of the promise of enlightenment, however, burdened by the patent misogynist requirement to transform into a man, but also as a spectre and an embodiment of the suppressed female-dominated ritual and spiritual authority. This is further fortified by casting the ghost of the serpent woman or her reborn self as the *shirabyōshi*, a gender-bending erotic performer.

The Ritualist Snake – Shirabyōshi

The first thing we learn about the *shite* in the first act is that she is a *shirabyōshi* and that she wishes to perform a dedication ceremony for the temple bell to ameliorate karma incurred by an unnamed sin. This reminds the audience of a few traits typically attributed to female entertainers: firstly, that "sin" (*tsumi*) or transgression (especially its sexual aspect due to the Buddhological view of women as temptresses) is frequently associated with their profession, and secondly, that female performers can act as ritualists. In the above discussion, we saw how, on the symbolic level, the serpentine aspect of the character of the shite is multifaceted and polysemic, with multiple overlapping layers. This also resonates with her aspect as a performer.

The layer of the *shite*'s character in *Dōjōji* pertaining to her identity as a performer is, to a large extent, reflective of the views of women in medieval Japan, particularly those who made a living as entertainers or performers. The woman introduces herself as a performer, declares that she came specifically to perform a ritual, and during her ritual dance, she enchants the men in attendance; it seems that it is both her erotic allure *and* her mesmerizing ritual power that enchanted the monk attendants and granted her way to the bell. Indeed, medieval female performers have had the perceived characteristics of their profession (performance), their bodies (their female sexuality), and their origins as ritualists conflated in the literary and artistic representations and understanding of their persons, with serious ramifications.

Examining this issue, Michele Marra established the concept which he termed the "shamaness/courtesan /bodhisattva" paradigm,[28] which united these distinct female identities and treated them as different aspects of a singular imagined female identity. This paradigmatic woman was constructed by piecing together characteristics of different groups of women who existed and made their living in the real world largely on the margin. Among these women were various types of sex workers – "courtesans" – as well as various types of female performers, and the two sometimes overlapped. Furthermore, female performers earned an association with religious performance both due to their dancing, which recalled female shrine ritualists, as well as their songs, which recalled the female shrine oracles. Finally, these activities were reframed within the Buddhist eschatological schema:

> Buddhist thinkers assimilated the courtesan's performing act into their dialectic of skilful devices (hōben), interpreting the woman's locutions as an expression aimed at the realization of the supreme truth. The doctrine justified the courtesan's song as an expedient provided by the Buddha for the enlightenment of common people [...] The transformation of the courtesan's song into a medium for enlightenment was the Buddhist version of a more ancient religious practice in which female priests were believed to lend their voices to a deity to convey sacred messages to the common people who were unable to communicate with the god.[29]

Marra argued that the ritualistic origins of female performers were combined with Buddhist discourse to portray entertainers as vehicles of salvation. In the context of Buddhist doctrines such as expedient devices and "passions equal to enlightenment" (*bonnō soku bodai*), this role was exercised in such a way that transgressive actions (such as sexual enticement) could and would be interpreted as paths to enlightenment.

---

[28] Michele Marra "The Buddhist Mythmaking of Defilement: Sacred Courtesans in Medieval Japan", in *The Journal of Asian Studies* 52.1 (1993), 55.
[29] Ibid., 54.

In her inquiry into the workings of various modes of sex trade in medieval Japan, Janet Goodwin has largely debunked the long-standing and popular assumption of equating sexual activity with religious service and thinking of shamanesses' activities in sexual terms.[30] While Marra's paradigm does operate within these repudiated assumptions, his model is nevertheless helpful in illuminating a representation of intertwining concepts of female sexuality and religious activity, both Buddhist and kami-related. Namely, while female ritual activity may not have necessarily included sex, and while not all female performers engaged in sex or ritual, the imaginary construct that conflated female performance, sex, ritual activity, and spiritual authority was absolutely present in the medieval discourse, which Goodwin herself acknowledges:

> Overlapping these three dimensions of the woman's being is coopted within the Buddhist context to simultaneously condemn the female as defiled and an impediment to enlightenment, and an intruder from the margin into the normative, and on the other hand, vest her with power to aid the exact opposite – be a mouthpiece for the sacred, ritually handle it, and ultimately facilitate achievement of enlightenment.[31]

As the discourse of female religious authority was intrinsically connected with the discourse of her transgressive nature, in the medieval period, female performers experienced a great decline in status, the most consistent disapproval coming from the Buddhist clergy, who especially denigrate female entertainers, referring to them as "base women" (*bonbi no onna*).[32] Being religious ritualists did not help women achieve a more elevated status; at best, their status was ambiguous:

> In the thirteenth and fourteenth centuries, miracle tales, saints' hagiographies, and noh plays portrayed asobi specifically as prostitutes. They presented them as obstructions to the religious practice of both monks and laymen [...] When Asobi became a Buddhist instructor, this transgression was turned on its head. Female sexuality was first used as a tool to win men's attention, then devalorized as the women themselves were transformed from seducers into agents of salvation.[33]

In the above quote, Goodwin focuses her argument on performers known as *asobi*. Still, the same principle applies to *shirabyōshi*, who also frequently

---

[30] Janet R. Goodwin, *Selling Songs and Smiles* (Honolulu: University of Hawaii Press, 2006), 85-119.

[31] Janet R. Goodwin "Shadows of Transgression: Heian and Kamakura Constructions of Prostitution", in *Monumenta Nipponica* 55.3 (2000), 327–68.

[32] Ibid., 348.

[33] Ibid., 355

appear in *setsuwa*, Noh, and other medieval literary genres. Therefore, the entertainers were viewed as a threat to salvation due to their association with sex (even if this was an imaginary perception propelled by medieval Buddhist literature). Still, the same association found them celebrated as guides to enlightenment. Marra explains how the complexity and the allure of this concept made performers' favourite topic of medieval Noh:

> The paradigm of the shamaness/courtesan/bodhisattva became a common topic in one strain of anecdotal literature of the Japanese Middle Ages that asked the courtesan to play the role of spokeswoman for the Buddha. Kan'ami combines the threads developed by Buddhist mythographers in a theatrical unity that perfectly answers the Buddhist need for an exorcising performance in which the threat of defilement is domesticated and assimilated into the structure of the sacred.[34]

As an example of this, Marra cites the play *Eguchi*. A priest on a pilgrimage disembarks at the village of Eguchi. Seeing a gravesite, he learns a courtesan, known as the Lady of Eguchi, was buried there. She has a reputation for being a poet and a manifestation of the Bodhisattva Fugen. She was known for once denying overnight lodging to the monk and poet Saigyō (1118 – 1190) so as not to allow him to be corrupted by dwelling in her home. As the priest recalls Saigyo's poem, a mysterious woman appears and recites the reply. In the course of their conversation, it is revealed that she is the ghost of Lady Eguchi, and she vanishes. In the interlude, a local villager narrates a story of the lady's encounter with another famous monk, Shōkū (910 – 1007), a devotee of Bodhisattva Fugen who was instructed in a dream to visit the courtesan, Lady Eguchi. As he looked at her, he saw her in the earthly form of a beautiful woman; when he closed his eyes, he saw her as Fugen. The second act brings the Lady back to the stage aboard a boat floating in the moonlight, reenacting a scene entertaining a customer. In her monologue, she reveals a deep understanding of the Buddhist Truth, and with that, the play concludes.[35] Lady Eguchi, therefore, is a being of transgression, but that very feature vests her with the contrasting but corresponding role of the teacher of the Buddhist Law and an aide to achieving enlightenment.

Marra's paradigm cannot be applied as straightforwardly in *Dōjōji* as in *Eguchi*, but the ritualist *shite* still draws on these schematic elements. Whereas the character of Lady Eguchi neatly reflects the entirety of the paradigm as envisaged by Marra, Kiyohime may need to rely on disparate elements of her characterizations over time. The eroticism and sexual

---

[34] Mara, "Mythmaking", 58.
[35] *Eguchi*. Sanari, ed. *Yōyoku taikan*, 471-487.

attraction implied draw on the erotic imagination attached to the *shirabyōshi,* fortified with the early incarnations of Kiyohime that depict her as someone who potentially offers sex as entertainment (as the inn proprietor) and is at the very least familiar with the ways of male/female intimacy (being a widow). The more recent Kyohime, on the other hand, is an innocent peasant girl, reducing the sexual component and amplifying the salvific one. These elements then all converge in her Noh stage incarnation as a *shirabyōshi.* As such representation, the *Dōjōji* woman demonstrates how all the disparate identities are a part of the paradigm, as she assumes all these ambiguous roles. Finally, the serpent mythology is introduced into this context in an astonishing move that places the serpent into the position of a ritualist (along with being the object of ritual). The formulation of her character as the Noh *Dōjōji* ritualist, therefore, is extraordinarily complex, with each of these separate identities carrying complexities all of their own.

Competing Rituals: Subject/Object Dichotomy

There are two major rituals taking place in *Dōjōji*: the *ranbyōshi*[36] cum *kaneiri* (bell-entering) in the first act and the Buddhist exorcism ritual in the second. As noted earlier, the very first appearance of the *Dōjōji* woman already betrays that she is somehow different or extraordinary. She alerts the audience that a specific sin burdens her, and there is a feverish urgency of an "impatient heart" (*isogi kokoro*)[37] in her efforts to arrive at the temple. Shite proceeds to introduce herself as a *shirabyōshi,* and announces herself as a ritualist:

> *Kore ha kono kuni no katawara ni sumu shirabyōshi nite sōrō. Kane no kuyō ni soto mai wo mai sōrō beshi. Kuyo wo ogamasete tamawari sōrō he.*[38]

> I am a shirabyōshi living in the vicinity of this province. I intend to perform a dance at the bell dedication ceremony. Please allow me to pay my obeisance at the ceremony.

Following brief hesitation, the temple servant relents, as he concludes aloud that she is "not an ordinary woman" (*tada no nyonin to ha chigai*).[39] Indeed, as the audience is about to learn, she is not; there is more to her than meets the eye. Her insistence on arriving in a hurry and her impatience to attend the ceremony betray a restless heart and disturbed spirit. On the surface, the

---

[36] "Disordered rhythm"; an action piece with flexible rhythms controlled by the drummer watching the movements of the dancer. Brazell 1999: 42.
[37] *Dōjōji.* Sanari, ed. *Yōyoku taikan,* 1793.
[38] Ibid.
[39] Ibid, 1794.

woman seems anxious to reap the karmic benefits of attending a grand ceremony, such as the consecration of the temple bell. However, having tricked her way near the bell, it becomes clear that this bell is of particular significance to the woman. With this, the *shite* moves into her first ritual, the r*anbyōshi*.

Dōjōji's Ranbyōshi is a famous scene in which the *shite* dances in a serpent-like style corresponding to each sound of the drum, which is hit vigorously as if to show the violent pounding of her heart. To represent the costume of actual *shirabyōshi*, who performed dressed as men, the *shite* puts on a courtier's cap and begins the dance, starting to slowly stomp her feet, moving towards the bell as if climbing.[40] Initially, the *shite* performs the usual dedication dance, recalling the origins of the temple, stomping feet at increasing speed, culminating in a rapid dance (*kyū no mai*). She then starts moving closer to the bell, which is also where her mood begins to shift, and her emotion towards the bell irrupts as she exclaims, "Oh how I remember this hateful bell!" (*omeba kane urameshiya tote*).[41] What ensues is, arguably, the most "theatrical" moment in Noh performative tradition – the shite leaps into the falling bell, completely disappearing inside it before the bell touches the ground. This concludes the first act, and during the interlude, the Abbot narrates the story of the Kiyohime, revealing her identity and connection to the bell. His recount is confirmed when the bell is lifted, and the *shite* reemerges in the form of the furious demonic serpent.

How is the *shite* as the ritualist positioned within this performance? The scene in which she leaps into the great bell on the surface seems like a desperate action, and it could be said that the *shite*'s vigorous dance hints at her true identity as a serpent demon as she expresses her pent-up agony, sadness, and fury. However, the *shite* is both a *shirabyōshi*, and the serpent-demon. Both these identities, as discussed above, carry their own set of ambivalences: *shirabyōshi* as a type of female entertainer with an ambiguous ritual function, and the serpent as a deity that traditionally carries both negative and auspicious connotations, in either case requiring ritual handling. Furthermore, taking these two identities into account, the shite is either a shape-shifting serpent demon or a religious ritualist possessed by one; in other words, she could either be a demon pretending to be a *shirabyōshi*, or a *shirabyōshi* transformed into a demon by way of possession, meaning that either of these identities can be "true" or "false" (or both).

In her psycho-analytic reading of the play, which focuses on phallic symbolism, Susan Blakeley Klein suggests that it may be that the woman, on

---

[40] This particular "climbing" movement is a specific feature of the *Dōjōji's ranbyōshi*. Fukuzawa 2012: 263-270.

[41] *Dōjōji*. Sanari, ed. *Yōyoku taikan*, 1796.

some level, represents the monk himself,[42] and this would be nothing new in Noh. In fact, continuous spiralling gender inversions - a man "performing" a woman "performing" a man - are seen elsewhere in plays.[43] Even the pre-serpentine form of the shite, the *shirabyōshi*, carries similar gender ambivalence, as these types of performers were famous for performing in male attire, sometimes carrying swords. If we add to this the Buddhist concepts of non-dualism, prominent in medieval Japan, and the strong karmic bond between the original couple, the shite emerges as a yet new complex identity, with the male, female, and serpentine meshed together. Furthermore, suppose we observe the trajectory of the transformation in Dōjōji. In that case, we can note that *Dōjōji* transformation works like the transformation of the Dragon Princess in the Lotus Sutra in reverse. Whereas a serpent in the form of a woman transforms into a man to escape her serpentine form and achieve Buddhahood, in the case of *Dōjōji*, there is Kiyohime, who had within the tradition already been granted enlightenment, and having assumed the *shirabyōshi*'s ritualist role, transforms (symbolically) into a man, only to return to the serpentine form. In this way, the Buddhist soteriological concerns and its ritual efficacy seem to be brought into question, especially considering the counter-ritual performed by the monks of the temple directed at the serpent demon.

Led by the Abbot, the monks invoke a number of Buddhist protector deities and vigorously chant at the serpent demon before them. The incantations of the monks in their battle against the serpent are straightforwardly posited as an exorcism of the evil demon in the form of the serpentine monster, aiming to break her shameful attachment and bring her to the Path. As such, from the Buddhist viewpoint, this would be the central ritual of the play. However, the serpent demon retreats as "her body burns in her fire" (*iki ha myōka to natsute sono mi wo yaku*), and she disappears into the rapids of the Hidaka river, her final destiny unknown, clearly indicating that the exorcism only worked partially, at best. This suggests that the exorcism is there to serve as the foil for the central rite of *Dōjōji* – the *ranbyōshi*, and what ostensibly was supposed to be a narrative concluding in Buddhist salvation is rather an interplay of two ritual regimens, both resting on their respective structural and ideological objective.

The woman is performing the dance to trick the monks and get closer to the bell, but at the same time, she is performing an exorcism/pacification for herself. Like a shamanic ritualist, the *shirabyōshi* invites in and embodies/enacts

---

[42] Jane Marie Law, ed., *Religious Reflections on the Human Body* (Bloomington: Indiana University Press, 1995), 107-112.

[43] Plays such as Kakitsubata, or Matsukaze, for example.

the demonic serpent-monster. Through her overlapping identities, she is able to act simultaneously as both the performer and the target of the exorcism/pacification. As the *shirabyōshi*, the *Dōjōji* woman performs the ambiguous, alluring dance that both seduces the monks and performs a religious function; she declares to be suffering due to unnamed "transgressions", moving towards the bell to atone for them, but really to assume her rightful place in the religious regimen which had pushed her away and relegated to the margin. As the serpent, she, on one level, represents a protector of the Buddhist Law, but she also has strong Chtonic connotations as a deity of old with unclear ambivalent intentions. Bergen notes that *Dōjōji* is the kind of play where kami-worship and Buddhism "join forces in their complementary goals of pacification and enlightenment (...) effecting a collision of past and present".[44] However, while this is certainly in line with the medieval Japanese *shinbutsu* (kami/Buddha) episteme, we see the two rituals going against rather than hand-in-hand with each other. The play concludes with a revelation of what is real, but what eventually is "real" remains a question. So, yes, the *Dōjōji* woman`s trials and tribulations are an expression of the damning consequences of desire and attachment, or even an unfortunate story of one-sided love presented as a Buddhist morality tale. Still, beyond that, they symbolize and perform the tension between the overlapping religious (Buddhist and kami-worshipping) codes and male- and female-centred ritual authority.

As noted before, the serpent motif is embedded in the long line of mythical and literary narratives with negative and horrific associations. However, it also betrays kinship with powerful non-Buddhist deities,[45] and in Dōjōji, these aspects converge. Furthermore, thinking of the shite's words and actions while taking into account the complexity of her layered identities discussed above it makes it somewhat uncertain for us to ascribe a gender (or, ultimately, even species) to her. For example, when *Dōjōji's* shite enters and proclaims that she needs to have her evil deeds cancelled out, she says: "My sin will surely be erased" (*tsukurishi tsumi mo kienu beshi*).[46] Who is coming and saying this? The *shirabyōshi*? The ghost of the original woman? The serpent? All three?

I want to suggest that the way the *Dōjōji* shite is constructed, as a web of spiralling dichotomous identities, renders the ritual treatment she is subjected to equally directed to all these identities. Taking that to the level of actual staged Noh performance, all these facets are embodied in the figure of woman-serpent-demon-*shirabyōshi* because of its ambiguity/ambivalence. Casting the

---

[44] Doris G. Bargen, *A Woman's Weapon: Spirit Possession in the Tale of Genji* (Honolulu, Hi: University of Hawai'i Press, 1997).

[45] Kelsey, "Salvation", 84-85.

[46] *Dōjōji.* Sanari, ed, *Yōyoku taikan*, 1793.

protagonist in this way catalyzes all these orders (gender/religious/biological) as if this constructed entity belongs to all of them but to none completely.

Conclusion

Uniting the religio-ritual frameworks of Buddhist and non-Buddhist traditions by navigating interaction between Buddhist concepts and non-Buddhist mythologies in a dialectical process, *Dōjōji* problematizes the efficacy of the salvific efforts ostensibly at the basis of the tradition and offers up an alternative rooted in and born out of this interaction. The performative nature of the genre allows it to maximize the narrative potential of the Kiyohime legend, transforming it from a seemingly straightforward cautionary tale about the danger of carnal lust for Buddhist monks into a complex and layered piece about suffering and salvation, transgressing boundaries, and overlapping religious frameworks.

The way in which the play *Dōjōji* constructs its *shite* wrests her from the confining and subjugating conceptualizations of a being to either be desired and scorned, loathed and destroyed, or saved and delivered, but only under the Buddhist androcentric conditions. Instead, it neutralizes those conceptualizations and resurrects and brings back the chthonic deity and the shamanic ritualist to square off against the Buddhist establishment represented by the monks of the temple. And while the play stops short of granting her the final victory, it leaves the door open for her to resurface from the Hidaka river because, as Cohen reminds us, the monster always escapes but not without a promise of return.

Bibliography

Brazell, Karen. Ed., *Traditional Japanese Theater*. Revised edition. New York: Columbia University Press, 1999.

Dix, Monika. "Saint or Serpent? Engendering the Female Body in Medieval Japanese Buddhist Narratives". In *The Body in Asia*, n.d.

Dumas, Raechel. "Historicizing Japan's Abject Femininity: Reading Women's Bodies in Nihon Ryōiki". *Japanese Journal of Religious Studies* 40, no. 2 (2013): 247–75.

Dykstra, Yoshiko K., "Miraculous Tales of the Lotus Sutra. The Dainihonkoku Hokkegenki". *Monumenta Nipponica* 32, no. 2 (1977): 189–210.

Ekū, Kokan, and Masato Sone. *Genkō Shakusho Wage*. Zoku Shintō Taikei. Ronsetsu Hen 8–10. Tōkyō: Shintō Taikei Hensankai, 14.

Faure, Bernard. *The Red Thread: Buddhist Approaches to Sexuality*. Princeton, N.J: Princeton University Press, 1998.

_____. *The Power of Denial: Buddhism, Purity, and Gender*. Buddhisms. Princeton, N.J: Princeton University Press, 2003.

_____. *Gods of Medieval Japan: Protectors and Predators.* Univ of Hawaii Pr, 2015.

Fukuzawa, Nozomi. *Nō ⟨dōjōji⟩ ranbyōshi no denshō o meguru – kōsai: konparu tayūie to kotsuzumi yukiie no kakawari o chūshin ni.* Hōsei daigaku daigakuin kiyo. No. 69 (2012): 270–262.

Goodwin, Janet R. "Shadows of Transgression: Heian and Kamakura Constructions of Prostitution". *Monumenta Nipponica* 55, no. 3: 327–68, 2000.

———. *Selling Songs and Smiles.* Honolulu: University of Hawaii Press, 2006.

Inoue, Mitsusada, and Shōsuke Ōsone, eds., *Ōjōden, Hokke Genki.* Nihon Shisō Taikei 7. Tōkyō: Iwanami Shoten, 49.

Kaminishi, Ikumi. *Explaining Pictures: Buddhist Propaganda and Etoki Storytelling in Japan.* Honolulu: University of Hawaii Press, 2006.

Kimbrough, R. Keller. *Preachers, Poets, Women, and the Way: Izumi Shikibu and the Buddhist Literature of Medieval Japan.* Ann Arbor, MI: U of M Center For Japanese Studies, 2008.

Law, Jane Marie, ed. *Religious Reflections on the Human Body.* Bloomington: Indiana University Press, 1995.

Lim, Beng Choo. *Another Stage: Kanze Nobumitsu and the Late Muromachi Noh Theater.* Ithaca, NY: Cornell Univ East Asia Program, 2012.

Marra, Michele. "The Buddhist Mythmaking of Defilement: Sacred Courtesans in Medieval Japan". *The Journal of Asian Studies* 52, no. 1 (1993): 49–65.

Nagano, Jōichi, ed. *Konjaku Monogatari Shū.* Koten Nihon Bungaku Zenshū 10. Tōkyō: Chikuma Shobō, 35.

Nomura, Shinichi. *Higashi shina kai: hebisei no genshō.*

Sanari, Kentarō. *Yōkyoku Taikan: [A Comprehensive Study of Nō Texts].* Tōkyō: Meiji Shoin, 5.

Turner, Bryan S., and Zheng Yangwen, eds. *The Body in Asia.* NED-New edition, 1. Berghahn Books, 2009.

Waters, Virginia Skord. "Sex, Lies, and the Illustrated Scroll: The Dojoji Engi Emaki". *Monumenta Nipponica* 52, no. 1 (1997): 59–84.

Wilson, Liz. *Charming Cadavers: Horrific Figurations of the Feminine in Indian Buddhist Hagiographic Literature.* Women in Culture and Society. Chicago, IL; London: University of Chicago Press, 1996.

Yoshida, Kazuhiko. "The Enlightenment of the Dragon King's Daughter in The Lotus Sutra. In *Engendering Faith: Women and Buddhism in Premodern Japan,* edited by Barbara Ruch. Michigan Monograph Series in Japanese Studies, no. 43. Ann Arbor, Mich: Center for Japanese Studies, University of Michigan, 2002.

Chapter 6

The Old Woman and the Mountains: Recentering the Monstrous in Japanese *Yamauba* Tales

Laura Nuffer

Colby College

Abstract

Yamauba, or "mountain hags," rank among the most iconic monsters of Japanese folklore. Imagined as grotesque old women who lurk in wild places, *yamauba* pose a deadly threat to unwary humans, but they can also act as fairy godmother-like helpers, bestowing magical gifts on virtuous heroines. Modern feminist scholars have sought to reclaim the *yamauba* by reframing her as a subversive figure who rejects the constraints of patriarchal society. However, as I argue in this essay, premodern sources do not support the interpretation of the *yamauba* as a liberatory archetype of female power. On the contrary, tales of *yamauba* reinscribe cultural norms, presenting female ageing as a monsterizing force and teaching women that safety and happiness lie within the bounds of the household.

My analysis centres on two premodern narratives, both of which hinge on a fraught encounter between a mountain hag and a young woman. In an episode from the twelfth-century tale collection *Tales of Times Now Past (Konjaku monogatarishū)*, a mountain-dwelling demoness—commonly regarded as a precursor to the *yamauba*—deceives and nearly devours a young mother who has gone into the wild to abandon her newborn child. In *Lady Hanayo (Hanayo no hime)*, a fairytale-like novella from the sixteenth century, the *yamauba* assumes a more benevolent role, giving aid to a young noblewoman cast out by her wicked stepmother. However, whether she is a predator or a benefactor, the *yamauba* polices boundaries: the women who cross paths with her in the wilderness quickly reverse course and return to their proper social and spatial place. Although the *yamauba* herself exists outside the strictures of human society, her outsider status marks her as sinister or pitiable rather than enviable.

Keywords: Japanese folklore, Monsters, Setsuwa, Otogizōshi, Fairy tales

* * *

Introduction

Driven by dire necessity, a young woman leaves her home and journeys deep into the mountains. She wanders, lost in the wilderness, until by good fortune she stumbles across the dwelling of a kindly old woman. With nowhere else to turn, the young woman gratefully accepts the old woman's offer of shelter…

Because this is a book about monsters, you already distrust the old woman, and you are right to do so: she is a *yamauba*, or "mountain hag," a sinister being believed to lurk in the wild places of Japan.[1] Over the centuries, many tales have been told about *yamauba*, and some of the best known involve encounters of the sort outlined above, in which a young woman finds herself at the dubious mercy of an old woman who is something other than human. The heroines of the narratives examined in this chapter escape safely, but they are lucky to do so. *Yamauba* have frequently been compared to witches in European lore, and while the analogy is imperfect—*yamauba* do not cast spells, and they have no association with heretic religious practices—it does offer some sense of the danger that they pose. Like the witch in *Hansel and Gretel* or Baba Yaga in Russian fairy tales, *yamauba* are notorious cannibals whose presence always elicits at least a frisson of fear. Quick-thinking humans often succeed in outwitting *yamauba*, and worthy heroes or heroines might even win their aid; however, some tales make good on their threat and end with a crunch and a gulp.

Also like European witches, *yamauba* emerged as a constellation of sometimes contradictory archetypes over the course of a long, tangled, and now-fragmentary history that blurs the notional distinction between literature and folklore. Japanese tradition boasts a fantastic array of uncanny beings, ranging from the broadly familiar (ghosts, water sprites) to the hallucinogenically bizarre (one-eyed paper lanterns with lolling tongues, sickle-wielding weasels that cause lethal whirlwinds).[2] *Yamauba* have received more scholarly attention than most of their fellow monsters, in part because they rank among the most enduringly culturally prominent, but also because the sheer diversity of ways

---

[1] Here and throughout, I use the term "monster" as a hypernym of *yamauba*, demons, and other imaginary entities believed to pose a threat to humans. In modern Japanese, beings of this sort would collectively be referred to as *yōkai*, a word frequently if imperfectly translated as "monster." *Yōkai* are typically construed as being supernatural and in some way rooted in Japanese tradition; the term does not apply to monsters such as Godzilla whose origins were conceptualized in scientific terms. *Yamauba* may be contracted to *yamanba*; the two terms are in most contexts functionally interchangeable.

[2] Japanese water sprites, or *kappa*, are amphibian-like creatures that share with their Western counterparts the unfortunate habit of drowning the incautious. One-eyed lantern spirits are *chōchin-obake*, and sickle weasels are *kamaitachi*.

in which they have been imagined seems to demand explanation: what exactly *are* they?

Like all truly compelling monsters, *yamauba* tantalize with the possibility that they are not entirely monsters after all. From the earliest days of Japanese ethnography, folklorists speculated that the seemingly demonic figure of the man-eating crone in fact held deep ties to the divine. Orikuchi Shinobu (1887-1953) theorized that the original *yamauba* were priestesses who served a mountain god, first as nursemaids (*uba*, homophonous with the word meaning "hag"), then as wives.[3] This role required them to live in the wilderness, entering the village only to engage in ritual performances; as they grew old in the mountains, they became *uba* in the other sense of the word. Yanagita Kunio (1875-1962), perhaps the single most influential figure in Japanese folk studies, granted *yamauba* an even loftier pedigree: he held that they were one-time goddesses, ancient mother deities demoted to boogeywomen as a shifting religious landscape left them behind.[4]

More recently, feminist scholars have contributed to the ongoing recuperation of the *yamauba* by reframing her as a model of resistance to patriarchal values. This turn can be traced back to Baba Akiko, a pioneer of Japanese monster studies, whose writings explore the link between the sociopolitical creation of marginalized groups and the literary invention of demons (*oni*, a category to which *yamauba* are generally understood to belong). Building on Orikuchi's work, Baba views *yamauba* as mythologized descendants of mountain-dwelling women who "inherited the bloodlines of priestesses, which were connected to the lineages of ancient local deities."[5] However, Baba grants these women an agency that Orikuchi withholds; by her account, they were not *chosen* to live in the mountains but rather *chose* to live there: "By no means did these women of the mountains wish for a life outside the mountains."[6]

The prominent literary critic Mizuta Noriko amplifies Baba's vision of the *yamauba* as a self-determined outsider, citing the very qualities that mark her as marginal and monstrous—her advanced age, her estrangement from human

---

[3] Although *uba* meaning "nursemaid" and *uba* meaning "hag" are homophonous, they are written with different ideographic characters.

[4] Yanagita Kunio, *Yama no jinsei* (Tokyo: Kyōdo Kenkyūsha, 1926), 144-145. Yanagita regarded not only the *yamauba* but many other folkloric monsters as "fallen gods," a paradigm is most famously articulated in a 1934 essay: "Among all peoples, when an old faith is suppressed and defeated by a new faith, its gods must fall and become monsters [*yōkai*]. 'Monster' is another word for an unauthorized god." (Yanagita, *"Hitotsume kōzō," Teihon Yanagita Kunio zenshū* vol. 5 (Tokyo: Chikuma Shobō, 1968), 125.)

[5] Baba Akiko, *Oni no kenkyū* (1971; reis., Tokyo: Chikuma Shobō, 1988), 179.

[6] Ibid.

society—as the source of her power: "Refusing to be forced into a constrained role, rather than settle in the village, the *yamauba* is a woman who wishes to choose her place freely. She is a woman who cannot be tamed by the men of the village."[7] For modern women, Mizuta continues, the *yamauba* presents "an alluring figure, who as she ages is for the first time liberated from culturally constructed womanhood."[8] Several Anglophone scholars have followed Mizuta in celebrating the *yamauba* as an icon of female rebellion, among them Rebecca Copeland, who argues that the *yamauba* "represents all that lies outside the social norm, beyond the boundaries of the civilized. She is a woman without family, a woman who does not conform . . . Her freedom figured as terror. She turns the world upside down, inverting expectations and the comfort of the assumed."[9]

Here, I do not seek to reclaim or reframe the *yamauba*; rather, I attempt to re-monster her. Although I do not deny the *yamauba*'s subversive and empowering potential (just as Baba, Mizuta, Copeland, and other scholars do not deny the misogyny woven throughout *yamauba* lore), I find that much of this potential emerges only when she is viewed as a composite figure and approached with a hermeneutic of subversion that might colloquially be termed "sympathy for the devil." Reading individual narratives about *yamauba* in accordance with intratextual cues tends to produce a less inspirational interpretation: more often than not, the *yamauba* is not an escapee but an exile, not an alluring figure but an abjected one, not an invitation to a life of freedom in the wild margins of the world but a warning to remain within the safety of the centre. Far from presenting a liberatory vision of female ageing, the *yamauba* reinforces the cultural paradigm—as pervasive throughout premodern Japanese history as it is here and now—that values youth and beauty while positioning elderly women as pathetic and threatening others.

I make my case for interpreting the *yamauba* as a cautionary figure enforcing social norms and encoding a negative valuation of elderly women through a close reading of two premodern narratives, both of which hinge on an encounter between a young woman who travels into the mountains and a monstrous old woman who offers her lodging. The first of these narratives appears in a collection of short tales known as *Tales of Times Now Past* (*Konjaku monogatarishū*), compiled in the mid-twelfth century by an unknown

---

[7] Mizuta Noriko, "*Yamauba no yume: joron to shite,*" in *Josei no genkei to katarinaoshi: yamaubatachi no monogatari*, ed. Mizuta Noriko and Kitada Sachie (Tokyo: Gakugei Shorin, 2002), 11.

[8] Ibid., 37.

[9] Rebecca Copeland, "Mythical Bad Girls: The Corpse, the Crone, the Snake," in *Bad Girls of Japan*, ed. Laura Miller and Jan Bardsley (New York: Palgrave Macmillan, 2005), 23.

anthologist.[10] (The tale in question, which predates the first known occurrence of the word *yamauba* by roughly two centuries, refers to the monstrous old woman only by the generic term for "demon"; however, scholars frequently view the character as a kind of proto-*yamauba*.) The second narrative examined in this chapter, a fairytale-like illustrated volume entitled *Lady Hanayo* (*Hanayo no hime*), dates to the late sixteenth or early seventeenth century, although it is thought to have roots in medieval storytelling traditions.[11] These works differ strikingly in their construction of the monstrous old woman in the mountains. In *Tales of Times Now Past*, she is a predator who lures in the unwary with a kindly guise; by contrast, in *Lady Hanayo*, she offers sincere assistance to her human guest. Nevertheless, in both tales, the *yamauba* (or *yamauba*-like figure) ultimately functions to bring about a reinstatement of the status quo: the young woman who encounters her in the lawless and liminal realm of the mountains quickly reverses course, returning to the strictures and structures of patriarchal society.

Taking the Measure of the Mountain Hag: Proto-*Yamauba* as Generic Monsters

On a strictly lexical level, the literary history of the *yamauba* begins just before the turn of the fifteenth century, when the word makes its first known appearance in the temple chronicle *The History of Daisenji Temple in Hōki Province* (*Hōki no kuni Daisenji engi*, 1398). The relevant episode is extremely laconic and more than a little mystifying. A *yamauba*, who is identified by this term but not otherwise described, approaches the Buddhist priest Kongōbō as he is performing ascetic training near a mountain cave. She begs for medicine for her breasts, upon which he offers her hot stones. (Why the *yamauba* needs medicine for her breasts is unclear, but it is worth noting that the specifically female features of her body have been singled out as a source of suffering.) Believing that the stones are medicine, the *yamauba* swallows them and is incinerated; after that, the faithful are able to visit the location unharassed. A more detailed account of the same event appears in an earlier chronicle of the same temple, *The History of Daisenji Temple* (*Daisenji engimaki*, ca. 1316).

---

[10] Modern scholars use the term *setsuwa* to refer to the brief, anecdotal stories in *Tales of Times Now Past* and similar anthologies. Because *setsuwa* is an anachronistic designation— the people who originally wrote and told these tales would not have referred to them as such—I will forgo it here in favor of maximizing readability for a broad audience.

[11] *Lady Hanayo* belongs to a group of roughly five hundred works of medieval and early modern narrative fiction known as *otogizōshi*. Like *setsuwa*, *otogizōshi* is a term of convenience adopted by modern scholars to denote a highly heterogeneous group of works, and I avoid it here.

Here, however, Kongōbō's adversary is referred to as a "hag" (*uba*) rather than a "mountain hag"; she is also labelled a "demon woman" (*kijo*) and described as "fearsome," although the text offers no explanation as to *what* makes her fearsome.[12]

Taken together, the Daisenji temple chronicles suggest that the term *yamauba* attached itself to preexisting narratives about menacing old mountain-dwelling women, who were originally classed under the more expansive label of *oni*, or demon.[13] Arguably, the distinction between *yamauba* and *oni* never entirely solidified, as suggested by one of the several alternate names for *yamauba*, *onibaba* or "demon granny."[14] Folklore recorded by Japanese ethnographers in the early twentieth century frequently treats *yamauba* and female *oni* as allomotifs, meaning that one can replace the other without altering the substance of the narrative.[15] In some instances, the conjoined figure of the *yamauba*/female *oni* blurs together with an even broader supercategory of monsters. Here, the tale of the hot stones from the Daisenji temple chronicles offers an instructive example. Numerous orally transmitted variants of this narrative persisted into the twentieth century; however, while the tales

---

[12] Tokuda Kazuo, "*Nō to setsuwa, denshō yamauba o megutte: Zeami jidai no yamauba denshō* (2)," *Kanze* 83, no. 10 (October 2016), 42-44. This early appearance of the word *yamauba* is not written as the standard two-character compound 山姥 (ideographically, "mountain" + "hag") but rather as the three-character compound 山優婆 (ideographically, "mountain" + "gentle" + "crone"). The characters 優婆 are taken from the Buddhist term for a female parishioner, *ubai*, which is written 優婆夷 and derived from the Sanskrit word *upāsikā*. The characters of *ubai* were chosen for their phonetic rather than ideographic value, but in the context of the Daisenji temple chronicle, it is significant that the *ba* is written with a character denoting an old woman.

[13] *Kijo* is written with the characters meaning "demon woman"; the character read as *ki* in this compound is read as *oni* ("demon" or "ogre") when it stands alone.

[14] Tellingly, the word *onibaba* lacks a masculine equivalent; there is no "demon grandpa." *Yamauba* has a superficial counterpart in the more obscure *yamajiji*, or "mountain grandpa"; however, the *yamajiji* is typically envisioned as a one-legged creature with a single massive eye in the center of his forehead—his body is marked as monstrous by its impossibility, unlike the entirely possible (and eventually inevitable) body of the *yamauba*.

[15] Influential folk scholar Komatsu Kazuhiko sees the *yamauba* as the feminine counterpart of *oni*: "The word demon [*oni*] carries a masculine image. However, we must not forget there are also female demons. These may be called demonesses [*kijo*] or demon grannies [*onibaba*], but in folk society they are most often known as *yamauba*." (*Kamikakushi: Ikai kara no izanai* [Tokyo: Kōbundō, 1991], 156.) Here and throughout, I refer to orally transmitted folktales recorded by ethnographers active in the twentieth century. Although these narratives have not been handed down unaltered from centuries past, to a substantial degree they preserve premodern narratives.

documented by modern ethnographers bear an undeniable genetic relationship to their fourteenth-century antecedents—and share the sadistic edge likely to prick at modern sensibilities—the supernatural entity tricked into consuming the stones is often a shapeshifting raccoon-dog instead of a yamauba.[16] The monster, in other words, is at times an interchangeable part.

Most attempts to trace the development of the *yamauba* look beyond the relatively shallow history of the name itself. Some scholars see glimmers of the *yamauba* in eighth-century mythological texts, linking her to several female deities, among them the fearsome goddesses of the underworld known as *shikome* or "ugly women."[17] Other scholars extend their search deeper into the past, suggesting a connection between prehistoric pottery figurines that appear to have been ritually dismembered and folktales in which the body of a *yamauba* produces food or mysterious treasures.[18] However, these proposed proto-*yamauba* bear at most an ambiguous resemblance to later *yamauba* explicitly named as such, even accounting for the broad diversity encompassed by the term. The earliest figures to exhibit a core cluster of *yamauba*-like attributes—old age, femaleness, cannibalism, and mountain-dwelling—appear only in the twelfth century, in the tale collection *Tales of Times Now Past.*[19] Monsters matching this description feature in not one but two tales, which are respectively entitled "A Woman with Child Goes to South Yamashina, Meets a Demon, and Flees" (hereafter "A Woman with Child") and "The Hunters'

---

[16] Ikeda Hiroko, *A Type and Motif Index of Japanese Folk Literature* (Helsinki: Suomalainen Tiedakatemia, 1971), 227. From a scientific perspective, raccoon-dogs, or *tanuki*, are midsized omnivorous canids; from a folkloric perspective, they are shapeshifting tricksters whose pranks range from mischievous to murderous.

[17] Ōtō Tokihiko, *Nihon minzokugaku no kenkyū* (Tokyo: Gakueisha, 1979), 30; Yumiko Hulvey, "Myths and Monsters: The Female Body as the Site for Political Agendas," in *Body Politics and the Fictional Double*, ed. Debra Walker King (Bloomington: Indiana University Press, 2000), 75. Hulvey also draws a connection between the *yamauba* and the progenitor goddess Izanami, who dispatches the *shikome* to pursue her former husband when he comes to seek her in the underworld.

[18] Atsuhiko Yoshida, "*Yamauba to Kiki shinwa oyobi Jōmon jidai no shūkyō girei*," *Chōsa kenkyū hōkoku* 31 (1990), 65-69.

[19] Although the archetypal *yamauba* is envisioned as a haggard old woman, exceptions exist. Perhaps the most famous example of a youthful *yamauba* is the foster mother of the legendary hero Kintarō, said to have been abandoned in the mountains. Several eighteenth-century sources represent Kintarō's foster mother as a voluptuous beauty, including Chikamatsu Monzaemon's play *Yamauba with Child* (*Konochi yamauba*, 1712) and numerous woodblock prints by Kitagawa Utamaro (1753-1806). Although these glamorized depictions of Kintarō's foster mother may draw on folkloric conceptions of the *yamauba* as a bountiful mother goddess, they also reflect the tastes of eighteenth-century consumers of visual media. Simply put, sex sold.

Mother Becomes a Demon and Tries to Eat Her Children" (hereafter "The Hunters' Mother").[20] As these titles indicate, in both instances the presumed proto-*yamauba* is identified only as a demon.

Many of the scholars who have analyzed "A Woman with Child" and "The Hunters' Mother" have done so in search of literary precursors to the *yamauba*, meaning that the tales have often been interpreted with reference to later *yamauba* lore. Here, I adopt a different angle of approach, examining "A Woman with Child" primarily within the context of *Tales of Times Now Past*. (I focus on this tale because it showcases the female demon's interactions with a human woman, although my discussion touches on "The Hunters' Mother" as well.) A staggeringly compendious work, *Tales of Times Now Past* consists of more than a thousand thematically organized short stories. Although the focus shifts repeatedly and radically throughout the anthology, among the compiler's many aims is an elucidation of the patterns underlying human interactions with the supernatural. "A Woman with Child" and "The Hunters' Mother" are only two of more than forty tales dedicated to this monsterological project. Taken together, they may reflect an association between old women and mountains; however, the demon in "A Woman with Child" ultimately behaves in much the same manner as her conspecifics, who assume other guises and haunt other locations. Far from constituting a distinct subtype of monster, she in many ways represents the demonic default in *Tales of Times Now Past*: a malevolent *genius loci* embodying the danger of liminal spaces.

The unnamed protagonist of "A Woman with Child" discovers this danger for herself through near-fatal experience. The tale opens not in the mountains but in the capital, where she works as a servant in an aristocratic household. She has no high rank, no parents to support her, and no husband, but nonetheless she has found herself pregnant. (Twelfth-century Japanese mores placed a relatively low premium on female chastity, so the protagonist's pregnancy does not put her at risk of harsh repercussions; however, it does carry some degree of stigma—the narrator states that she is too ashamed to confess her condition to her employer—and the tale's contemporary audience would have understood that she lacks the resources to care for the child.) At a loss, she resolves to deliver the child deep in the wilderness and abandon it.

The protagonist puts her plan into action when she enters labor, slipping away from her employer's estate accompanied by only a single serving girl. At last, she comes to a dilapidated house on a mountainside—a good place to give

---

[20] The Japanese title of "A Woman with Child Goes to South Yamashina, Meets a Demon, and Flees" is *Ubume Minami Yamashina ni yukite oni ni aite nigeshi katari* (Volume 27, Tale 15). "The Hunters' Mother Becomes a Demon and Tries to Eat Her Children" is *Ryōshi no haha oni to narite ko o kuwamu to seshi katari* (Volume 27, Tale 22).

birth, she decides, assuming the house to be unoccupied. When she enters, however, she is greeted by an old woman. Luckily—or so it seems—the protagonist quickly wins the sympathy of the house's elderly inhabitant, who assists with the delivery and encourages her to stay on during her period of postpartum ritual pollution. The child proves to be a beautiful baby boy, and the protagonist finds herself unable to abandon him, so she nurses and cares for him instead. All is well until, as she is dozing one afternoon, she faintly hears a voice saying, "My, what a yummy mouthful."[21] When she opens her eyes, she sees the old woman staring hungrily at her newborn son. Her kindly host now appears fearsome, monstrous. Realizing that she has come to the house of a demon, the protagonist flees with her son and the serving girl, running until they reach human habitation. Only many years later, when she has become an old woman herself, does she tell the story of the old woman she met in the mountains.

To a modern reader, "A Woman with Child" seems ripe for interpretation as a psychological allegory. The evidence of the old woman's sinister nature is filtered entirely through the protagonist's perception, and even then, it never rises above the level of insinuation; there is only a sinister utterance faintly overheard, a seeming aura of menace. And isn't it a strange coincidence that as soon as the protagonist resolves *not* to kill her newborn son—a resolve that she puts into action by breastfeeding him—she is confronted by a woman who wants to kill and eat him? The scenario looks very much like an inner conflict externalized: in the process of rejecting her infanticidal urges, the woman projects them onto a monstrous other, whom she then abandons in the mountains where she previously planned to abandon her child. Many critics have indeed read the tale in this vein. According to Hijikata Yōichi, "The demonic old woman is a mirror reflecting the heart of the woman herself, who sees her beloved child as a burden."[22] Meera Viswanathan likewise views the two women as mirrors of one another, "represent[ing] the dialectic of female resistance, in which we see not so much an opposition between female characters

---

[21] The old woman's utterance is doubly sinister in Japanese, as it alludes to the phrase *oni hitokuchi*, meaning "a demon's mouthful." Still in use today, this phrase can be traced back to the sixth chapter of the tenth-century poem tale *The Tales of Ise* (*Ise monogatari*). Although most of the work's chapters are dedicated to interactions between humans, the atypical sixth chapter recounts a tryst gone supernaturally wrong: a man carries his lover away to an abandoned storehouse, where she is devoured by a demon. A version of this story appears in the twenty-seventh volume of *Tales of Times Now Past*.

[22] Hijikata Yōichi, "*Fūjirareta gūi: Konjaku sezoku setsuwa ichimen*," *Kokugo to kokubungaku* 64 no. 2 (February 1987), 54.

as an internal struggle between production and consumption, between the sacrifice of self and the assertion of self."[23]

But of course, "A Woman with Child" was not written for modern readers. (In the strictest sense, it was probably not written for readers at all; a widely accepted theory holds that *Tales of Times Now Past* was intended as a stock of material with which Buddhist preachers could "enliven their sermons."[24]) Presumption of hidden depth and hyperfocus on the motivations and mental states of characters are not universal modes of engaging with narrative. Arguably, texts can produce meaning on levels that their creators and consumers do not consciously apprehend; in all likelihood, however, the intended audience of "A Woman with Child" would not have approached the tale with the hermeneutic of suspicion that treats revelations as the opening of false-bottomed drawers. When we read in accordance with narratorial and contextual cues, "A Woman with Child" turns on the straightforward unmasking of a monster: the kindly old woman is really a demon. There is no secret beneath the secret (the demon is really the protagonist's guilty conscience!) discoverable only by the attentive reader. Just as importantly, the intended audience of *Tales of Times Now Past* likely held greater interest than we do in monsters *qua* monsters. Modern academics, for the most part, have little personal concern with the question of how best to avoid harm from malign supernatural entities; it is not the same sort of question as "How do I avoid becoming ill?" or "How do I avoid becoming the victim of a crime?" If it feels flat and flaccid to concede that a text's meaning does in fact lie on its surface, then the monster is a particularly difficult surface to reconcile ourselves to, because in its literal sense it does not even exist. But in twelfth-century Japan, ghosts and demons inhabited the same domain of worrisome realities as disease and violent assault. "A Woman with Child" spoke directly to and about the visceral anxieties of its audience.[25]

---

[23] Meera Viswanathan, "In Pursuit of the Yamamba: The Question of Female Resistance," in *The Woman's Hand: Gender and Theory in Japanese Women's Writing*, ed. Paul Schalow and Gordon Walker (Stanford: Stanford University Press, 1996), 245.

[24] Marian Ury, *Tales of Times Now Past: Sixty-Two Stories from a Medieval Japanese Collection* (Berkeley: University of California Press, 1979), 2.

[25] Much debate has surrounded the question of whether premodern audiences would have held literal belief in supernatural entities as they were represented in literary sources. In her book *A Woman's Weapon* (Honolulu: University of Hawaii, 1997), Doris Bargen makes a compelling case that Murasaki Shikikbu's *The Tale of Genji* (*Genji monogatari*, ca. 1008)—a monument of classical court literature—employs spirit possession as a device to dramatize female discontent in a polygamous society. However, the possessing spirits that bedevil aristocrats in *The Tale of Genji* are a different sort of entity than demons, ghosts, and foxes of *Tales of Times Now Past*, and the two works belong to distinct literary traditions. Ultimately, I believe that Marian Ury

Most of the tales in *Tales of Times Now Past* close with explanatory commentary and a formulaic assertion that the story has been told as it was passed down, thus framing it as a factual if secondhand account. Crucially, in the final passage of "A Woman with Child," the narrator validates the protagonist's assessment of the danger posed by the old woman:

When one thinks about it, old places like that always have *things* living in them. No doubt the old woman who called the child "a yummy mouthful" was also a demon (*oni*) or something of that sort. And so people have passed the tale down, saying that this is why you should never go into places like that alone.[26]

The addition of "or something of that sort" introduces a note of ambiguity; however, several other tales also end with the narrator professing uncertainty as to the precise identity of an uncanny creature. At a minimum, the narrator seems certain that the old woman is a "thing," or *mono*, *Tales of Times Now Past's* most general category of sinister supernatural being. Thus, the tale concludes with a threefold emphasis on the monstrous: a confirmation that the old woman is a demon or something akin to one; a review of the evidence indicating her demonic nature (calls a child a yummy mouthful, inhabits a decaying house); and advice on avoiding similar encounters with demons (don't go into decaying houses). In short, whether or not the old woman of "A Woman with Child" meets the definition of a *yamauba*, she is undeniably a monster—and therein lies the point of the tale.

Hidden Faces, Hazardous Bodies: The Cautionary Functions of "A Woman With Child"

Although "A Woman with Child" portrays its monster as a solitary being, she is not *sui generis*. As the narrator's closing lines make clear, the story of the sinister old woman is worth telling not because it is anomalous, but because it models the behaviour of the many other dangerous entities inhabiting the demon-haunted world of premodern Japan. Each of the thirty-one volumes in *Tales of Times Now Past* centres on a particular theme; "A Woman with Child" hails from the twenty-seventh volume, which consists entirely of episodes involving ghosts, demons, and other such entities. Although tales of uncanny creatures appear in other volumes of *Tales of Times Now Past*, elsewhere they are subordinated to the agenda of the volume that contains them. By contrast,

---

is correct when she asserts that for classical audiences, "supernatural creatures possess[ed] an independent and alarming reality" ("A Heian Note on the Supernatural," *The Journal of the Association of Teachers of Japanese* 22, no. 2 [1988], 189).

[26] Satō Kenzō, ed. *Konjaku monogatarishū: Honchō sezokubu jōkan* (Tokyo: Kadokawa Shoten, 1995), 353.

the twenty-seventh volume seeks to construct a systematized overview of all things sinister and supernatural—a unified theory of monsters.

The first and most vital point in *Tales of Times Now Past*'s theory of monsters is this: if you are not careful, they will kill you. In literature and lore around the world, including in Japan, monsters tend to fare poorly; they are outwitted and overcome, constructed as an opposite but unequal force carefully weighted to prop up that which it pushes against. But the twenty-seventh volume of *Tales of Times Now Past* largely rejects the comfort of the triumphal narrative. It cultivates unease. As demonstrated by the closing commentary of "A Woman with Child," even when the protagonist of a tale emerges unscathed, the narrator adopts a cautionary tone: *she* got away, but if you enter a place like that, *you* might not. As literary historian Marian Ury astutely notes, "there is a resemblance here to modern folklore of urban crime."[27] Out of the forty-four complete tales in the twenty-seventh volume, ten end with at least one human death. However, not all supernatural entities pose an equal threat. Unlike the encyclopedic catalogues of the weird that would come into vogue several centuries later, the twenty-seventh volume of *Tales of Times Now Past* is interested in establishing patterns rather than entertaining with variety; the compiler does not devise an elaborate taxonomy of the supernatural, instead dividing the bulk of his attention among ghosts, demons, and foxes. (Foxes, like raccoon-dogs, were mischievous and at times malicious shapeshifters.) Demons are by far the deadliest of these three, claiming human victims in eight out of the twelve complete tales in which they appear. The survival of the protagonist of "A Woman with Child" is by no means a foregone conclusion.

Why, then, *does* she survive? Mori Masato, an eminent scholar of *Tales of Times Now Past*, argues that the twenty-seventh volume attaches exorcistic power to the act of identification; in his words, "To learn the true form of an extraordinary being is to overpower that being."[28] I would further posit that learning does not occur as an instantaneous process; rather, knowledge is preceded by suspicion, the dawning awareness that one has crossed paths with something strange and dangerous. Suspicion is the foundation of self-preservation, although by itself it produces only partial victory, not conquest but the reinscription of boundaries temporarily disrupted; the human escapes from a space (s)he ought not to have ventured into, or the monster is driven out from a space it ought not to have intruded upon. In such tales, the monster—foiled but not vanquished—retains some measure of mystery, and its identity remains a matter of conjecture rather than direct knowledge. This pattern, exemplified

---

[27] Ury, "A Heian Note on the Supernatural," 189

[28] Mori Masato, "'Konjaku Monogatari-Shū': Supernatural Creatures and Order," *Japanese Journal of Religious Studies* 9, no. 2/3 (1982), 165.

by "A Woman with Child," predominates throughout the twenty-seventh volume. Some tales, however, allow for a more heroic progression of events, in which suspicion is followed by judicious violence. (Although the twenty-seventh volume features several bloodthirsty female demons, among humans, violence is the sole province of men; human women who encounter the supernatural must flee rather than fight.) For the supernatural, defeat means exposure, as is demonstrated in the tale entitled "A Fox Transforms Itself into a Giant Cedar Tree and is Shot to Death."[29] While travelling through the mountains at night, the protagonist notices an improbably massive cedar tree. Although he does not know exactly what manner of being it is, he suspects supernatural mischief, and so he and his attendant shoot arrows at it. In the morning, a dead fox, so old that it is bald, is found lying where the tree had stood, with arrows in its body and a branch in its mouth.

Here, we should note a critical exception to Mori's maxim that learning the true form of an extraordinary being is tantamount to overpowering it. Although defeat unmasks the supernatural, the supernatural unmasks *itself* in its moment of victory—in which case revelation comes too late. A particularly chilling example of a monster's triumphant self-disclosure occurs in one of the best-known tales from the twenty-seventh volume, "The Demon of Agi Bridge in Ōmi Province Eats a Man."[30] The protagonist, a brash young man, accepts a dare to cross a bridge haunted by a demon and narrowly escapes. Warned by a diviner that the demon will continue to pursue him, the man goes into ritual seclusion, but relaxes his caution enough to admit his brother. The lapse proves fatal. Once inside the house, the man's "brother" bites off his head and, with a gleeful exclamation, turns to look at his wife; to her horror, she finds herself face-to-face with the green-skinned, yellow-eyed demon that her husband had described meeting on the bridge. There is a crucial distinction here between seeing the monster and the monster showing itself. All of this is to say that the protagonist of "A Woman with Child" survives not only because she realizes the old woman's demonic nature, but because she realizes *in time*. She senses danger where a less wary observer, like the unfortunate victim in "The Demon of Agi Bridge," might overlook the subtle signs—and having sensed danger, she exercises the same sort of self-preserving savvy that prompts the man in "A Giant Cedar" to shoot at a disquieting tree. Her suspicious mind is not the mirror of her guilty heart, as several modern commentators have suggested; it is simply proof of her intelligence.

---

[29] The Japanese title of "A Fox Transforms Itself into a Giant Cedar Tree and is Shot to Death" is *Kitsune ōsugi no ki ni henjite shasatsu sareshi katari* (Volume 27, Tale 37).
[30] The Japanese title of "The Demon of Agi Bridge in Ōmi Province Eats a Man" is *Ōmi no kuni Agi no hashi no oni hito o kuishi katari* (Volume 27, Tale 13).

The audience would have known that the protagonist of "A Woman with Child" is intelligent for the same reason that they would have known that the old woman is a demon: the narrator says so. She is praised for her cleverness once near the end of the tale, after she has completed her escape, but also once near the beginning, when she has resolved to secretly deliver and desert her child in the wilderness:

> Being a clever person, this woman thought, "When it seems that the time has come [for me to give birth], I will take a single serving girl to accompany me, go somewhere deep in the mountains, and give birth under a tree or something of that sort. If I die, then it will all be over without anyone knowing; if I live, then I will return [to the capital] as if nothing happened."[31]

To modern readers, this planned abandonment likely stands out as the most chilling aspect of the tale, and the narrator's apparent approval is jarring; we are tempted to read it as ironic, to take *clever* as a cipher for *coldly calculating*. However, the simpler explanation is the better one: the narrator approves because the protagonist is making a sensible choice. Roughly the first two-thirds of *Tales of Times Now Past* is dedicated to Buddhist didactic narratives; after this, the axis of didacticism undergoes a radical realignment, shifting from virtue-vice to cleverness-foolishness.[32] Pragmatics, not ethics, dictate meaning—and the original audience of "A Woman with Child" would have pragmatically recognized infant abandonment as one of the limited options available to overburdened parents.[33] The practice was not openly sanctioned—indeed, it had been prohibited by imperial edict since 867—but it remained a perennial last resort, as demonstrated by the many subsequent edicts repeating the initial prohibition.[34] Even wanted children died with grim regularity; infant mortality in the twelfth century approached or even exceeded fifty per cent.[35] Simply put, babies came and babies went, and so it is perhaps unsurprising that "A Woman with Child" shows little interest in the question of maternal obligations to a newborn child. The protagonist's flight from the old woman's house seems

---

[31] Satō, *Konjaku monogatarishū honchū sezoku bu jōkan*, 351.

[32] Nagano Jōichi, *Konjaku monogatarishū ronkō* (Tokyo: Kasama Shoin, 1979), 181.

[33] A tale in the nineteenth volume of *Tales of Times Now Past*, "A Dog Comes to Tacchi Gate and Secretly Suckles an Abandoned Infant," presents infant abandonment as an unfortunate but unavoidable social fixture. For discussion of and other contemporary narratives of infant abandonment, see Michelle Osterfield Li, *Ambiguous Bodies: Reading the Grotesque in Japanese Setsuwa Tales* (Stanford: Stanford University Press, 2009), 188-189.

[34] Moriyama Shigeki and Nakae Kazue, *Nihon kodomo shi* (Tokyo: Heibonsha, 2002), 35.

[35] William Wayne Farris, *Japan's Medieval Population: Famine, Fertility, and Warfare in a Transformative Age* (Honolulu: University of Hawai'i Press, 2006), 10.

motivated more by self-interest than by protective instinct; when she spies the old woman staring hungrily at her child, her immediate fear is that *she* will be eaten.[36] And once she has made her escape, she gives her child away to be raised by an unspecified person.

For the original audience of "A Woman with Child," the protagonist's pregnancy would have carried as much significance as anything that happened to the resulting child. The protagonist departs the capital just as she goes into labour. This timing is, so to speak, pregnant with significance. As in many other times and places, childbirth in twelfth-century Japan provoked anxieties extending beyond the objective risk to the mother; it was "an event charged with uncertainty," during which "the space inhabited by the living was believed to momentarily overlap with the realms of the dead, unseen malevolent spirits, and Buddhist, Shinto and other deities."[37] Like death, birth brought the literal and figurative leakiness of the body into distressingly clear focus, and the resulting fluids were a potent source of ritual pollution. In addition to defiling the parturition chamber and those within it, afterbirth attracted hungry ghosts, or *gaki*—karmically burdened souls ubiquitous but unseen in the human realm, doomed to feed insatiably on corpses, faeces, and other organic filth.

Ordinarily, spirit mediums and Buddhist priests would be in attendance to mitigate the spiritual hazards associated with delivery. However, the protagonist of "A Woman with Child" chooses to give birth without ritual intercession— and in doing so, she also accepts the risk of dying without ritual intercession. The consequences of such a death would be dire. Women who perished in childbirth became ghosts known as *ubume*, fated to wander the world with the spirits of their lost infants in their arms, begging passersby to hold their babies for a moment. (Acquiescing to this request was a potentially fatal error.) We can be certain that the *ubume* had already emerged as a distinct class of monster by the time of *Tales of Times Now Past*, as a later tale in the twenty-seventh volume features a ghost referred to by this term. Crucially, however, *ubume* has a double meaning: its literal translation is "birthing woman," and it is used in this sense in the title of "A Woman with Child." This is not to imply that the protagonist of "A Woman with Child" is actually a ghost herself—*Tales of Times Now Past* does not deal in plot twists of this sort—but rather to highlight the ominous potential attached to pregnancy in particular and the

---

[36] Vishwanathan states that "neither the young woman nor her maid is at risk of being eaten by the yama[u]ba" ("In Pursuit of the Yamamba," 245), while Hulvey states that "the mother and maid may feel threatened by the old woman, but clearly the only object of her sinister gaze is the male baby" ("Myths and Monsters," 78). Both of these claims, I believe, overinterpret the text.

[37] Anna Andreeva, "Childbirth in Aristocratic Households of Heian Japan," *Dynamis* 34 no. 2 (2014), 358.

female body in general. Underlying the *ubume* is a logic of guilt by conceptual association, a hypervigilance that elides the thing under threat with the threat itself. Childbearing kills women; therefore, childbearing women kill. (Perhaps the *yamauba* derives some of her terror from a similar process of metonymy: age causes death, and therefore the aged cause death.)

Although "A Woman with Child" explicitly invokes the threat of dying in childbirth, the possibility is discarded not long after it is raised, when the protagonist safely delivers her son. Contemporary listeners, however, would have known that the supernatural dangers of parturition outlasted the event itself. The new mother remained ritually polluted for seven days after giving birth—a condition that spread, contagion-like, to the occupants of any spaces that she entered.[38] Nevertheless, the old woman invites her guest to stay on during her period of postpartum pollution, preemptively dismissing worries about defilement: "I'm old, and I live out in the country, so I don't bother with taboos."[39] The term denoting taboos, *monoimi*, literally translates to "avoidance of things"—not things as in material objects, but things of the sort that go bump in the night. The old woman, of course, does not need to worry about supernatural menaces, inasmuch as she is one herself. Her seeming incaution does not rouse the protagonist's suspicion; in reality, prolonged and highly restrictive regimens of avoidance and seclusion were a luxury of aristocratic culture, and even among the elite of the capital, taboos might at times bend to the dictates of convenience. But neither were taboos empty pretense; recall that in "The Demon of Agi Bridge," the protagonist is decapitated by a demon when he prematurely terminates his ritual seclusion (which is referred to by the same word, *monoimi*, as the postpartum taboos in "A Woman with Child").[40] Like many of the preventive measures that permeate our own twenty-first-century lives, the taboos intended to ward off supernatural misfortune were subject to various sorts of circumvention while at the same time being accepted as genuinely protective.

---

[38] For a detailed overview of the ways in which postpartum ritual pollution did and did not spread, see Hitomi Tonomura, "Birth-giving and Avoidance Taboo: Women's Body versus the Historiography of 'Ubuya,'" *Japan Review* 19 (2007), 15-16.

[39] Satō, *Konjaku monogatarishū honchū sezoku bu jōkan*, 352.

[40] Conversely, a later tale in the twenty-seventh volume, "A Demon in Harima Province Comes to a Man's House and is Shot" (27.23) demonstrates the lifesaving power of properly observing *monoimi*. Warned by a diviner that a demon will come to his house on a particular day, a man enters ritual seclusion. As predicted, the demon appears outside the gate of his house, and then—much to the consternation of the house's occupants—disappears and reappears *inside* the house. One of the man's sons summons up the courage to shoot the demon with an arrow, upon which it vanishes. Although *monoimi* is not sufficient to ward off the demon entirely, the man survives the incident, unlike his incautious and ill-fated counterpart in "The Demon of Agi Bridge."

Pregnancy and childbirth unsettle in part because of their liminal quality; a woman in labour inhabits a fraught midground between being one person and two people, while at the same time acting as a gateway through which her unborn child must pass. Perhaps the demonic old woman of "A Woman with Child" is drawn to the protagonist's betwixt-and-between state as well as her improperly managed ritual pollution. As many scholars have noted, *Tales of Times Now Past* persistently links the monstrous and the liminal, a tendency exemplified by the previously mentioned demon of Agi Bridge.[41] In addition to favouring bridges, uncanny beings gravitated to old, uninhabited houses and temples, which straddled the divide between culture and nature, order and chaos. More than any other location, abandoned buildings dominate the twenty-seventh volume as the archetypal topos of the sinister. They also provoke the greatest share of overtly articulated anxiety. Although bridges are repeatedly depicted as the hunting grounds of demons, ghosts, and foxes, at no point does the narrator warn against crossing them; by contrast, numerous tales, including "A Woman with Child," conclude with an admonition not to enter abandoned buildings.[42] Much like the host of supernatural menaces believed to surround childbirth, the creatures imagined to inhabit deserted and decaying places amplified an entirely unimaginary danger. The twelfth century witnessed the erosion of imperial authority, a decline accompanied by broader political and economic destabilization and punctuated by a sequence of plagues and famines. This breakdown fed a growing population of beggars and thieves. Whether or not supernatural beings happened to lurk in an unoccupied structure, cutpurses and cutthroats very well might.

Although most of the tales in the twenty-seventh volume unfold in the capital and its outskirts, mountains also receive sustained attention as a haunt of the uncanny. Revered in both Buddhist and Shinto tradition, mountains possessed a liminal aspect inasmuch as they bridged the worlds of the mortal and divine. Within the context of this-worldly geography, however, mountains did not lay between but stood unambiguously *beyond*. Analogous to forests in the European tradition, they epitomized wilderness at its most wild, the elsemost elsewhere of the city. Like abandoned houses, mountains posed a real danger, particularly when they were unfamiliar terrain; interlopers such as the protagonist of "A Woman with Child" risked falling victim to bandits or simply losing their way. (Several tales in the twenty-seventh volume associate mountains

---

[41] Mori, "Supernatural Creatures and Order," 154-156; Kawashima Miki, "*Nihon no oni no kenkyū*," *Tamayura* 18 (1986); 7-8; Sahara Sakumi, "*Konjaku monogatarishū ni okeru reikitan no kōzō: dai nijūnana o chūshin ni*," *Komazawa tandai kokubun* 19 (1989), 9.

[42] In "The Demon of Agi Bridge," the narrator condemns the protagonist's poor judgment in crossing a bridge that he knew to be haunted by a demon, but there is no suggestion that bridges should be avoided altogether.

with a figure known as *mayowashigami,* or "god of misdirection.") But mountains also figured as a locus of anxiety in that they offered refuge to absconders, itinerants, outlaws, and others who produced nothing and paid no taxes. Significantly, the protagonist of "A Woman with Child" returns to her employer's household immediately after her sojourn in the mountains. Her encounter with the demon woman does not inspire a reconciliation to motherhood—recall that she gives her child away—but in a different sense, she has been driven back into her proper social place as well as her proper spatial place.

The Making of a Monster: Age, Sex, and Other Risk Factors

The would-be cannibal in "A Woman with Child" is not the only sinister old mountain-dwelling woman to lurk among the pages of *Tales of Times Now Past.* The second such *yamauba*-like figure appears later in the twenty-seventh volume, in a tale entitled "The Hunters' Mother Becomes a Demon and Tries to Eat Her Children." The hunters in question, a pair of brothers, make their living ambushing deer in the mountains. One moonless night, as they are out hunting, they realize that something is hunting *them*: a bony hand reaches out of the darkness to grab one of the brothers by the hair. The other brother manages to sever the hand at the wrist by shooting a forked arrow, and the shaken pair take their dubious trophy and return home. There, they hear agonized groans coming from the room of their elderly mother. When they light a torch to examine the hand, it looks suspiciously like their mother's hand—and when they open the door to their mother's room, she lunges at them, cursing. "Is this yours?" the brothers ask, throwing a hand at her. Then they slam the door shut and lock their mad, mutilated mother in the room to die. As in "A Woman with Child," the narrator concludes by eliminating any doubt about the old woman's demonic nature:

> The hunter's mother had grown old and demented, and so she became a demon and tried to eat her children; this is why she went into the mountains. When people's parents grow old like this, they inevitably become demons and try to eat their own children.[43]

"A Woman with Child" closes with actionable advice: do not enter abandoned buildings. "The Hunters' Mother," by contrast, leaves its listeners with a grim prediction that their parents will, in time, transform into devouring monsters. What would the tale's original audience have made of this pronouncement? Even presuming a literal belief in the supernatural—a commonsense understanding that disappearances, illnesses, and other sorts of misfortune arose from the workings of malign forces—listeners would have known that

---

[43] Satō, Konjaku monogatarishū honchū sezoku bu jōkan, 352.

elderly parents did not regularly become demons. However, elderly parents *did* regularly become burdens, consuming more resources than they provided.

"The Hunters' Mother" poses a revealing contrast to a tale from the thirtieth volume of *Tales of Times Now Past*, "The 'Abandoned Crone' Mountain in Shinano Province,"[44] which also grapples with the problem posed by elderly relatives. A certain man, surrendering to the nagging of his cold-hearted wife, carries his much-loved but geriatric aunt into the mountains and leaves her there to die; however, he is soon overcome by regret and goes back to retrieve her. Thereafter, the mountain became known as "Abandoned Crone" Mountain, or Obasuteyama. Unlike infanticide, geronticide was never a widespread or tacitly accepted practice in premodern Japan. Nonetheless, it loomed large in literature and folklore, and twentieth-century ethnographers recorded variants of the Obasuteyama legend in oral traditions throughout Japan. Historian Laurel Cornell suggests that narratives of this sort channelled common animus toward elderly female relatives, who tended to outlive their male counterparts and often came into conflict with daughters-in-law: "While geronticide may not have existed in people's behaviour, it did exist in their hearts and minds . . . The peasant husband and his wife must have wished, often, that they could abandon grandmother on the mountain."[45] However, most Obasuteyama-type narratives conjure up the spectre of geronticide only to banish it; the fantasy of disposing of aged relatives is acknowledged in one breath but condemned in the next. "The Hunters' Mother," by contrast, takes the geronticidal fantasy to its grim extreme and presents the hunters' murder of their mad old mother as entirely justified.

As Sahara Sakumi observes, the hunters' once-human mother stands apart from the other demons in the twenty-seventh volume, which may appear to be human but are nothing of the sort.[46] However, several later narratives— including *Lady Hanayo*, to be discussed below—present *yamauba* as women who have aged out of humanity and into monstrosity, connecting to a larger body of lore in which the passage of time breeds monsters.[47] Foxes and raccoon-dogs were believed to gain magical powers as they grew old; recall that in "A Giant Cedar," the fox that attempted to lead the protagonist astray is bald with age. Cats, too, eventually graduated from ordinary feline mystique

---

[44] The Japanese title of "The 'Abandoned Crone' Mountain in Shinano Province" is *Shinano no kuni no obasuteyama no katari* (Volume 30, Tale 9).

[45] Laurell Cornell, "The Deaths of Old Women: Folklore and Differential Mortality in Nineteenth-Century Japan," in *Recreating Japanese Women, 1600–1945*, ed. Gail Lee Bernstein (Berkeley: University of California, 1991), 87.

[46] Sahara, "*Konjaku monogatarishū ni okeru reikitan no kōzō*," 8.

[47] Tokuda Kazuo, "*Nō to setsuwa, denshō yamauba o megutte: Zeami jidai no yamauba denshō* (1)." *Kanze* 83, no. 6 (June 2016), 41.

to supernatural menace, becoming two-tailed cat demons known as *nekomata*.
Even inanimate objects succumbed to the monsterizing force of time:
discarded household items such as pots and umbrellas bedevilled their former
owners as "ninety-nine-year gods," or *tsukumogami*. Men, however, were
conspicuously immune to such transformations. Premodern literary works do
not treat ageing in either sex as a cause for unambivalent celebration, but as a
general rule, male senescence inspires pathos rather than horror or contempt.
In the words of religious scholar Yamaori Testuo, "While the image of the [old
man] is wrapped in an aura of elegance and spirituality, by contrast, there is a
tendency for the old woman to be tied to the traditions of the demon woman
and the *yama[u]ba*, and to be made an object of fear and dread."[48]

The old women in "A Woman with Child" and "The Hunters' Mother" are
undoubtedly objects of fear and dread, but are they *yamauba*? Or, phrased
more precisely, do they reflect a stable conception of a distinct sort of monster,
and can we posit a genetic link between these tales and later narratives whose
monsters are explicitly named as *yamauba*? Perhaps unsurprisingly, these
questions resist definitive answers. As mentioned above, the twenty-seventh
volume assigns most of its monsters to a limited number of broad categories
and shows little interest in granular classification. However, there are hints of
incipient speciation of the generic class of "demon" into recognizable subtypes
prefiguring the more narrowly defined monsters of subsequent centuries. The
tales "A Demon Appears as a Plank, Comes to a Man's House, and Kills Him"
and "A Demon Appears as an Oil Jar and Kills Someone"—which unfold
exactly as their titles imply—have been interpreted as early depictions of
tsukumogami-like entities.[49] Similarly, the demon of Agi Bridge, which initially
manifests as a beautiful young woman, closely resembles a figure identified in
later works as Hashihime, or "bridge lady."[50] If we accept that not-yet-named
proto-monsters are lurking beneath the surface of *Tales of Times Now Past*, then
yamauba may well number among them.

To be sure, the demonic old women of "A Woman with Child" and "The
Hunters' Mother" do not seem to be wholly of a kind, nor do they fulfil quite
the same cautionary function. "A Woman with Child" marks the mountains as
an unsafe space, overlaying their danger with the danger of abandoned

---

[48] Yamaori Tetsuo, "The Image of 'Rōjo' or Elderly Women in Japanese Legend," *Japan Review* 9 (1997), 30.

[49] Yamauchi Hisashi, *Mononoke* (Tokyo: Hōsei Daigaku Shuppankyoku, 2004), 294.

[50] Terry Kawashima, *Writing Margins: The Textual Construction of Gender in Heian and Kamakura Japan* (Cambridge, MA: Harvard Asia Center Publications, 2001), 254. Despite the high value attached to female youth and beauty, these qualities could become signifiers of monstrosity just as readily as female age and ugliness.

buildings. By contrast, although "The Hunters' Mother" presents the mountains as a place of hunting and killing, the human protagonists emerge as the top predators; ultimately, the real danger resides in their hearth and home. Nevertheless, both tales emphasize their montane setting, and the association of old women with mountains by itself carries significance. The demons of the twenty-seventh volume do not take this form in other locations—they may appear elsewhere as young women, but not as elderly ones—and they tend to prefer cities and their surrounding environs; in most of the tales set in wild places, the monster's part goes to foxes or raccoon-dogs.[51]

The baby-eating old woman in "A Woman with Child" and her filicidal counterpart in "The Hunters' Mother" are further united by their grotesque inversion of the maternal ideal, a characteristic not shared by the other demons in the twenty-seventh volume. (Although the old woman in "A Woman with Child" is not herself the mother of the infant she wishes to devour, she does assume the allomaternal role of midwife-cum-nursemaid, as signified by the fact that she gives the child its ritually important first bath.[52]) In later lore, too, *yamauba* sometimes masquerade as mothers. A particularly grisly example of this occurs in the folktale *O Sun, the Chain* (*Tentō-san, kane no kusari*), in which three young boys at home by themselves make the mistake of opening the door to a *yamauba* posing as their mother. (There is a macabre truth at the heart of this deception: the *yamauba* has recently killed and eaten the boys' mother, and so is in some sense merged with her.) The elder two brothers survive the ordeal, but the youngest does not. Intriguingly, the motif of the telltale hand—a crucial plot point in "The Hunters' Mother"—appears twice in *O Sun, the Chain*. The brothers initially deny entry to the *yamauba* because her hairy hands give her away; she assuages their suspicions by shaving her hands, but then gives herself away again when she serves the severed hand of the youngest brother (whom she has surreptitiously butchered) as dinner. While there is no unambiguous genetic relationship between *O Sun, the Chain* and "The Hunters' Mother," there is a shared orbit around the mother as an object of anxiety, a common fear that the woman who ought to feed her children may one day start feeding *on* them.

---

[51] Sahara, "*Konjaku monogatarishū ni okeru reikitan no kōzō*," 8, 20. The word that I translate here as "raccoon dog" is *kusainagi*; the meaning of the word is debated, and other translators might render it as "wild boar." See Ikegami Jun'ichi, *Setsuwa to sono shūhen* (Osaka: Izumi Shoin, 2008), 177.

[52] Herein lies another possible tie to the *yamauba*: as previously mentioned, *uba* not only means "hag" but is a homophone of "nursemaid," a meaning perhaps originally embedded in the compound word *yamauba*.

As demonstrated by *O Sun, the Chain*, the *yamauba* brings monstrosity and maternity into messy entanglement: she is both a menacing mother and a menace *to* mothers. These dual roles are showcased with lurid clarity in the legend of the *onibaba* of Adachigahara Moor. (Recall that *onibaba*, or "demon granny," is a near-synonym of *yamauba*.) Supposedly an episode in the history of Kanzeji Temple in Fukushima, the legend lacks a clear date of origin; it incorporates elements of the fifteenth-century Noh play *The Black Mound* (*Kurozuka*), but most closely resembles an act from the 1762 puppet play *Adachigahara Moor in Ōshū Province* (*Ōshū Adachigahara*).[53] A woman named Iwate serves as a nursemaid to a girl suffering from a disease curable only by the liver of an unborn child. Determined to save her young mistress, Iwate takes up residence in a house in the wilderness and waits for a suitable victim. At last, a pregnant woman happens by and requests lodging; Iwate offers to assist with the delivery, but instead cuts the fetus out of her guest. Only after she has committed this gruesome deed does she realize that she has killed her long-lost daughter, who was travelling in search of her. Driven mad with remorse, she becomes an *onibaba*, haunting Adachigahara Moor until she is finally vanquished by a Buddhist priest armed with a magical bow.

The legend of Adachigahara Moor distantly echoes the legend of the *yamauba* from Daisenji Temple; both tales valorize Buddhism as a source of masculine authority and assert its ascendancy over malevolent supernatural forces, which are represented as female. But at its core, the Adachigahara legend turns on the conflict between two women, one young and fertile and the other old and barren—the same juxtaposition of opposites that underpins "A Woman with Child." Also as in "A Woman with Child," the old woman initially assumes the symbolically charged role of midwife, acting in tandem with her younger counterpart as a giver of life, only to abruptly become a bringer of death. No line of direct influence links "A Woman with Child" to the Adachigahara legend. However, it is not an accident that both narratives envision the *yamauba* (broadly defined) as a kind of anti-midwife, who preys on women and infants amid the medical and ritual practices surrounding childbirth. "The Hunters' Mother" constructs mothers and monsters as conjoined entities, converging with advancing age. *Yamauba* threaten all who cross their path, but for pregnant and postpartum women, the threat is doubled: the demonic hag represents not only a clear and present danger, but also a dark and foreboding future.

---

[53] Kondō Yoshihiro, *Nihon no oni: Nihon bunka tankyū no shikaku* (Tokyo: Oᵁfuᵁsha, 1967).

From Predator to Protector: The Kinder, Gentler *Yamauba*

Five hundred years after the compilation of *Tales of Times Now Past*, man-eating hags still haunted the mountains of Japan's imaginary geography. However, they were perhaps less fearsome than in centuries past. During Japan's medieval era, generally understood as the years between 1185 and 1603, literary depictions of the monstrous increasingly took on a sympathetic note; although demons and other such creatures retained their menace, many were now a breed apart from the inscrutable and malicious supernatural entities that troubled the world of *Tales of Times Now Past*. Endowed with psychological interiority and imbued with Buddhist moral significance, they recognized their own abject status and yearned for future salvation.[54] *Yamauba* were early beneficiaries of this humanizing turn, as most famously exemplified by a fifteenth-century Noh play entitled *The Mountain Hag* (*Yamanba*). Attributed to the great dramatist Zeami (1363-1443), *The Mountain Hag* presents its titular figure as a lonely wanderer in the wilderness; she may or may not eat humans (Zeami is coy on this point), but she also offers aid to travellers while eternally longing for release from her rounds of the mountains.

Although Zeami's kinder, gentler *yamauba* cast a long literary shadow, she also represents a uniquely aestheticized example of her kind; like all of Zeami's works, *The Mountain Hag* draws heavily on classic poetry and esoteric Zen philosophy. Not all *yamauba* were so rarefied. *Lady Hanayo*, a popular illustrated tale from the late sixteenth century, features an earthier but also narratively meatier *yamauba*—a pitiful but mostly benevolent figure who presents an illuminating contrast to the female demon in "A Woman with Child." To be clear, no line of direct influence links these two tales; both belong to a broad and fuzzily bounded category of narratives about frightening old women in the mountains, and both cast the frightening old woman opposite a frightened young woman. Like the protagonist of "A Woman with Child," the eponymous heroine of *Lady Hanayo* meets this old woman at the turning point of her journey into and out of the wilderness. However, where the protagonist of "A Woman with Child" ends up exactly where she began, in service at a noble household, Hanayo transitions from maidenhood to wifehood—a forward and upward trajectory, but one that nonetheless restores her to her prescribed social station.

Lady Hanayo forms a trio with two other closely related tales, *Hagskin* (*Ubakawa*) and *The Bowl-Wearer* (*Hachikazuki*). Extant manuscripts of all three works date to the sixteenth and seventeenth centuries, when they were

---

[54] Michelle Osterfield Li, "Human of the Heart: Pitiful Oni in Medieval Japan," in *The Ashgate Research Companion to Monsters and the Monstrous*, edited by Asa Simon Mittman and Peter Dendle (London: Ashgate Publishing, 2012), 173-174.

produced for sale to a growing class of literate consumers; however, they are thought to have historically deeper roots in the oral performances of itinerant storyteller-preachers.[55] Scholars frequently note the similarity between the *Lady Hanayo/ Hagskin/ Bowl-Wearer* triad and the Western fairy tale *Cinderella*, although in many respects the three works bear a closer resemblance to related but lesser-known Western tales such as Charles Perrault's *Donkeyskin* and the Grimm Brothers' *All-Kinds-of-Fur*.[56] What precisely constitutes a fairy tale, and whether or not *Lady Hanayo* qualifies as one, are questions that lie beyond the scope of this chapter; suffice it to say that readers conversant with Western fairy tales would find much that is familiar in *Lady Hanayo*. Indeed, some scholars, most prominently Chieko Irie Mulhern, hypothesize that *Lady Hanayo* and its congeners ultimately derive from *Cinderella*-type stories brought to Japan by Jesuit missionaries in the mid-sixteenth century.[57]

Whatever its origin, the core plot of *Lady Hanayo* and its sister tales begins with a beautiful young lady being driven from her home by a cruel stepmother. All three works agree that the heroine is of noble birth, although they do not agree on her name: in both *Lady Hanayo* and *The Bowl-Wearer*, she is the title character, while in *Hagskin*—the shortest and simplest of the three tales and possibly the closest to the ancestral form[58]—she is referred to only as "the

---

[55] Monika Dix, "Hachikazuki: Revealing Kannon's Crowning Compassion in Muromachi Fiction," *Japanese Journal of Religious Studies* 36, no. 2 (2009), 280-281; Chigusa Steven, "Hachikazuki: A Muromachi Short Story," *Monumenta Nipponica* 32, no. 3 (1977), 305-306.

[56] The widely used Aarne-Thompson-Uther tale-type index classifies *Cinderella* as Type 510A ("The Persecuted Heroine"), whereas *Donkeyskin* and *All-Kinds-of-Fur* are assigned to Type 510B ("The Unnatural Father"). Although *Lady Hanayo* and its sister tales lack the most shocking aspect of Type 510B tales—the incestuous desires of the heroine's father—they otherwise form a very close parallel.

[57] For a discussion of the possible connection between *The Bowl-Wearer / Hagskin / Lady Hanayo* trio and Western *Cinderella*-type tales, see Chieko Irie Mulhern's articles "Cinderella and the Jesuits: An Otogizōshi Cycle as Christian Literature," *Monumenta Nipponica* 34, no. 4 (1979), 409-447 and "Analysis of Cinderella Motifs, Italian and Japanese," *Asian Folklore Studies* 44, no. 1 (1985), 1–37. Mulhern identifies highly specific similarities between these three tales and Italian *Cinderella*-type tales, making an intriguing (if not conclusive) argument for the influence of the latter on the former; however, her suggestion that *Lady Hanayo* and its sister tales were authored in direct connection with Jesuit evangelism is more provocative than persuasive.

[58] Sachi Schmidt-Hori, "Symbolic Death and Rebirth into Womanhood: An Analysis of Stepdaughter Narratives from Heian and Medieval Japan," *Japanese Language and Literature* 54 no. 2 (October 2020), 454. Schmidt-Hori concludes that *Hagskin* "exhibits common characteristics of an orally transmitted folk tale, including its brevity and lack of details." By contrast, Fukuda Akira concludes that although Lady Hanayo is more narratively complex and more self-consciously literary than *The Bowl-Wearer* and

girl." Disguised by a supernatural object that renders her grotesque, the heroine works as a lowly fire-tender at the mansion of a lord, until the lord's youngest son sees through the illusion and falls madly in love with her. In *The Bowl-Wearer* and *Lady Hanayo*, the lord and his wife contrive to humiliate the seemingly hideous servant woman to whom their son has pledged himself, demanding that she present herself alongside the accomplished and elegant wives of their older sons. However, during the gathering meant to demonstrate her unsuitability as a bride, the heroine not only removes her disfiguring disguise to unveil her beauty, but at the same time reveals a dowry of gold and other valuables. This symbolic equation of physical attractiveness and material wealth foregrounds the principle that underlies all three tales: a woman's looks are her fortune. For the (hopefully) fairer sex, beauty, prosperity, and marital success constitute an indissociable trinity.

The bare-bones summary above elides significant points of difference between the three works, among them the nature of the heroine's magical disguise and the means by which she acquires it. All of the tales attach religious significance to the narrative, attributing the heroine's good fortune to the blessing of the bodhisattva Kannon and promising the audience similar rewards for faith. In *The Bowl-Wearer*, the farthest outlier of the trio, the heroine's dying mother—a devoted worshipper of Kannon—entrusts her daughter to the bodhisattva and places a large wooden bowl over her head. The bowl mysteriously sticks fast, obscuring the girl's face and earning her the moniker Hachikazuki, or "bowl-wearer." Luckily, on the eve of Hachikazuki's contest against her sisters-in-law, the bowl suddenly falls off, releasing a trove of hidden riches. Where Hachikazuki's bizarre accessory renders her freakish, the heroines of *Hagskin* and *Lady Hanayo* become ugly in a more conventional sense: they appear to be old women thanks to a magical garment referred to respectively as a "hagskin" (*ubakawa*) and a "hag robe" (*ubakinu*). The heroine of *Hagskin* receives the titular garment directly from Kannon soon after she flees from her stepmother. The tale is candid about the reason for this disguise; Kannon warns the heroine that if she does not conceal her beauty, "some man will take you for himself."[59] *Lady Hanayo* is less straightforward; the purpose of the hag robe goes unstated, and its wearer does not receive it from Kannon but instead through an unlikely intermediary: a *yamauba* who lives deep in the mountains.

Hagskin, the high density of folkloric motifs hints that it most closely resembles the source tale (*Mukashibanashi kara otogizōshi e: Muromachi monogatari to minkan denshō* [Tokyo: Miyai Shoten, 2000], 189).

[59] "*Ubakawa*," in *Shinchū Muromachi monogatarishū*, ed. Hamanaka Osamu, (Tokyo: Benseisha, 1989), 16.

Hanayo stumbles across the *yamauba* in a moment of crisis. Born as the beautiful and beloved child of a wealthy provincial governor, she leads a charmed life—that is until her mother dies and her father remarries. The new wife is predictably wicked; tales of abusive stepmothers have a long history in Japan as well as the West.[60] Unlike her counterpart in *Cinderella*, however, Hanayo's stepmother has no daughters of her own whose prospects she seeks to advance. Rather, she resents the affection that her husband lavishes on Hanayo and so devises a plan to rid herself of her perceived rival. Her opportunity comes when Hanayo's father leaves to consult with his former mother-in-law about a suitable match for his daughter, who will be unable to inherit his estate without a husband. (The purpose of this errand is significant: from the first, the tale makes clear that Hanayo's fate rides on her future marriage. Indeed, the man identified as a fitting fiancé for Hanayo is the same man she will eventually marry; destiny and paternal will converge.) Seizing the moment, Hanayo's stepmother hires a man to take her into the mountains and leave her there.

In both *The Bowl-Wearer* and *Hagskin*, the heroine's journey to the manor of her future husband takes her through a symbolically charged location where she undergoes a transformative event (respectively, attempted suicide in a river and a visitation from Kannon at a Buddhist temple). Hanayo is the only one of the three heroines whose path leads through the mountains—and, narratively speaking, it is a long path indeed. Although all of the tales in the trio tacitly construe long-suffering endurance as a feminine virtue, *Lady Hanayo* underscores the point through repetition. Hanayo's travels are not a single trial but a series of trials, which begin even before the henchman abandons her in the wilderness: eager to maximize his profit, he first brings her to his house and orders his wife to strip her of her fine robes. Although powerless to openly defy her husband, the henchman's wife aids Hanayo by dressing her in travellers' garb, concealing her beauty with a humble hempen garment and a reed hat.[61] With only this scant protection, Hanayo is deserted on a mountain known as Ubagamine, or "Hag Peak"—a pointed foreshadowing.

Having been forbidden to retrace her path, Hanayo presses onward into the wilderness. As night falls, she sees firelight in the distance and hurries toward it, thinking that it will lead her to a house; to her horror, she instead finds a cave with a hag squatting inside. Unlike the seemingly human demon in "A

---

[60] For an overview of Japanese tales of abused stepdaughters, or *mamako mono*, see Sachi Schmidt-Hori, "Symbolic Death and Rebirth into Womanhood."

[61] The reed hat given to Hanayo by the henchman's wife distantly recalls the wooden bowl that Hachikazuki's mother places over her head; indeed, some scholars have suggested that Hachikazuki's odd headgear was intended to mimic the conical, broad-brimmed rush hats worn by female travelers, including the itinerant storyteller-nuns who may have originally disseminated the tale. See Steven, "*Hachikazuki*," 311.

Woman with Child," the creature that Hanayo encounters is nakedly monstrous: "She did not look human ... Her face was [square] like a wooden serving tray, with sunken eye sockets and bulging eyeballs. Tusks protruded from her wide mouth up as far as her nose, which was pointed like a bird's beak. Her forehead was furrowed with wrinkles."[62] The corresponding illustration shows a horned, gargoyle-faced old woman seated before a fire with her legs akimbo and her open robe revealing sagging breasts; her body is immodestly displayed, but in the mode of the freakshow rather than the peepshow. Despite her fearsome appearance, the cave's occupant welcomes Hanayo warmly and, weeping, assures her guest of her good intentions:

> I was human once, but I lived too long. After my children passed away, my grandchildren and great-grandchildren took care of me, but they came to hate me and did not allow me in the house. So I made the mountains my home, spending my days gathering nuts to feed myself. One day, a man came down from the peak of this mountain and fell in love with me. He came to me regularly from the peak of Mount Fuji, but then he brought me to this cave and placed me here. During the day, he cuts firewood and piles it up by the mouth of the cave, and at night I build a fire to warm my old bones. Even as I am now, my human heart has been roused, and I feel compassion for you.[63]

The *yamauba* then announces that she has worms on her scalp, which cause her to itch; like her counterpart in the Daisenji temple chronicles, she is afflicted by her own flesh. Hanayo is ordered to pluck the parasites out with a pair of fire tongs. Despite her terror, she complies, and the *yamauba* eagerly devours the worms as they are extracted—a detail that establishes her as an antisocial creature of unclean appetites. After a miserable night in the cave, dawn breaks, and Hanayo is repaid for her assistance: the *yamauba* gives her a small bag, with instructions to open it only after she has found a man to marry, and then places three grains of sacred rice in Hanayo's mouth with the promise that they will sustain her for many days.

Hanayo's initial interaction with the *yamauba* follows a classic pattern of trial and reward, paralleling the Proppian progression of functions whereby a hero receives a magical item from a donor.[64] At this juncture, we might expect Hanayo to continue on her journey—but instead, the sequence of trial and reward repeats itself when the *yamauba's* demon husband makes a sudden

---

[62] "*Hanayo no hime*," in *Muromachi jidai monogatari taisei* vol 10, ed. Yokoyama Shigeru and Matsumoto Ryūshin (Tokyo: Kadokawa Shoten, 1982), 530.

[63] Ibid., 530-531.

[64] Vladimir Propp, *The Morphology of the Folktale*, trans. Laurence Scott (Austin: University of Texas Press, 1968), 39-44.

arrival. The tense scene that follows both echoes and amplifies the earlier episode in which the henchman's wife surreptitiously shields Hanayo from her husband's cruelty. Fearing that Hanayo will be devoured, the *yamauba* hides Hanayo in a pit at the back of the cave, although the ruse is not entirely successful: as soon as the demon enters, he complains of the smell. Like the giant's wife in *Jack and the Beanstalk*, the *yamauba* lies to protect her human guest from her keen-nosed and bloodthirsty husband.[65] In the process, however, she reveals her own cannibalistic tendencies: she claims that the odour is from a head (presumably human) that she recently discarded. Mollified, the demon departs, and the *yamauba* instructs Hanayo to walk upstream along a nearby river and remain at the first human residence that she encounters. Before Hanayo sets out, the *yamauba* clothes her in a magical robe that makes her appear to be an old woman—a reprisal of the scene in which the henchman's wife gives Hanayo her hempen robe. As before, the stated purpose of the disguise is merely to render Hanayo inconspicuous; unlike in *Hagskin*, the exact nature of the danger associated with being visibly young, beautiful, and female remains unspecified.

The treatment that Hanayo receives in her disguised state represents another point of departure from *Hagskin*. Wearing the *yamauba*'s magical robe and following her guidance, Hanayo arrives at the mansion of a nobleman. As instructed, Hanayo does not leave the spot, and a maidservant named Akino takes pity on the old lady sitting outside the gates and gives her work tending the fire. By contrast, *Hagskin* depicts a world with far less sympathy for the elderly; as the heroine travels, she is mocked for her ugliness, and she is offered employment at the manor only because the lord's son is struck by the curious discrepancy between her apparent age and her melodic voice. Hachikazuki likewise suffers abuse for her unsightly appearance and finds work in the mansion only because the lord considers her an amusing oddity. In inventing the character of Akino to grant the heroine entry into the lord's household, *Lady Hanayo* introduces an element of realism; after all, a lord would not be directly responsible for appointing servants to menial tasks. But at the same time, this alteration obscures the power dynamics made visible in *Hagskin* and *The Bowl-Wearer*, in which the heroine's fate is decided not by the compassion of a low-ranking woman but rather by the caprice of a high-ranking man.

---

[65] The motif of a monster's wife concealing a human visitor from her husband also features prominently in the Japanese folktale *Kozuna, the Demon's Child*, in which a girl is kidnapped by a demon and becomes his wife. When her father comes to look for her, she must hide him and invent a story to explain his scent. See Fanny Hagin Mayer, *Ancient Tales in Modern Japan: An Anthology of Japanese Folk Tales* (Bloomington: Indiana University Press, 1985), 102.

Although *Lady Hanayo* places greater narrative weight on interactions between female characters than either of its sister tales, Hanayo's happiness ultimately depends on her ability to win the heart of the lord's youngest son, Saishō. She succeeds in doing so, albeit unwittingly; in an act of voyeurism reminiscent of classical courtly romances, Saishō catches a glimpse of Hanayo while she is disrobed and is immediately smitten. The pair overcome the opposition of Saishō's parents, aided in part by the contents of the mysterious bag that Hanayo received from the *yamauba*. When she opens it at the designated time—that is, *after* she has found a man to marry—it contains a five-coloured jewel that turns into fine robes for her to wear when she presents herself alongside her sisters-in-law. (Contemporary audiences would have no doubt connected this to the Buddhist wish-granting jewel, or *nyoi hōju*, associated with Kannon.) However, like the riches eventually released from the bowl on Hachikazuki's head, the contents of the *yamauba*'s bag are in effect a dowry, and thus never fully in the possession of their supposed owner; they cannot be directed toward ends other than securing Hanayo's marriage. In short, Lady Hanayo constructs wifehood as a natural and necessary extension of womanhood— the final destination of the heroine's journey. Even the *yamauba*, bound to her demon husband, cannot break free from the marital imperative.

Blessing, but not Blessed: The Mountain Hag as Abject Fairy Godmother

On its surface, *Lady Hanayo* consciously imitates classic court literature, not only by embroidering its prose with stylistic flourishes but also by expanding its cast to include a host of secondary characters.[66] In true aristocratic fashion, the households of both Hanayo's father and her future father-in-law are populated with servants who act as confidants and go-betweens; thus, in one sense the *yamauba* is merely one of several female helper figures who assist Hanayo at various stages of her journey. In another sense, however, the *yamauba* stands strikingly apart. Alien to the world of aristocratic hierarchies and aesthetics, she is as much a folkloric borrowing as a literary invention, rooted in a body of orally transmitted folktales that cast the *yamauba* as a quasi-divine benefactor.[67]

---

[66] Despite its provincial setting, *Lady Hanayo* depicts the kind of rarefied lifestyle emblematic of the imperial court, perhaps reflecting the displacement of aristocrats and their culture to the provinces during the turbulence of Japan's Warring States Era (1457-1573); indeed, one function of the work may have been to "[instruct] affluent provincial lords to emulate certain customs." (Noriko Reider, "'Hanayo No Hime,' or 'Blossom Princess': A Late-Medieval Japanese Stepdaughter Story and Provincial Customs," *Asian Ethnology* 70, no. 1 (2011), 72.)

[67] Fukuda, *Mukashibanashi kara otogizōshi e*, 189.

Two folktales in particular stand out as close cousins of *Lady Hanayo: Millet Fortune, Rice Fortune* (*Awabuku Komebuku*) and *Hagskin* (*Ubakawa*, not to be confused with the sixteenth-century text of the same name). Although both were first recorded in the twentieth century, they are presumed to be considerably older; the history of their development relative to *Lady Hanayo* remains obscure, but the genetic connection is unmistakable. In both tales, the *yamauba* plays a role roughly comparable to that of the Western fairy godmother, while at the same time presenting a figure more pitiable than enviable.

Like *Lady Hanayo*, *Millet Fortune, Rice Fortune* enlists the *yamauba* as the ally of a persecuted stepdaughter—in this case, a peasant girl named Komebuku, who is sent into the mountains with her stepsister Awabuku to gather chestnuts. Awabuku quickly fills her bag and returns home, but Komebuku has been given a bag riddled with holes and cannot complete her task.[68] A familiar sequence follows: lost in the mountains, Komebuku happens upon a *yamauba*'s house, where she is offered shelter and asked to pick lice from the hair of her horrifying host. (This trial obviously corresponds to Hanayo's deworming of the *yamauba*'s scalp; the motif may have its roots in an eighth-century myth in which the god Okuninushi must pluck centipedes from the hair of his future father-in-law in order to win his bride.[69]) After Komebuku has completed this task, the *yamauba* rewards her with a mysterious box. Komebuku makes her way back to her stepmother's house but receives no better treatment than before; while Awabuku goes to a festival, Komebuku is left to do chores. Opening the box from the *yamauba*, she finds a sumptuous robe and decides that she will attend the festival too. There, a rich man sees her and asks for her as a bride. The stepmother attempts to smuggle her daughter into the wedding palanquin but does not succeed; the pair fall into a ditch and become mud snails, while Komebuku marries and lives happily ever after.

The commonalities between *Lady Hanayo* and *Millet Fortune, Rice Fortune*, require little elaboration. Further heightening the resemblance, some versions of *Millet Fortune, Rice Fortune* include a scene that closely mirrors Hanayo's narrow escape from the *yamauba*'s demon husband: the *yamauba*'s two demon sons come home and detect Komebuku's scent, but their mother manages to divert their attention. Unlike *Lady Hanayo*, which exists in a definitive form

---

[68] Komebuku and Awabuku respectively mean "rice fortune" and "millet fortune," reflecting the high prestige accorded to rice; like an ugly stepsister, millet ranked a poor second. The names of the sisters are not constant across all tellings; among other possible variations, Komebuku's stepsister may be named Nuwabuku ("Rice Bran Fortune"), and the suffix -*buku* may be written with the character meaning "bag" instead of "fortune." See Ikeda, *A Type and Motif Index of Japanese Folk Literature*, 138-139.

[69] Arakawa Rie, "*Yamauba no kawa o megutte: nugu koto to kiru koto,*" *Gakushūin Daigaku jōdai bungaku kenkyū* 30 (2005), 8.

with only minor discrepancies among manuscripts, *Millet Fortune, Rice Fortune* is not so much a singular tale as a mosaic of variants. Some tellings end with Awabuku refusing to pluck lice from the *yamauba* and receiving a bad gift— sometimes worthless, sometimes actively punitive—in contrast to the good gift granted to the virtuous Komebuku.[70] Most frequently, however, Komebuku's ultimate reward is not the *yamauba's* gift itself but rather the match that it facilitates. Awabuku's Kafkaesque metamorphosis after she is ejected from her stepsister's wedding palanquin further highlights the premium placed on marriage: she fails to become a bride, and so she becomes a bug.

The folktale *Hagskin* holds a different cluster of motifs in common with *Lady Hanayo*, but the similarities are no less striking. As the title suggests, the heroine, who goes unnamed in most tellings, receives a magical garment that makes her appear to be an old woman. Thus disguised, she tends the fire in a rich man's house until the rich man's son discovers her true beauty and takes her as his wife. When told as self-contained narratives, *Hagskin*-type folktales parallel *Lady Hanayo* from the outset; the heroine sets out on her journey after being evicted by her cruel stepmother. However, the folktale *Hagskin* more commonly attaches as a kind of second act to a folktale known as *The Snake Bridegroom (Hebi mukoiri)*.[71] In keeping with its title, *The Snake Bridegroom* opens with the heroine's father betrothing her to a snake, either in exchange for agricultural labour or to save the life of a frog that the snake has captured. Like her counterpart in Western *Beauty and the Beast*-type tales, the heroine dutifully consents to the match. But the similarity ends there: while she is an obedient daughter, she is anything but an obedient wife, and she immediately devises a plan to kill her reptilian husband.

In its simpler and unquestionably older form, *The Snake Bridegroom* ends with the heroine freed from her animal spouse and returning home not happily wed but happily widowed. However, rather than circling back to the status quo, some tellings instead set the heroine on a by-now familiar path: she acquires a hagskin garment (often but not always from a *yamauba*), finds employment as a fire-tender while in disguise, and in the end gains a second, more satisfactory husband. This addition not only extends the tale but fundamentally redirects its course. In its original form, *The Snake Bridegroom* takes a flatly unromantic view of marriage; the heroine's task is not to find a good husband but to rid herself of a bad one. But when the tale is hybridized

---

[70] Senno Michiko, "'*Komebuki Awabuki' ni miru kankeisei*," *Kyōto Kōka Joshi Daigaku kenkyū kiyō* 48 (2010), 13. This shorter, simpler version of the tale—which Senno speculates may be its original form—resembles ATU 410 ("The Kind and the Unkind Girls").

[71] Ikeda, *A Type and Motif Index of Japanese Folk Literature*, 139.

with the *Hagskin* narrative and the figure of the *yamauba* is introduced, a happy ending requires a husband after all. Far from embodying untameable female independence, the *yamauba* domesticates the husband-murdering heroine of *The Snake Bridegroom*, shepherding her into the role of wife.

Perhaps because the serpent-husband plays the part of the monster, the *yamauba* in hagskin-type *Snake Bridegroom* tales tends to lack the menacing aspect of her counterparts in *Lady Hanayo* and *Millet Fortune, Rice Fortune*, granting the magical garment to the heroine without demanding a delousing or some other boon. In some tellings, the *yamauba* is replaced by or combined with a frog, who rewards the heroine as thanks for defeating the snake. (Snakes and frogs were imagined to be natural enemies.) The theme of a grateful animal offering repayment to a human benefactor occurs frequently in Japanese lore. However, there is also a specific symbolic logic at work here: as "a magical object used to enact a rite of death and rebirth,"[72] the hagskin evokes the dramatic metamorphosis of the amphibian life cycle. The construction of the frog and the *yamauba* as alter egos also hints at a connection with a mountain goddess; folk-religious traditions in several regions of Japan worship a deity of the mountains who comes down to the fields in spring and then departs in the autumn in the form of a frog. (The logic behind this belief derives in part from wordplay, as the word for "frog" is homophonous with the verb meaning "to go back.") Within this paradigm, the young woman who receives the hagskin garment mirrors the mountain god descending to bring fertility to the spring fields; like the barrenness of winter, her haggard appearance will eventually blossom into beauty.[73]

Like her counterparts in *Millet Fortune, Rice Fortune* and the hagskin-type folktales—and also like fairy godmothers in Western stories—the *yamauba* of *Lady Hanayo* looks very much like a goddess writ small. She dispenses miraculous gifts that facilitate the heroine's transition from daughter to wife, initiating her into the role signifying female adulthood. Many scholars see in the *yamauba* mythic strands tied to both Buddhist and Shinto traditions. Perhaps she is an avatar of the bodhisattva Kannon, whom the tale names as Hanayo's protector.[74] Perhaps her demon husband is a mountain god and she is a priestess in his service, keeping a sacred fire.[75] A solid case can be made for these interpretations, but—as with readings that impute a benevolent dimension to the demon woman in "A Woman with Child"—there is an imperfect alignment between

---

[72] Arakawa, "*Yamauba no kawa o megutte*," 16.

[73] Okada, *Hachikazuki kenkyū* (Tokyo: Ōfū, 2002), 26-27.

[74] Okada, *Hachikazuki kenkyū*, 63; Reider, "'Hanayo No Hime,' or 'Blossom Princess,'" 68.

[75] Okada, *Hachikazuki kenkyū*, 24-25, 53-54.

the presumed hidden depths of the text and what is visible on its surface. Contemporary audiences would have come to *Lady Hanayo* with the cultural knowledge necessary to make connections of the sort described above, but they were presumably not reading as an exercise in indexing folkloric motifs; as Hotate Michihisa writes, it is impossible to know to what degree readers were consciously aware of the tale's mythic substrate.[76] When we attend to the *yamauba* as she is explicitly described, she emerges as a figure more abject than divine.

Lady Hanayo closes with a lengthy happily-ever-after sequence, which not only affirms the lasting good fortune of Hanayo and her husband but also enumerates the rewards and punishments meted out to the supporting characters. Hanayo's father remarries; her stepmother vanishes into self-imposed exile; the henchman is beheaded with a dull saw, while his compassionate wife is pardoned; Akino receives a house and a monthly stipend; and so on for several pages. Amid all this tying up of loose ends, the *yamauba's* story trails off into uncertainty. Only the fate of her robe is revealed:

> Lady Hanayo's father revered and made offerings to the hag robe that the *yamauba* had bestowed upon his daughter. A mound was built near the temple of Kannon to inter the garment, and memorial tablets were erected so that the *yamauba's* demonic nature would be transformed and she would attain salvation in the next life.[77]

This proxy funeral rite is curiously disconnected from its supposed beneficiary; insofar as readers know, the *yamauba* is still alive in the mountains. Although the *yamauba's* miraculous robe is enshrined as a kind of sacred relic, this veneration of the garment does not fully extend to its owner; the tale's final word on the *yamauba* is that she is a demon in need of salvation, contradicting (or at least complicating) interpretations that take her to be an avatar of Kannon.

The *yamauba's* account of her own history likewise paints a less-than-divine picture. Although she acts as a guide to Hanayo, directing her back to civilization, her course is determined by forces that propel her inexorably into the wilderness. She does not, as Mizuta writes, "freely choose her residence." Her residence is doubly chosen for her: she enters the mountains because her grandchildren have cast her out—a clear borrowing from the Obasuteyama legends—and inhabits the cave because her demon husband has brought her there. Her relationship with the demon reproduces the sexed hierarchy of human society; she is dependent upon and unequal to him, as demonstrated by her

---

[76] Hotate Michihisa, *Monogatari no chūsei: shinwa, setsuwa, minwa no rekishigaku* (Tokyo: Tokyo Daigaku Shuppankai, 1998), 327.

[77] "*Hanayo no hime,*" *Muromachi jidai monogatari taisei* vol. 10, 556.

inability to openly shield her human guest from his hunger. This is not to say that *Lady Hanayo* depicts absolute female disenfranchisement: the tale endows its secondary female characters with agency and interiority, gesturing towards a complex network of relationships among women in elite households and acknowledging female influence in certain spheres of decision-making. By comparison, the fearsome *yamauba* ironically stands out as an embodiment of female choicelessness.

Lady Hanayo is not alone in its depiction of the *yamauba* as a fundamentally tragic figure. The slippage from old woman to demon inevitably leads downward; the hunters' mother in *Tales of Times Now Past* and the *onibaba* of Adachigahara, both formerly human, inspire horror rather than envy. They are monsters of the sort that demand to be slain, as indeed they eventually are. Although the comparatively benign *yamauba* in *Lady Hanayo* does not become the target of violent conquest, she is rendered symbolically deceased by an *in absentia* funeral—a well-intentioned act, but one that nonetheless aims to end her existence as a *yamauba*. And it is an unhappy existence indeed. The *yamauba*'s implied cannibalism, her ugliness, and the squalor of her dwelling do not gleefully flout the norms prescribing female self-restraint, beauty, and domesticity; a straightforward reading of the text suggests that she is entirely as miserable as she first appears.

Herein lies a crucial paradox: the *yamauba* blesses but is not blessed. She bestows treasures upon Hanayo but lives a life of bare survival. She feeds Hanayo sacred rice, but her own diet is marked by deprivation and defilement. She guides Hanayo to an ideal marriage with a handsome young lord, but she herself is wed to a monster. Even at her most goddess-like, the *yamauba* does not represent an aspirational figure: readers might fantasize about receiving her aid, but they would not want to assume her place. *Lady Hanayo* takes it as given that it is better to be a beautiful young bride than an ugly old woman; after all, the heroine gains her happy ending only after she sheds the *yamauba*'s hag robe.

Out of the Mountains

"The monster polices the borders of the possible," declares Jeffery Jerome Cohen in his seminal essay "Monster Culture: Seven Theses."[78] The outwardly demonic but selflessly benevolent *yamauba* of *Lady Hanayo* and her outwardly human but hungrily malevolent counterpart in "A Woman with Child" are very different sorts of monster—one might say their border policing is of the good

---

[78] Jeffrey Jerome Cohen, "Monster Culture (Seven Theses)," in *Monster Theory: Reading Culture*, ed. Jeffrey Jerome Cohen (Minneapolis: University of Minnesota Press, 1996), 12.

cop/bad cop variety. However, they both function to return women who have gone astray to their proper places, both spatially and socially: the protagonist of "A Woman with Child" resumes service in her employer's household, while Hanayo assumes her predetermined role as a wife. For both women, this restoration to civilization is a desirable outcome; there is no implication that the mountains offer an escape from the constraints of human society. On the contrary, human society offers an escape from the danger of the mountains, where those who linger too long may well be eaten.

Monsters are polysemous, palimpsest creatures with no fixed form or meaning, rewritten and reread to meet many needs, and the *yamauba* signifies more capaciously than most. In the twenty-first century, she seems to entice across boundaries rather than enforce them; scholars see in her an unrepentantly ugly woman of unrestrained appetites, undiminished by old age. Interpretations in this vein put the *yamauba* to worthy use—but not to her intended use. There is little reason to believe that the original audiences of "A Woman with Child," *Lady Hanayo*, and other premodern narratives about *yamauba* saw the ancient cannibal woman in the mountains as a subversive or seductive figure. Whether cast in the role of predator or benefactor, she affirmed the values of the people who told her story.

Bibliography

Primary Sources

"Hanayo no hime." In Muromachi jidai monogatari taisei vol 10, ed. Yokoyama Shigeru and Matsumoto Ryūshin, 515-559. Tokyo: Kadokawa Shoten, 1982.

Satō Kenzō, ed. Konjaku monogatarishū: Honchō sezokubu jōkan. Tokyo: Kadokawa Shoten, 1995.

Satō Kenzō, ed. Konjaku monogatarishū: Honchō sezokubu gekan. Tokyo: Kadokawa Shoten, 1995.

"Ubakawa." In Shinchū Muromachi monogatarishū, ed. Hamanaka Osamu, 13-21. Tokyo: Benseisha, 1989.

Secondary Sources

Arakawa Rie. "Yamauba no kawa o megutte: nugu koto to kiru koto." *Gakushūin Daigaku jōdai bungaku kenkyū* 30, 1-17, 2005.

Baba Akiko. *Oni no kenkyū.* Tokyo: Chikuma Shobō, 1988. First published in 1971 by San'ichi Shobō.

Bargen, Doris. *A Woman's Weapon: Spirit Possession in the Tale of Genji.* Honolulu: University of Hawaii, 1997.

Cohen, Jeffrey Jerome. "Monster Culture (Seven Theses)." In *Monster Theory: Reading Culture*, ed. Jeffrey Jerome Cohen, 3–25. Minneapolis: University of Minnesota Press, 1996.

Copeland, Rebecca. "Mythical Bad Girls: The Corpse, the Crone, the Snake." In *Bad Girls of Japan*, edited by Laura Miller and Jan Bardsley, 15-32. New York: Palgrave Macmillan, 2005.

Cornell, Laurell. "The Deaths of Old Women: Folklore and Differential Mortality in Nineteenth-Century Japan." In *Recreating Japanese Women, 1600–1945*, ed. Gail Lee Bernstein, 71-87. Berkeley: University of California, 1991.

Dix, Monika. "Hachikazuki: Revealing Kannon's Crowning Compassion in Muromachi Fiction." *Japanese Journal of Religious Studies* 36, no. 2, 279–94, 2009.

Farris, William Wayne. *Japan's Medieval Population: Famine, Fertility, and Warfare in a Transformative Age*. Honolulu: University of Hawai'i Press, 2006.

Fukuda Akira. *Mukashibanashi kara otogizōshi e: Muromachi monogatari to minkan denshō*. Tokyo: Miyai Shoten, 2000.

Hijikata Yōichi. "Fūjirareta gūi: Konjaku sezoku setsuwa ichimen." *Kokugo to kokubungaku* 64 No. 2 ,46-64, February 1987.

Hotate Michihisa. *Monogatari no chūsei: shinwa, setsuwa, minwa no rekishigaku*. Tokyo: Tokyo Daigaku Shuppankai, 1998.

Hulvey, Yumiko. "Myths and Monsters: The Female Body as the Site for Political Agendas." In *Body Politics and the Fictional Double*, ed. Debra Walker King, 71-88. Bloomington: Indiana University Press, 2000.

Ikeda Hiroko. *A Type and Motif Index of Japanese Folk Literature*. Helsinki: Suomalainen Tiedakatemia, 1971.

Ikegami Jun'ichi. "Kusainagi no shōtai: 'Konjaku monogatarishū' no nango kōshō." In *Setsuwa to sono shūhen*, vol. 4 of *Ikegami Jun'ichi Chosakushū*, 177-189. Osaka: Izumi Shoin, 2008.

Kawashima Miki. "Nihon no oni no kenkyū." *Tamayura* 18, 1-9, 1986.

Kawashima, Terry. Writing Margins: *The Textual Construction of Gender in Heian and Kamakura Japan*. Cambridge, MA: Harvard Asia Center Publications, 2001.

Komatsu Kazuhiko. *Kamikakushi: Ikai kara no izanai*. Tokyo: Kōbundō, 1991.

Kondō Yoshihiro. *Nihon no oni: Nihon bunka tankyū no shikaku*. Tokyo: Ōfūsha, 1967.

Li, Michelle Osterfield. *Ambiguous Bodies: Reading the Grotesque in Japanese Setsuwa Tales*. Stanford: Stanford University Press, 2009.

_____. "Human of the Heart: Pitiful Oni in Medieval Japan." In *The Ashgate Research Companion to Monsters and the Monstrous*, ed. Asa Simon Mittman with Peter Dendle, 173–96. London: Ashgate Publishing, 2012.

Mayer, Fanny Hagin, trans. and intr. *Ancient Tales in Modern Japan: An Anthology of Japanese Folk Tales*. Bloomington: Indiana University Press, 1985.

Mizuta Noriko. "Yamauba no yume: joron to shite." In *Josei no genkei to katarinaoshi: yamaubatachi no monogatari*, ed. Mizuta Noriko and Kitada Sachie, 7-37. Tokyo: Gakugei Shorin, 2002.

Mori Masato. "Kodai shinsei hyōgenron josetsu." *Kokugo kokubungaku kenkyū* 49, 20-36, 2014.

_____. "'Konjaku Monogatari-Shū': Supernatural Creatures and Order." *Japanese Journal of Religious Studies* 9, no. 2/3, 147-70, 1982.

Moriyama Shigeki and Nakae Kazue. *Nihon kodomo shi.* Tokyo: Heibonsha , 2002.

Mulhern, Chieko Irie. "Cinderella and the Jesuits. An Otogizōshi Cycle as Christian Literature." *Monumenta Nipponica* 34, no. 4, 409–47, 1979.

_____. "Analysis of Cinderella Motifs, Italian and Japanese." *Asian Folklore Studies* 44, no. 1, 1–37, 1985.

Okada Keisuke. *Hachikazuki kenkyū.* Tokyo: Ōfū, 2002.

Orikuchi Shinobu. "Okina no hassei." In *Orikuchi Shinobu zenshū* volume 2, ed. Orikuchi Shinobu zenshū kankōkai, 371-415. Tokyo: Chūō Kōronsha, 1995. First published in 1929 in Minzoku Geijutsu.

Ōtō Tokihiko. *Nihon minzokugaku no kenkyū.* Tokyo: Gakueisha, 1979.

Propp, Vladimir. *The Morphology of the Folktale.* Trans. Laurence Scott. Austin: University of Texas Press, 1968.

Reider, Noriko. "'Hanayo No Hime,' or 'Blossom Princess': A Late-Medieval Japanese Stepdaughter Story and Provincial Customs." *Asian Ethnology* 70, no. 1, 59–80, 2011.

_____. *Mountain Witches: Yamauba.* Logan: Utah State University Press, 2021.

Sahara Sakumi. "Konjaku monogatarishū ni okeru reikitan no kōzō: dai nijūnana o chūshin ni." *Komazawa tandai kokubun* 19, 1-21, 1989.

Schmidt-Hori, Sachi. "Symbolic Death and Rebirth into Womanhood: An Analysis of Stepdaughter Narratives from Heian and Medieval Japan." *Japanese Language and Literature* 54 no. 2, 448–475, 2020.

Senno Michiko. "'Komebuki Awabuki' ni miru kankeisei." *Kyōto Kōka Joshi Daigaku kenkyū kiyō* 48, 11-31, 2010.

Steven, Chigusa. "Hachikazuki: A Muromachi Short Story." *Monumenta Nipponica* 32, no. 3, 303–31, 1977.

Tokuda Kazuo. "Nō to setsuwa, denshō yamauba o megutte: Zeami jidai no yamauba denshō (1)." *Kanze* 83, no. 6, 36-41, June 2016.

_____. "Nō to setsuwa, denshō yamauba o megutte: Zeami jidai no yamauba denshō (2)." *Kanze* 83, no. 8, 42-48, August 2016.

_____. "Nō to setsuwa, denshō yamauba o megutte: Zeami jidai no yamauba denshō (3)." *Kanze* 83, no. 10, 42-47, October 2016.

_____. "Nō to setsuwa, denshō yamauba o megutte: Zeami jidai no yamauba denshō (4)." *Kanze* 83, no. 12, 34-39, December 2016.

Tonomura, Hitomi. "Birth-Giving and Avoidance Taboo: Women's Body versus the Historiography of 'Ubuya.'" *Japan Review* 19, 3-45, 2007.

Ury, Marian. "A Heian Note on the Supernatural." *The Journal of the Association of Teachers of Japanese* 22, no. 2, 189–194, 1988.

_____. trans. and intr. *Tales of Times Now Past: Sixty-Two Stories from a Medieval Japanese Collection.* Berkeley: University of California Press, 1979.

Viswanathan, Meera. "In Pursuit of the Yamamba: The Question of Female Resistance." In *The Woman's Hand: Gender and Theory in Japanese Women's*

Writing, ed. Paul Schalow and Gordon Walker, 239-261. Stanford: Stanford University Press, 1996.

Yamaori Tetsuo. "The Image of 'Rōjo' or Elderly Women in Japanese Legend." *Japan Review* 9, 29-40, 1997.

Yamauchi Hisashi. Mononoke. Tokyo: Hōsei Daigaku Shuppankyoku, 2004.

Yanagita Kunio. "Yama no jinsei." In *Teihon Yanagita Kunio zenshū* volume 4, 59-171. Tokyo: Chikuma Shobō, 1963. First published in 1926 by *Kyōdo Kenkyūsha.*

_____. "Hitotsume kōzō." In *Teihon Yanagita Kunio zenshū* volume 5, 117-159. Tokyo: Chikuma Shobō, 1962. First published in 1934 by Oyama Shoten.

Chapter 7

Enlightening Monsters: Collecting and Displaying *Yōkai* Relics in Early Modern Japanese Buddhism

Kevin Bond

University of Regina

Abstract

The last few decades have seen a burgeoning interest in *yōkai*, one of the most influential categories of the "monstrous" in Japanese religious and folkloric cultures. Such supernatural entities, often zoological in appearance, have become well known to academic discourse and the public imagination via their depictions in early modern (seventeenth to nineteenth centuries) illustrated media such as encyclopedic catalogues.

However, much less known and understood is the manufacture of taxidermic and osseous remains of *yōkai,* which were simultaneously employed among early modern Buddhist institutions as cryptid-like relics.

This chapter examines such purported *yōkai* remains as understudied "monstrous" oddities that were adopted as atypical religious objects and threaded into the Buddhist world of relics, legends, and corresponding practices of display. It approaches *yōkai* relics as imaginative products whose accumulation became a form of spiritual wealth to bolster the auspicious history and status of Buddhist temples. To do so, I draw on recent monster theory and method by scholars such as cultural anthropologist and folklorist Komatsu Kazuhiko, to examine several early modern legends concerning the confrontation, subjugation, and enshrinement of *yōkai* and their relics within Buddhist sites. I investigate the particular cosmological ambiguity and, thus, characteristic polyvalence that made them attractive candidates for adoption into a unique subclass of divine agents, which today remains largely ignored by Buddhist scholarship. I contend that the extraordinary nature of their physical remains was employed as a new form of fashionable spiritual currency, one that can be understood as the products of distinctive developments in early modern material culture, as instruments of cultural power and exchange among intellectual, commercial, and political spheres, which still resonate across Japanese religion today.

Keywords: Japanese Buddhism, local legends, *yōkai*, relics, cryptids, material culture, display culture, Material Culture of Relics

*** * ***

Introduction

In the autumn of 2014, the Japanese public was treated to an exhibition of supernatural creatures known as *yōkai* 妖怪, an amorphous class of mysterious, creepy, often monstrous entities that for centuries have remained fixtures in religious, artistic, and intellectual discourse. The event was held in Osaka's commercial and entertainment district of Umeda. It featured two hundred pieces, many from the famous Yumoto Kōichi 湯本豪一 Collection[1] in the form of illustrated scrolls, coloured woodblock prints, and various handcrafts, objects, and texts depicting *yōkai*, dating mostly from the Edo or early modern period (1603–1868), a golden age of Japanese monster culture.[2] The month-long event dubbed the largest of its kind in Japan, capitalized on the recent burst of similar exhibitions across the country's museums and galleries catering to the public's current fascination with Japan's folkloric, supernatural past but also the contemporary popular media culture—*manga, anime*, live-action film, and video games—in which *yōkai* creatures increasingly feature.

What distinguished the Osaka exhibition, however, was the display of purported physical remains of specimens described as "mummies" (*miira* ミイラ) of *yōkai* "cryptids" (*genjū* 幻獣, lit., "imaginary beast").[3] Such so-called mummified relics were composed of odd, occasionally grotesque, taxidermic and osseous composites of small suspect animals such as fish, birds, cats, and monkeys, providing extra visceral materiality and physical presence compared to their more common two-dimensional representations. The morbid, albeit fascinatingly creative craftsmanship offered up displays of anatomic parts

---

[1] Japan's largest private collection of *yōkai* artworks and objects. See Yumoto Kōichi, *Konjaku yōkai taikan* (Tokyo: PIE International, 2013), *Konjaku yōkai ruirui* (Tokyo: PIE International, 2017*)*, and *Yōkai ezōshi* (Tokyo: PIE International, 2018) for reproductions of the collection. The Yumoto Collection is now housed in the Yumoto Kōichi Memorial Japan *Yōkai* Museum (Miyoshi Mononoke Museum), Japan's first public *yōkai* museum, which opened in Miyoshi City, Hiroshima Prefecture, in 2019.

[2] The exhibition homepage, http://kudanchan.jp/, is unfortunately no longer available. Limited images and promotional material from the event's corporate organizers, Knowledge Capital Association and KMO Corporation, can be found at https://kc-i.jp/Content/263.

[3] Like the English term "cryptid" which emerged in the 1980s, "*genjū*" is a recent neologism that, according to Itō, seems to have appeared in the 1970s (Itō 2010: 14).

(such as heads and arms) and even complete corpses of well-known *yōkai* such as the *kappa* 河童 (turtle-like water goblins), *ningyo* 人魚 (merpeople), and *karasu tengu* 烏天狗 (hybrid human-crow mountain spirits). The collection was promoted as "Japan's first public exhibition of *yōkai* cryptids" and attracted media and folklorists weighing in on the nature of such an odd menagerie of purported *yōkai* remains, including collector and scholar Yumoto Kōichi himself.[4]

Headlining the event was the preserved corpse of a *kudan* 件, a small bovine-human hybrid composed of a strange-looking human face stitched to a calf-like body. Much like the recent *yōkai* Amabie merperson invoked to fight Coronavirus in 2019,[5] the *kudan* is considered gifted with prophetic ability and has, therefore, long been an auspicious *yōkai* since Edo times. Images of the beast are known to have been treated as a type of protective talisman in the hopes of dispensing protective blessings and warding away the very misfortune it portends.[6] The *kudan*'s body was therefore deemed appropriate for placement on an altar before a small Shintō shrine complete with a traditional red *torii* gate. Though a temporary construction for the event, the shrine housing suggests the *yōkai* something akin (or equal) to the traditional sacred Shintō spirit manifestations known as *kami* 神, and so considered worthy of veneration. Event organizers presented the *kudan* as an animate creature imbued with personality and interest in social interaction. It was affectionately called "little baby *kudan*," and given a less morbid, cutesy cartoon appearance in advertising. Promotional materials depict the calf-human hybrid standing upright and wide-eyed, announcing (in a familiar

---

[4] Knowledge Capital, "'Yōkai genjū hyakumonogatari' kaisai: Nihon hatsukōkai no yōkai genjū no miira ga tōjō" 「妖怪幻獣百物語」開催: 日本初公開の妖怪幻獣のミイラが登場! August 20, 2022, https://kc-i.jp/Content/263. The exhibition was called "One Hundred Tales of *Yōkai* Cryptids" (*Yōkai genjō hyakumonogatari* 妖怪幻獣百物語). Not the first of its kind, the Osaka exhibition was preceded in 2006 by a more modest *yōkai* cryptid exhibition held at the National Museum of Nature and Science in Tokyo. A similar exhibition, *Genjō miira daihakurankai: oni kara ningyō made* 幻獣ミイラ大博覧会-鬼から人魚まで (Cryptid Mummy Exposition: From Demons to Merpeople, stylized in promotional material as "Remains of Cryptids Expo: Various Cryptids, from Demon to Mermaid"), was held more recently in summer 2021 at the Yumoto Kōichi Memorial Japan Yōkai Museum (Miyoshi Mononoke Museum), and featured several of the same yōkai cryptids (homepage with images can be found at: https://miyoshi-mononoke.jp/2021/07/1423/).
[5] For an examination of the Amabie viral internet phenomenon, see Takayashi and Fujii.
[6] See Murakami. Also see Yamaguchi, 2010: 104–111 and 2014: 172–175 for details and images of Osaka *kudan*.

Osaka dialect), "I'm no cow, I'm a *kudan!* I have a cow's body and a human head. Come witness my strange and prophetic self!"[7]

While perhaps an unexpected sight, the *kudan*'s enshrinement, along with the display of its less-animate siblings, is particularly revealing about the status and function of *yōkai* and their purported remains as lesser-known sacred objects and even divine (or semi-divine) agents in the history of Japanese religion. For centuries, *yōkai* have existed on the peripheries of religious spaces as strange, otherworldly outsiders that were typically excluded, but at times included, among local pantheons, rituals, and official Buddhist temple and Shintō shrine histories. Within religious spaces, they have comprised a small class of benevolent, even enlightened, entities that, despite a lower-order status, may still dispense community blessings alongside the more common *kami* and Buddhist divinities. While museum and gallery exhibitions have become a primary space in which the contemporary public may gain access to the visual and material culture of Japan's *yōkai* history, religious sites have long been important proprietors of purported *yōkai* remains. Since at least the early modern period, a high proportion of taxidermic and osseous *yōkai* objects (such as teeth, claws, horns, skulls, and bones, but occasionally entire mummified corpses) have been owned by Buddhist temples and Shinto shrines, and often on display for public viewing. Today, many have found their way into the hands of private collectors, families, and museums, but a significant number (an accurate count of which remains unknown) remain in the possession of temples and shrines. Recent fieldwork by folklorist Yamaguchi Naoki cataloguing nearly sixty examples show common groups to be the mountain ogre or demon (*oni* 鬼) and *karasu tengu*, the aquatic *ningyo*, *kappa*, and dragon (*ryū* 竜) or serpent (*daija* 大蛇), as well as a miscellany group of "beasts" (*kemono* 獣) that includes the *kudan*, with a number preserved by temples and shrines as thaumaturgical objects.[8]

In this chapter, I examine *yōkai* and their purported physical remains as understudied "monstrous" oddities that were adopted as atypical religious objects and threaded into the larger, especially Buddhist, world of relics, legends, and corresponding practices of display. The relatively small number of such extant remains should not be dismissed, however, as an aberration in the footnotes of Japanese Buddhist history. Rather, they should be appreciated as imaginative products whose accumulation became a form of "spiritual wealth" to bolster a site's auspicious history and status in order to dispense miraculous benefits to its community and its ability to secure patronage. To

---

[7] Knowledge Capital, "'Yōkai genjū hyakumonogatari' kaisai: Nihon hatsukōkai no yōkai genjū no miira ga tōjō" 妖怪幻獣百物語」開催:日本初公開の妖怪幻獣のミイラが登場! August 20, 2022, https://kc-i.jp/Content/263.

[8] Yamaguchi.

do so, I draw on recent monster theory and method by scholars such as cultural anthropologist and folklorist Komatsu Kazuhiko to examine several early modern legends concerning the confrontation, subjugation, and enshrinement of *yōkai* and their relics within Buddhist sites. I investigate the particular cosmological ambiguity and, thus, characteristic polyvalence that made them attractive candidates for adoption into a unique subclass of divine agents that today remains largely ignored by Buddhist scholarship.[9] I contend that the extraordinary nature of their physical remains was employed as a new form of fashionable spiritual currency, one that can be understood as a product of distinctive developments in early modern material culture, as instruments of cultural power and exchange among wider intellectual, commercial, and even political spheres within and beyond the religious precinct, and that still resonates across Japanese religion today.

Yōkai and the Monstrous

Japan has long played host to all manner of supernatural phenomena ranging from the bizarre and humorous to the malevolent and monstrous. A wide spectrum of these strange presences and frightful creatures are today collectively known as "*yōkai*," an umbrella term composed of Sino-Japanese characters meaning "eerie," "mysterious," or "ominous."[10] The late eighteenth-century illustrated encyclopedic catalogues of artist Toriyama Sekien 鳥山石燕 (1712–1788) famously depict a vast assortment of over two hundred such strange entities: cannibalistic predators, shapeshifting animals, spectres of the human dead, phantom mirages and ghost lights, fantastic spirits borne from flora and fauna, and mischievous housewares sprung to whimsical animate life.[11]

Despite their great number and variety, a defining characteristic of *yōkai* is their commonly amorphous natures that, as folklorist Michael Dylan Foster notes, "Defy definitive categorization—they are ambiguously positioned beyond (or between) good and evil."[12] In early modern text and images, they are found to shift along ontological, behavioural, and iconographical spectrums easily. They may move about the world without restraint and across boundaries, separating the human world from the otherworld of spirits and gods. Some appear as malevolent creatures haunting the dark recesses of a forest, and others as protective neighbours bringing blessings to a community. The form in

---

[9] Faure similarly notes how Japanese and Western scholars continue to overlook Buddhist demons and their fluid relationship with the gods (Faure, 5).

[10] For a history of the term and its polemical use in Meiji-period (1868–1912) academia toward modernization efforts in Japan, see Figal, 40–52.

[11] See Toriyama for a modern reprint. For an English translation with annotations, see Yoda and Alt.

[12] Foster, 15.

which *yōkai* so behave is accordingly subject to easy change and adaptability: they may be unformed, inhabit natural or manufactured objects, or transform into anthropomorphic or animal forms on a whim, often undetected by the human realm. In early modern times, many *yōkai* were consequently known as *bakemono* 化物, a term comprised of characters meaning "thing" or "being" (*mono* 物) that "changes," "disguises," or "takes form" (*bake* 化). This unpredictable, often unknowable, nature of the *yōkai* is a prime example of the fundamental transmutable character of all beings in Japanese cosmology, including humans, spirits, animals, and gods.[13]

Any blanket definition of *yōkai* as Japanese "monsters," then, is entirely problematic. "*Yōkai*" is too broad and varied a term in practice to consider it populated by any monolithic species. (The more specific Japanese term "*kaibutsu*" 怪物 is perhaps a more apt analogue for the Western term "monster.") Their penchant for mutability further frustrates taxonomic strategies toward a coherent structural classification, and so does not satisfy any certain definitions of "monster," "evil," "foe", and so forth. The conceptual label of "monster" is here, as Mikles and Laycock write in their work on monster theory, a "second-order category,"[14] a non-native convention imposed by power structures (such as academia) looking outward from a presumed centre to periphery.

Nonetheless, many *yōkai* certainly behave "monstrously" in their disruption of these very power structures. In his influential 1996 essay on monster theory, Jeffrey Jerome Cohen suggests that monsters commonly refuse easy taxonomic efforts and so elude and disrupt the conventional classificatory "order of things" and that as their "incoherent bodies resist attempts to include them in any systematic structuration...the monster is dangerous, a form suspended between forms that threatens to smash distinctions."[15] Drawing on J.Z. Smith's study of religion as a taxonomic category, Mikles and Laycock propose a modified, and here more useful, process of definition: the ontological ambiguity of an entity that threatens (and paradoxically reinforces) categorical distinctions (such as good versus evil or god versus monster) is, rather, what makes it "monstrous." Conversely, such ambiguity may just as easily render an entity as "godly."

A useful demonstration of such a "godly monstrosity" recognizable to Western audiences is the iconic Godzilla (Jpn. Gojira), the king of "*kaijū*" 怪獣 or "strange beasts" who operates as a close analogue to *yōkai*. A slumbering ancestor rising from his otherworldly watery abode, Godzilla invades the human realm in the role of the traditional angry spirit (*goryō* 御霊) meting out (indiscriminate)

---

[13] Papp, 39.
[14] Mikles and Laycock, 6–7.
[15] Cohen, 6.

divine punishment on society for its (nuclear) transgressions. In the original 1956 film, Godzilla is simultaneously revered as a *kami* by clergy and feared as an apocalyptic enemy of the nation. His destructive wrath plays within both categories of "friend" (a desperate rally call against the proliferation of nuclear weapons) and "foe" (mass annihilation of life and property), smashing distinctions between god and monster to elicit a combination of celebration and horror that has become an entertaining staple of the franchise.

Periphery and Centre: *Yōkai* as Buddhist Outsiders and Insiders

Central to the audience's fear and fascination of Godzilla's monstrosity is the *kaijū*'s unchecked mobility. Godzilla exists freely outside human institutions in an unpredictable, uncontrollable state and so enjoys independence from human authority. His ebb and flow between his abode in the ocean depths and urban centres like Tokyo offers a modern cinematic depiction of two fundamental divisions of Japanese cosmology: first, the undomesticated, wild spaces inhabited by otherworldly entities like spirits, gods, and *yōkai* (typically located in inhospitable terrain like mountains, forests, water bodies, and caves); and second, an opposing domesticated, ordered space of cultivated lands and human villages. Monsters, *yōkai* scholar Zília Papp notes, historically occupy such "terrain helping to demarcate the concepts of *uchi* (内, inside) and *soto* (外, outside), the physical and psychological categories that differentiate insiders and outsiders."[16] Religious sites, as social and intellectual historian Federico Marcon also notes, commonly stand at the confluence of these spaces as boundary markers and negotiating agents mediating any wayward supernatural traffic like *yōkai* that might cross over unannounced and unchecked.[17]

Like Godzilla, then, *yōkai* may be shunned or welcomed by the human realm. In his study of *yōkai* culture, anthropologist and folklorist Komatsu Kazuhiko draws on Yamaguchi Masao's conceptual theory of boundaries and offers helpful insight into the spatial behaviour of the Japanese supernatural. Yamaguchi considers images, symbols, and practices devalued or deemed taboo by society to be ostracized to the periphery of ordered space in order to maintain a stabilized, coherent (human) worldview. This chaotic periphery remains, however, active and dynamic, and discontent to forever insulate normative civilization and order from the taboo, which eventually gravitates toward and revitalizes the centre.[18] Komatsu considers strange phenomena like *yōkai* as examples of such outsiders that may approach the centre. Similarly,

---

[16] Papp, 87.
[17] Marcon, 3–4.
[18] Komatsu, 165–166.

Mikles and Laycock contend that while monsters are often quarantined to the periphery, they tend to return to the ordered centre, where they transform outsider to insider, monster to god, to be granted citizenship by a community.[19]

Understanding this supernatural dynamic between centre and periphery requires a few words on the relationship between *yōkai* and their closest and oldest divine relatives, the *kami*. The father of modern Japanese folklore studies, Yanagita Kunio 柳田国男 (1875–1962), considered *yōkai* as "ruined" or "downfallen" (*reiraku* 零落) *kami* whose divinity had diminished over time as new power structures emerged. *Yōkai*, he states, are essentially former *kami* no longer recognized as such.[20] For instance, a *kami* of water (*suijin* 水神) may be reduced to the *yōkai* status of a *kappa* (water goblin), or a *kami* of the mountain (*yama no kami* 山の神) relegated to an existence as a mountain hag (*yamauba, yamanba* 山姥).[21] Such *yōkai* are the "losers" stripped of their ritual support networks and pantheonic memberships and exiled as orphans to join the wilds on the edges of human civilization.

Contemporary scholars like Komatsu, however, consider Yanagida's well-known theory on the supernatural somewhat limited by not fully considering the complexity of *yōkai*. Komatsu acknowledges that *kami* may certainly "degrade" into *yōkai* and be abandoned to the periphery. He notes instances of unworshipped *kami* left neglected in an abandoned house or dumped by the roadside or in a field.[22] However, he also considers the inverse: that *yōkai* may (again) be elevated in status to proper divinities where they are invited to return to the civilized centre to (re)join a pantheonic order and (re)gain divine status.[23]

A key indicator differentiating the two supernatural states of insider and outsider is an entity's positive or negative worth to a community. Komatsu considers the status and function of supernatural entities like *yōkai* and *kami* in terms of value systems and commodities. He notes that *kami* possess some commodity of human value, and so enjoy the trust and worship of a community expressed via enshrinement and deification (*matsuri age* 祀り上げ). *Yōkai* typically enjoys no such favourable treatment or positive value, and so are denied enshrinement (*matsuri sute* 祀り棄て) as mistrusted, unaffiliated outsiders and potential dangers. Such dynamic systems of enshrinement/worshipped (*yōkai* to *kami*) and abandonment/unworshipped

---

[19] Mikles and Laycock, 13.
[20] Yanagita, 16.
[21] Komatsu, Ch. 2.1.
[22] Komatsu, Ch. 2.1.
[23] Komatsu, Ch. 2.1.

(*kami* to *yōkai*) have fundamentally shaped traditional Japanese attitudes toward divinities.[24]

Komatsu further explores a second and related strategic approach long employed to deal with harmful *yōkai* that proves especially useful here. This falls into the more familiar monster-killing category, which he calls the "slaying" (*taiji* 退治) of dangerous *kami* and *yōkai*. He examines folktales of monster hunting and dragon-slaying by famous heroes in which malevolent gods and *yōkai* were feared as monstrous outsiders and so considered antagonists to be punished and defeated in order to save the community from, for instance, demands of human sacrifice.[25] Importantly, his analysis evidences that slaying *yōkai* was not always an absolute or finite process but, at times, a *precursor* to an eventual enshrinement, with the act of slaying more pronounced in narrative and enshrinement expressed by real-world ritual performance. For example, he notes a case in the mountain village Monobeson in Kōchi Prefecture of a monstrous serpent that, once killed, was enshrined and deified by villagers for fear of it spreading retaliatory curses. These two seemingly contradictory treatments of the supernatural antagonist— destruction and deification—coexist as part of a larger parallel system to, first, subjugate malevolent spiritual entities and, second, pacify any lingering resentment and thus retribution by those potentially angry forces.

As we will see in detail below, *yōkai* became prominent targets of this subjugation-enshrinement process among esoteric Buddhist (Mikkyō 密教) temples that, in concert with political, artistic, and material developments of the early modern age, are found operative in the pantheonic adoption of *yōkai* and curation of their sacred relics by temple sites. It should be of no surprise that esoteric temples figure prominently among curators of *yōkai* remains. The esoteric forms of Japanese Buddhism, primarily represented by the Shingon 真言 and Tendai 天台 traditions, have long promoted a complex demonology and rich pantheon replete with evil beings brought under control by magico-religious rituals. Such esoteric designs over the monstrous, and the cosmological, geographical jurisdiction consequently imposed by Shingon and Tendai sites are embodied by the *maṇḍala*, iconographical, geometric depictions of esoteric

---

[24] Komatsu, Ch. 2.1.

[25] Komatsu, Ch. 2.1. The slaying of *yōkai* may also have roots in early modern concepts of "outsiders" (*ijin* 異人) and legends of "outsider-murders" (*ijin goroshi* 異人殺し) by villagers which emerged in the early modern period. Scholars like Komatsu have considered *yōkai* as examples of Japanese concepts of *ijin* outsiders as otherworldly, strange travelers who cross over into the human realm, whose ambiguity is variously resolved by rejection, discrimination, or even killing in order preserve order and bring blessings to the community (Komatsu, 150–163).

memberships and hierarchies in which the highest-ranking gods sit as kings and queens in the centre surrounded by increasingly-lower level, converted deities, placed around the periphery of the *maṇḍala* space.

I consider these esoteric methods of ritual and iconographical control and jurisdiction an example of what Foster calls an early modern "encyclopedic discourse" toward *yōkai*—taxonomic strategies employed by artists, writers, and intelligentsia since Edo times to reclassify and reorder *yōkai*, spurred by their problematic, but also alluring polyvalence and easy adaptability. As lesser beings considered in need of religious salvation, *yōkai* easily fell under the crosshairs of the (esoteric) Buddhist clergy, which often included them among the wide assortment of malevolent forces bringing fear and harm, such as demons, vengeful spirits (*mononoke* 物の気, *onryō* 怨霊), hungry ghosts (*gaki* 餓鬼), dragons, and unruly *kami*. However, esoteric Buddhist institutions also have a long and demonstrated history of ritual and iconographical subjugation (*chōboku* 調伏) in which spiritual rivals were converted in form and function to newly adopted allies of the *dharma*. *Yōkai*, in simple terms, presented temples with an exciting new cast of "free agents" who could be potentially pressed into (esoteric) Buddhist service.

In considering such an inherently composite, fluid, and syncretic nature of the Japanese divine realm, Teeuwen and Rambelli propose a category of "moot supernatural entities" or "moot deities"[26] to describe comparable (semi-)divine beings difficult to categorize that did not fully belong to the world of *kami* or as proper members of the Buddhist pantheon. Nonetheless, such anomalous sorts were of interest to both Shintō and Buddhist institutions, which often adopted them into their pantheons at tutelary deities or lower-order manifestations, though not always recognized in traditional understandings of Shintō-Buddhist syncretic paradigms such as *honji suijaku* 本地垂迹. Such "moot" entities, Teewen and Rambelli suggest, may include demons, witch animals, wrathful spirits, and even those associated with the *yōkai* class, such as the *tengu*.[27] Scholars have since proposed additional candidates, such as the *ningyo*[28] and the giant earthquake-inducing catfish *namazu*.[29]

I consider *yōkai*, like the *kudan* and those examined below, to be easy additions to this "moot" category of supernatural entities. Their "moot," that is, ambivalent and changing, status attracted Buddhist attention in the form of subjugation-enshrinement processes which, as we will see, worked to "stabilize" their otherwise unfixed natures as useful allies who could be conscripted into

---

[26] Teeuwen and Rambelli, 25, 28.
[27] Ibid., 29–30.
[28] Castiglioni, 36.
[29] Smits, 59.

religious structures as converted members who, along with their coopted remains, territorial domains, and powers, worked as agents of religious identity, community, and order.

Legendary Monster Relics

A central mechanism by which Japanese temples (and shrines) demonstrated authority over spiritual antagonists is the loose genre known as *engi* 縁起, short narrative literature focusing on the founding of sacred spaces by famous masters and their subsequent miraculous histories celebrating local divinities, saints, and numinous objects. *Engi* borrows heavily from related genres of literature, such as *densetsu* 伝説 (local legends), *reigenki* 霊験記 (tales of miraculous deity manifestations), *setsuwa* 説話 (didactic tales) and *denki* 伝記 (biographies), to the extent that it should be regarded as an amorphous and fluid genre, with differences often superficial and distinct only in function.

At the core of the Buddhist *engi* narrative drama is the confrontation between an eminent monk and local spirit, unruly and dangerous, which concludes in the victorious subjugation of the spirit and enshrinement of a deity to mark the origins of a temple the imposition or expansion of Buddhist space. Installation of temple space, in general terms, is achieved through the pacification and incorporation (or relocation) of unwanted spiritual rivals (often signified by new Buddhist nomenclature, imagery, and function), then superseded by a new population of Buddhist divinities and their corresponding clerical and ritual networks. Additional legends or miracle tales often supplement the initial *engi* origin story with the heroic exploits of subsequent Buddhist masters to demonstrate an ongoing and successful operation of temple space. Such Buddhist legends, moreover importantly, provide a narrative frame for the production and ownership of material culture of temple relics (*shari* 舎利) and "treasures" (variously termed *jihō* 寺宝, *reihō* 霊宝, *hōmotsu* 宝物, or *chinbō* 珍宝) and their ritual display, offering vestige proof and visceral, tactile demonstrations of a site's miraculous history. Treasures, and more frequently relics, operate within the wider class of sacred Buddhist objects, whether natural or manufactured, that may retain vestige powers of their former owners or spiritual sources and be considered spiritually "animate." Common examples include the personal belongings, ritual instruments, or physical remains of founders and saints, statues and iconographies, and physical objects associated with a site's miraculous history or local deity. These objects regularly function as spiritually-imbued agents offering "this-worldly benefits" (*genze riyaku* 現世利益) such as healing and protection and *kechien* 結縁, "karmic connections" with local divinities to ensure and accelerate a practitioner's petitions and prayers, and so are rolled out for public viewing, such as on auspicious festival days (*en'nichi* 縁日, "day of karmic [connection]), to attract worshippers and patronage.

Less commonly, but no less productive, relics and treasures may also include the purported remains of spiritual antagonists, subjugated and transformed into benign, protective, or enlightened members of the Buddhist community. As we will see below, temples at times regarded the physical remains of *yōkai* as such objects. As the Osaka exhibition suggests, these remains are of the zoological (and, to a lesser extent, anthropomorphic) variety, despite the immense diversity of *yōkai* flourishing since Edo times. This zoological focus, no doubt influenced by an intellectual and artistic "naturalization" of *yōkai* in the early modern period (discussed below), populated the otherworldly domains of mountains and rivers with the usual suspects of supernatural beings who might offer up dual service of spiritual adversary and ally.

Dismembering and Remembering the *Kappa*

A good place to begin examining these narrative, ritual, and material processes at work in the subjugation of *yōkai* and installation of their relics is the *kappa*. This infamous Japanese water goblin typically resembles a child-like amphibious creature with behavioural and anatomical elements drawn from animals such as the turtle. *Kappa* are ideal demonstrations of *yōkai* ambiguity: they can be mischievous, even deadly, tricksters (with a notorious propensity for drowning people and animals) but at times revered water deities bringing blessings to a community. This shifting nature is associated with its elemental character: its dangerous tendencies are an embodiment of destructive natural forces like rainstorms and floods. At the same time, its beneficial attributes are a product of its importance to fertility and agricultural communities.[30]

Bolstered by flourishing natural history studies in the eighteenth century, encyclopedic inquiry into strange phenomena and creatures produced anatomical sketches of *kappa*, typically with a focus on the elongated arms and outstretched webbed, clawed hands as a primary attribute of its dangerous strength.[31] Such "naturalization" of the *kappa*, with emphasis on its hands, was no doubt inspired by local sightings and the taxidermic manufacture of *kappa*. *Kappa* body parts, notably the arms and hands, are unsurprisingly among the most common *yōkai* remains in Japan.[32]

According to Japanese historian Nakamura Teiri, tales of severed *kappa* hands became popular around this time from the latter half of the eighteenth

---

[30] For an examination in English on the *kappa* see Foster. See also Nakamura Teiri's influential *Kappa no Nihonshi* 河童の日本史 *(A History of the Kappa in Japan)*.

[31] See, for instance, the 1712 encyclopedia *Wakan sansai zue* 和漢三才図会 (Terajima 1712: 461), Toriyama's *Gazu hyakki yagyō* 画図百鬼夜行 (Toriyama, 18), and the late Edo period illustration *Suiko jūni hin no zu* 水虎十二品之図 (Sakamoto).

[32] Yamaguchi, 37.

century. He notes a common narrative motif: caught attempting to drown a horse or person (or fondle a woman's buttocks), the *kappa* is punished with dismemberment, often by samurai officials. In submission, the defeated (symbolically slain) and now benevolent *kappa* begs for mercy and proposes a truce by way of exchange. In return for its severed hand, it promises to impart esoteric methods for mending broken appendages or concoctions for wonder drugs.[33] However, in some accounts, the *kappa*'s plea is refused, and the severed hand remains in possession of the family. There, it is regarded as a family heirloom or treasure (*kahō* 家宝). Despite a seemingly lifeless appendage, it is considered imbued with vestige healing properties derived from its previous owner.

Variants of these hand-severing legends, primarily of the second "heirloom" variety, were soon circulating among local legends of religious sites, with clergy in the active role of monster hunters meeting out justice and restoring peace. According to Edo-period legends of the Shingon temple Manzōji 満蔵寺 in Tsuchiura City, Ibaraki Prefecture, a mischievous *kappa* plagued the local river in the late fourteenth century, regularly drowning horses and children. When finally caught, the locals sought justice by execution. Manzōji's abbot intervened and pleaded mercy on behalf of the *kappa*, contenting the locals to corporal punishment by severing its hand. The abbot returned to the temple with the hand, treating it as though a corpse, offered funerary services, and enshrined it as a sacred object. Peace was then restored to the town. Later, when the area suffered a drought, the hand was unveiled in support of ritual petitions for rain, with immediate success. Given its miraculous power, the hand was kept carefully hidden at the temple for fear of it producing heavy rainfall and flooding. Since the temple's postwar destruction by fire, the hand has been housed in a local public museum, where it is unveiled every June at a festival honouring the *kappa* of Manzōji legend.[34]

A similar account is found in Japan's southern Fukuoka Prefecture, at another esoteric (Tendai) temple Seiryūin 清龍院 in Fukuoka City, which preserves both hands of a malicious *kappa* who enjoyed drowning locals in the river. According to temple accounts, a provincial lord named Kobayakawa Takakage 小早川隆景 (1533–1597) was pleasure boating when a *kappa* pulled a servant woman into the river. After a failed search, the lord petitioned the local abbot of Seiryūin for help, who conducted twenty-one days of esoteric rites until the *kappa*'s

---

[33] Such tales apparently functioned as promotional origins stories for healing techniques, purporting a secret transmission of medical knowledge such as salves and bone-setting (Nakayama, Ch.2; Foster, 8, 12). In some cases, gifts of fish are also offered by the apologetic *kappa*.

[34] Yamaguchi, 204; Yamaguchi, 66–67.

lifeless body surfaced in the river. Kobayakawa severed both its hands in an act of posthumous punishment, which were then enshrined in the temple, with funerary rites also provided for the *kappa*'s victim. Today, the hands are put on public display during a summer festival each August.[35]

Tokyo's Sōgenji 曹源寺 Zen temple provides an interesting case of a fully deified *kappa*, complete with formal iconography, pantheonic membership, titles, and ritual offerings. The *engi* states that in 1814, a wealthy raincoat merchant Kappaya Heihachi 合羽屋喜八 personally funded excavation work to prevent the constant flooding of the local river which had plagued its lowland environs. A resident *kappa*, whose life Heihachi had once saved, was inspired and assisted in the engineering work. Both merchant and *yōkai* became local heroes, with Heihachi as a saint-like figure interred at the temple, soon dubbed "Kappa Temple" by the community. Those lucky enough to catch sight of the *kappa* miraculously saw their fortunes overflow. So the *kappa* was formally enshrined as Kappa Daimyōjin 河童大明神, the "Great Illustrious *Kami*," a deity of fortune and guardian against disasters of fire and water. The Daimyōjin is still revered today in a small building before a shrine adorned with a hanging scroll depicting the *kappa*. The *kami*'s body is depicted unharmed with both hands intact, poised in a benevolent stance, with the right hand beckoning good fortune and the left holding a treasure bag. In recent years, Sōgenji has become somewhat of a popular mecca for *kawaii* (cutesy) *kappa* culture, with its small precinct adorned with a proud display of modern paintings and statues celebrating the *kappa*. The temple also preserves a fourteen-centimetre-long *kappa* hand, said to have been discovered by a businessman in the early twentieth century who then donated it to the temple.[36] The hand, however, remains more an anatomical curiosity than a formal treasure, not formally linked to any mischievous *kappa* legend, perhaps in favour of advertising the benevolent character of the *kappa* deity.

Shintō institutions also got in on the *kappa* action. The small shrine Shikihachimangū 志岐八幡宮 in Reihoku Town, Kumamoto Prefecture, is an interesting case of both hand-returning and hand-keeping motifs. According to shrine legend, a Shintō priest severed both hands of an evil *kappa* who had plagued the nearby river. The *kappa* pleaded for the return of its hands, but the priest granted only one and kept the other in possession of the shrine. The mummified hand is said to possess curative properties and ward off water-

---

[35] Yamaguchi, 57.
[36] Yamaguchi, 65.

related disasters such as cholera, and it is still used today to bless children each year during public festivals.[37]

In these examples, we see a common narrative pattern emerge that, whether formal *engi* or ancillary legend, casts the *yōkai* in the role of a wild spiritual outsider. *Kappa* roams the territorial fringes of Buddhist and Shintō space, at times a helpful neighbour but typically a threat to life and territory. Aggressively hunted or gently invited, its ultimate enshrinement concludes in a new peaceful order between human and supernatural with the simultaneous pacification of neighbouring space. Moreover, the enshrinement of *kappa* hands demonstrates not only vestige proof of victory over elemental forces but also a transactional culture of subjugated rivals giving up local sources of wealth and property in exchange for Buddhist (or Shintō) membership. Subjugation-enshrinement allows for incorporation into local pantheons where the *yōkai* may dispense protective benefits to the community, such as control over dangerous elemental forces and related misfortunes, whether by deification or, more typically, via a physical substitution by its reliquary remains as analogues of their (once) living owners.

A central mechanism of the subjugation-enshrinement process, especially prominent in Buddhist legends, is a posthumous funerary treatment of the *yōkai* and their bodily remains. These Buddhist funerary rites, typically known as *kuyō* 供養, have for centuries been provided to the recently (human) deceased, though, as we see here, they were at times extended to spiritual antagonists. By the early modern period, an individual's salvation rested less on personal *karma* and more on surviving kin to perform such memorial rites.[38] These memorials worked as a death management system for both the living and dead, and they had benefits for both parties. For the living, *kuyō* purifies any spiritual pollutants and appeases the spirit in order to avoid any possible retaliation against the living, especially in cases where its death involved acts of injustice or violence, so that it may become "fixed" in Buddhist space as a newly anointed and enlightened spirit. For the dead, *kuyō* enact a compassionate clerical intervention into the posthumous status of the departed spirit whereby a ritual transfer of merit (*ekō* 回向) from the living improves its karmic disposition so that they might attain salvation (such as heavenly rebirth in the Pure Land) with an improved body. These rituals often involve posthumous ordination (*jukai* 授戒), which confers upon the deceased permanent membership into the Buddhist family to ensure eventual salvation.

---

[37] Yamaguchi, 62; Yamaguchi, 206.

[38] On the development of Buddhist funerary and memorial practices in the early modern period, see Hur.

As suggested by the term *hotoke* 仏 ("*buddha*") used to describe spirits of the deceased, such salvation is often synonymous with or akin to, deification.

This entire funerary process—purification, pacification, and deification or salvation—became a central fixture in Buddhist narratives, rituals, and veneration of *yōkai* and their relics. Once defeated, the *kappa*'s corpse, if only a partial remnant, is given *kuyō* treatment in order to transform its status from *yōkai* to enlightened Buddhist entity or guardian spirit, appease any lingering resentment of its (violent) subjugation, and purify and transform its remains into relics or treasures to be enshrined. Early modern Buddhist productions of *yōkai* relics, then, and their ability to remain spiritually active as sacred objects safely dispensing miracles and blessings to their community, were maintained by this memorial system.

Yōkai of Mountains and Water: Fangs, Horns, and Gills

Subjugation-enshrinement, posthumous deification, and installation and display of *yōkai* relics at esoteric Buddhist sites reappear as a common design in early modern legends of other zoological *yōkai*. As identified above by Yamaguchi, these include common enemies of the *dharma* such as demons or ogres (*oni*), dragons or serpents, as well as *ningyo* merpeople that, like the *kappa*, commonly haunt wild spaces like mountains, rivers, and lakes, territorial borders with the otherworld. In this section, I examine Buddhist temple legends of such *yōkai* that further demonstrate that the accumulation and display of *yōkai* relics helped produce a "spiritual wealth" bolstering a site's auspicious history and reputation.

An ideal example is the Shingon temple Kikotsuji 鬼骨寺, "Temple of *Oni* Bones," in Naruto City, Tokushima Prefecture. According to extant Kikotsuji *engi* accounts dating from the early eighteenth to mid-nineteenth century,[39] the temple was founded by the famous Shingon founder Kūkai 空海 (774–835) but emphasised the serendipitous arrival of the later Pure Land (Jōdo)

---

[39] An illustrated account can be found in volume two of the 1818 Pure Land biography *Hōnen shōnin gyōjō ryakuden* 法然上人行状略傳 (*A Short Biographical Account of Saint Hōnen's Life and Travels*) (Shōyo Chōdō, 39 recto to 43 verso). See also the 1856 gazetteer *Awa no ochibo* 粟の落穂 (*Gleanings of Awa Province*) (Noguchi 32 recto–36 recto) as well as Fujisawa (1917: 171–177) for reproductions of the *engi* from the *Ashū kiji zatsuwa* 阿州奇事雑話 (*A Miscellany of Strange Events in Awa Province*, Kansei Era, 1789–1801) and the 1702 *Kikotsuji no engi* 鬼骨寺の縁起 (*Engi of Kikotsuji Temple*). See Yamaguchi, 31–33 for a modern account. The *engi* eventually circulated under the title *Kishin ōjō* 鬼神往生 (*The Salvific Pure Land Rebirth of Demons*) (see Honda, 39–42) and inspired a *noh* play by the same name by the end of the Edo period. See Tanaka, 462–472 for a reproduction of the *noh* text.

patriarch Hōnen 法然 (1133–1212) in 1207. At the time of Hōnen's visit, the temple had fallen under attack by a male and female pair of mountain *oni*, who confronted the monk, demanding he reveal the secrets of longevity so that they may prolong their evil lives. Hōnen presented them with an image of Amida 阿弥陀 or Muryōju Butsu 無量寿仏, the "*buddha* of infinite life," and taught the *nembutsu* 念仏 ritual prayer which promises eternal life in the *buddha's* heavenly Pure Land where they will be able to abandon their evil forms and attain the radiant golden bodies of enlightened celestial beings. Moved to tears, the *oni* returned to their mountain lair, installed the image of the *Buddha*, and engaged in *nembutsu* prayers with their two children, with the entire family dramatically ending their evil existence by leaping from the mountain peak. Auspicious purple clouds gathered around the summit, signalling to the locals that the evil family had attained the promised salvation of Pure Land rebirth.

As now posthumous members of the Buddhist family, temple clergy afforded their corpses funerary rites, and given their devotion and enlightened Pure Land rebirth, their fangs were formally enshrined as relics (*shari*). The Buddhist triumph over neighbouring evil delighted the local governor, who donated financial support to expand the temple's territory and inspired locals to devote themselves to Amida and the temple deity Yakushi Nyorai 薬師如来, the Medicine Buddha. The adoption of *oni* relics became synonymous with a period of temple revitalization and local patronage, commemorated by the temple's name change to its present "Kikotsuji." Legend also has it that *oni* horns were later discovered to possess healing properties.[40] Today, the fangs are enshrined within a small golden stupa reliquary, signifying their status as relics. Together with the horns, they remain open to the public with various artworks commemorating the local legend.

The central drama of the purported origins of Kannonshōji 観音正寺, a Tendai temple in Ōmihachiman City, Shiga Prefecture, contains a similar encounter between a *yōkai* and a Buddhist saint. According to the temple's *engi* legend in the *Saigoku sanjūsansho Kannon reijō ki zue* 西国三十三所観音霊場記図会 (*Illustrated Accounts of the Thirty-three Miraculous Saikoku Sites of Kannon*, 1804), the legendary Buddhist patron, Prince Shōtoku (574–622), encountered a tormented *ningyo* merperson in a river. The *ningyo* begged the Prince for mercy and confessed its sins: a fisherman in a former life, it cruelly took life without end and so was reborn into its present body as karmic punishment under constant attack by fish. The *ningyo* implored the Prince to carve and enshrine a statue of the *bodhisattva* Kannon 観音 nearby and perform memorial rites on its behalf so that it may escape its karmic

---

[40] Yamaguchi, 33.

suffering and attain a high rebirth in the celestial realm of the *bodhisattva*. The 1804 *engi* concludes thus:

> The Prince then carved a statue of Senju Kanzeon 千手観世音 [Thousand-armed Kannon] three *shaku* [approximately ninety centimetres] in height. He constructed for it a building which he named "Kannon Temple..." By such virtuous deeds, the *ningyo* obtained enlightenment. Soon after, the Prince beheld the *ningyo*'s floating corpse near the shore in a dream, a sign that it had indeed attained Buddhahood as a member of Kannon's divine family. He immediately set out for the beach and thereupon spotted the *ningyo*'s body washing toward him in the waves. The corpse was quickly removed and enshrined in the temple. It remains today [Kannonshōji's] most precious treasure.[41]

An 1859 coloured woodblock print by the famed Utagawa Kunisada (1786–1864) and Utagawa Hiroshige II (1826–1869) commemorates the *engi* legend by depicting the *ningyo* transforming into a beautiful enlightened being before the Prince.[42] Atop the print is a detail of Kannonshōji's precinct, illustrating the degree to which the public reputation of the temple was linked to the *ningyo* legend and its relics. According to Edo-period temple records, the *ningyo* mummy was put on public display during festivals to offer worshippers a chance at *kechien* to secure salvific ties with the enlightened being.[43] Today, the temple still enjoys such a reputation. It has adopted the *ningyo* as a PR mascot, with the temple advertised as "Kannonshōji, the legendary *ningyo* temple" and "Japan's only Buddhist temple founded by Prince Shōtoku for *Ningyo*."[44]

Similar instances of enshrined dragon or serpent relics are found at temples to the southwest. The Pure Land temple Hikarikyōji 光敬寺 in Yōrō Town, Gifu Prefecture, enshrines a "serpent skull," a gaping set of twenty-centimetre-wide animal jawbones with sharp teeth. According to temple legend, a young local woman fell in love with a handsome monk and, unable to control her

---

[41] Kōyo et. al, Vol. 5, 38 recto–39 verso.

[42] For a reproduction and transcription of the print, see Museum of Fine Arts, Boston, "Kannon-ji in Ōmi Province, No. 32 of the Saikoku Pilgrimage Route Saikoku junrei sanjūniban Kanonji Ōmi), from the series Miracles of Kannon (Kannon reigenki)" August 22, 2022. https://collections.mfa.org/objects/175728/kannonji-in-omi-province-no-32 of-the-saikoku-pilgrimage.

[43] Castiglioni, 27. Unfortunately, the *ningyo* mummy was lost in a fire in 1993. Photographs can be found in Yamaguchi, 77, 78–79 and 84–85. Until its destruction in 1993, it remained enshrined in the main hall, with toy figurines of the *ningyo* distributed to visitors (Ōmi Kyōdo Gangu Kenkyūkai, 158–160).

[44] "Introduction to Kannonshoji Temple." http://kannonshoji.or.jp/about/.

unrequited affections, threw herself into the rapids, where she transformed into a malevolent serpent from her karmic lust.[45] Hōnen's student and founder of the True Pure Land (Jōdo Shin) tradition, Shinran 親鸞 (1173–1262), passed through the area on pilgrimage and quelled the beast with the *nembutsu* along with a lecture admonishing its karmically inferior body that will not escape the torments of hell without the aid of Amida. The serpent bowed in obeisance and departed. Shinran and his disciples then performed memorial rites so that they might attain a superior rebirth and gain enlightenment. The serpent then rose from the water, transformed into a beautiful heavenly maiden, and ascended to the Pure Land. Its skull was soon discovered and eventually passed to Hikarikyōji in the late Edo period when it was enshrined as treasure commemorating the dragon's heavenly rebirth.[46] Today, its jawbones rest visibly alongside an image of Shinran in the temple's main hall.

At the Shingon temple Ishiteji 石手寺 in Matsuyama City, the capital of Ehime Prefecture, we find examples of the more aggressive monster-slaying motif. Two legends exist here. First, a temple monk, practised in the esoteric Buddhist ways of "slaying" (*taiji*) evil, defended locals from a male river dragon armed with *mantras*, *mudras*, and a stone sword with which he killed the beast. The monk returned its bones to the temple and enshrined them as treasure. Then, during the Gen'na Era (1615–1623), the area was again plagued by a second dragon, which transformed each night into a beautiful woman to lure passersby to a watery grave. A samurai lord hunted the dragon to its end with a rifle and took its skull as a family heirloom. In 1963, real estate developers built a new hotel resort downstream from the temple. They took ownership of the skull, building a shrine for it that is worshipped as the remains of the deified dragon princess, with memorial rites performed annually each summer.[47] The bones of the first dragon are also on public display today in Ishiteji's treasure hall (*hōmotsukan* 宝物館) alongside the sword, designated a Tangible Cultural Property of Matsuyama City in 1963.[48]

Another dragon-slaying tale can be found across the Seto Inland Sea at the Shingon temple Shōmokuji 青目寺 in Fuchū City, Hiroshima Prefecture. A thousand years ago, so the story goes, a male and female pair of mountain serpents terrorized the area by devouring people. After a samurai slew the male, its mate swore vengeance and hunted down the monks of Shōmokuji one by one. The temple abbot saved the temple by tricking the serpent into

[45] On the association between serpents, sexuality, lust, and the female body, see Klein.
[46] Yamaguchi, 142–145.
[47] Yamaguchi, 150–151.
[48] Matsuyamashi.

eating a straw decoy dressed in monk robes loaded with gunpowder. The abbot secured its jawbones from its bloody corpse, performed funerary rites so that its spirit would not return to curse the area, and enshrined it as a temple treasure. Today, it is unveiled to the public for veneration every seventeen years, along with the temple's main statue of Kannon.[49]

As we again observe in the legends of the ogres, *ningyo*, and dragons or serpents, Buddhist narratives and rituals facilitated the production of a material culture of relics and temple treasures, which could be put on display for the spiritual improvement of the public and ongoing demonstrations of temple authority. As demonstrated, osseous and taxidermic *yōkai* remains were considered appropriate, albeit potentially dangerous, objects for inclusion in the Buddhist world of relics and temple treasures and corresponding practices of display, worship, and festivities. Physical remains of the *kappa*, ogres, dragons, and *ningyo*, even if only partial remains, are essentially aberrant corpses requiring funerary treatment to eliminate possible impurities and avoid curses produced by their heretical or karmically inferior forms. The elevated, enlightened, or deified Buddhist status of the transformed *yōkai* rendered their anatomical remains now legitimate relics; once the bane of their communities, they are newly transformed into useful, spiritually potent objects safely dispensing both salvific and worldly benefits, with their territory and powers transferred to local authorities. Such funerary rites, which helped to populate a site's collection of relics or treasures, further worked to "stabilize" the amorphous bodies of *yōkai* and produce a new, workable form of Buddhist iconography that could be enshrined alongside more common imagery as spiritually animate objects. The allure of *yōkai* relics lies in their paradoxical status as "safely dead" (as monsters) and "practically alive" (as sources of divinity), helping to produce "spiritual wealth" to secure name, status, and patronage and expand and reinforce Buddhist space, networks, and practices.

The Cult of Monstrous Objects: Collecting and Displaying the *Yōkai* Specimen

Such "spiritual wealth," however, goes only so far as to explain the Buddhist accumulation of monstrous relics. Certainly, portable, three-dimensional *yōkai* remains worked as ideal material objects offering tactile, sensory demonstrations of (esoteric) Buddhist authority compared to more common supernatural depictions in text and image. Yet the manufacture of *yōkai* objects, and in particular their modularity, must be understood as understudied products of a wider burgeoning culture of craftsmanship and display in which

---

[49] Yamaguchi, 152.

objects were manufactured, accumulated, and deployed as instruments of cultural power and exchange among intellectual, commercial, and even political spheres.[50] In this final section, I focus on *yōkai* specimens as unique manufacturers of an early modern confluence of three distinct but interrelated intellectual, political, and artistic climates.

The first can be described as the "naturalization" of the supernatural as physical specimens and intellectual commodities. As suggested by the various taxonomic strategies employed toward otherworldly entities, prominent to Japan's early modern intellectual climate was its Neo-Confucian "investigation of things" (*kakubutsu chichi* 格物致知) to discern the structural reality of the natural world and the beings and objects which populate it. Such inquiry underlined an unprecedented age in studies of Japanese natural history, knowledge production and information exchange, literacy rates and publicly accessible printing, such as seen in the many compilations of encyclopedias, travel guides and guidebooks to famous places. As suggested by Toriyama's illustrated encyclopedias, *yōkai* became part of such intellectual investigations. In his examination of early modern studies of natural history (*honzōgaku* 本草学), Marcon argues epistemological shifts toward objectification and secularization of nature that transformed even the supernatural into tangible objects that could be grasped and manipulated.[51] Anatomical sketches of *kappa* and Toriyama's illustrations show how early modern *yōkai* were increasingly given a physical form and presence that occupied distinct geographical spaces as specimens. Any intellectual leap then, from two-dimensional representations of *yōkai* to purported physical specimens, would not have been regarded as ontologically significant. Such "naturalization" of *yōkai* like *kappa* and *ningyo* helped to collapse the gap between real and imagined zoological creatures, with both increasingly regarded as intellectual commodities and objects of curiosity that could be collected and put on display at spectacles. Marcon notes, for instance, that the late eighteenth century saw an increase in popular appetites for rare and exotic animals such as two-headed tortoises, giant crabs, and tiger skins, alongside which sat stuffed *ningyo*, *kappa* and *tengu* claws.[52]

Second, as suggested by the frequent intervention and clerical collaboration of aristocratic and military officials in subjugation accounts of *yōkai*, monstrous specimens can also be regarded as shared objects of religio-political transaction

---

[50] Such objects included *meisan* 名産 and *meibutsu* 名物 (famous objects and local specialty products), *kōbutsu* 好物 and *misemono* 見世物 (curiosities), *saikumono* 細工物 (craftworks), *tsukurimono* 作り物 (fabricated models) and *kazarimono* 飾り物 (decorative objects, ornamentation).

[51] Marcon, 7–9.

[52] Marcon, 224–225.

and power. In his study of early modern military material culture, Morgan Pitelka argues that "acquiring, stockpiling, activating, and displaying valuable things was ... one of the defining characteristics of sixteenth-century power"[53], which ultimately led to the subsequent early modern age of a "spectacular accumulation" of objects as expressions of power and authority. This accumulation of objects, Pitelka argues, became political demonstrations of the Tokugawa regime's power and wealth and tools of influence involved in conducting relationships or "sociability" with other power structures. For instance, objects such as swords and severed enemy heads recovered from the battlefield and prepared for display helped to reify the structural hierarchies of the government and impose Tokugawa dominance over the country's many territorial lords.[54]

I would contend that *yōkai* specimens operated on a similar register as instruments of political posturing by Buddhist temples as instruments of state power parading spoils of war. The unfixed nature of *yōkai* had always posed somewhat of a political conundrum or threat as spiritual forces unaligned with imperial or military authority. As "monstrous" embodiments of disorder and carnivalesque parody often allied with commoner interests,[55] ruling elites considered *yōkai* as potential disruptions to not only the spiritual order of Japan but the political, social, and economic stability of the realm. Komatsu proposes that for centuries, imperial and military governments maintained a display of power and authority by enacting symbolic control over the dangerous edges and otherworldly spaces of the realm where the chaotic supernatural, like *yōkai* may encroach to threaten peace and order.[56] In a fascinating recent study of *ningyo* mummies, Andrea Castiglioni offers similar insight into the particular cosmological and political challenges posed by *yōkai*. From the seventh century, the appearance of beached anatomical oddities like the hybrid *ningyo* were interpreted as potential aberrations of the natural world that, under the influence of correlative theories between heaven and earth, could admonish rulers for poor governance.[57] Castiglioni notes that "an essential quality for members of the Japanese governing elites in the classical and medieval periods was the capacity to properly interpret the political valence of natural omens such as the manifestation of a *ningyo* and to

---

[53] Pitelka, 5–6.

[54] Pitelka, 118–142.

[55] For instance, artists like Utagawa Kuniyoshi 歌川国芳 (1797–1861) famously seized on concepts of the grotesque monstrous body of chaotic supernatural creatures like *yōkai* to rally commoner support against oppressive military rule. For details and examples, see Hirano, chapters 2 and 4.

[56] Papp, 70.

[57] Castiglioni, 7.

calibrate human actions ... to assure the proper administration of the country."[58] These actions, familiar to the above *yōkai* legends, included corpse disposal, funerary rites, purification, and spirit pacification. Early modern Buddhist *yōkai* legends continued to idealize such clerical relationships with government powers under whose authority they operated as state-affiliated institutions. Buddhist clergy are cast as local heroes, often in cooperation with government officials (or doubling as public administrators) in meting out justice in the punishment and subjugation of malevolent entities, strategically reinforcing both the threat of the monstrous body and enacting authoritative control over it. Body parts like dragon bones, ogre horns, and *kappa* hands—physical objects embodying defeated antagonists from the spiritual battlefield—thus operated as part of a Buddhist loot system. Once dangerous but now made safe by defeat, such objects were gathered, prepared, and paraded as self-awarded trophies and transactional peace offerings celebrating high moments of Buddhist public service in pacifying and maintaining the realm.

Finally, the visceral sight and grotesque compositions of *yōkai* remain naturally made them regular objects at spectacular exhibitions and freakshows. Once safely neutered, *yōkai* remains, alongside other treasures and relics, offered locals a cabinet of curiosities that could paraded about during festivities and shore up patronage and local commercial interests. Specifically, this parading sits at the confluence of two related modes of commercial display culture that peaked in the eighteenth and nineteenth centuries: *kaichō* 開帳 (temple and shrine exhibitions) and *misemono* 見世物 (public spectacles and fairs). Commonly on display at *kaichō* were statues of a site's main object of worship in addition to ancillary relics and treasures, nominally held for the spiritual well-being of the nation but equally designed to solicit financial support. *Engi* publications were often distributed at the event, with visitors treated to guided tours and *dharma* lectures of the temple's statues, treasures, and *engi* history. Proximity to, and at times physical contact with, these objects is thought to promote *kechien* connections with their imbued power to improve blessings and salvation, as seen above.

Moreover, *kaichō* venues, often held within "temple towns" (*monzenmachi*) in major urban centres like Edo, became fused with commercial districts and entertainment zones, attracting an assortment of enterprises such as *misemono* spectacles and carnivals. These spectacles, organized by artisans, merchants, and entertainers, provided a regular side stage for all manner of curiosities like anatomical anomalies, exotic animals, and creative craftworks. The intricate taxidermic craftsmanship of *yōkai* specimens, which often involved

---

[58] Castiglioni, 12–13.

combining different animal parts, made them a feature at such events.[59] Their hybrid composition was possibly understood as artistic expressions of *tsukurimono* 作物, "artificial creations," that experimented with concepts of animate and inanimate,[60] making them of multivalent use to various actors and audiences. Here, we may observe what Foster identifies as a popular playfulness in early modern *yōkai* culture. Less serious an intellectual or political pursuit, this "ludic mode" nonetheless became a central characteristic of *yōkai* discourse in early modern Japan that flourished among new forms of entertainment, recreation, and commercial culture.[61]

Concluding Remarks

Gods and monsters, it would seem, are quietly by nature spiritual relatives whose apparent distinctions are largely structural and functional,[62] enacted by myths and legends and reinforced through geographical boundary, iconography, and ritual worship. As Mikles and Laycock have recently put it rather concisely, what may determine any social hierarchy that places a god above a monster is good representation by a "dedicated PR team."[63] *Yōkai*, as we have seen, are ideal—that is loud—demonstrations of this kinship and manufacture of difference within Japanese cosmology. They proudly wear both monstrous and godly qualities on their sleeves, both feared and revered, chaotic and civilized. Yet despite subjects of esoteric Buddhist subjugation-enshrinement, they are never fully subverted and integrated; as their grotesque remnants are intended to remind us, they remain interstitial "moot" supernatural entities, simultaneously offering up dual service as insider and outsider, friend and foe, as objects of religious authority, identity, and community. And though the *kappa, ningyo*, dragon, and ogre may be granted Buddhist enlightenment, their monstrous bodies—once again forced upon their communities by the enshrined preservation of their spectacular relics— remain explicitly at the fore, admonishing the continued to overfocus in (Buddhist) scholarship on the cosmological "divine" to the exclusion of the "monstrous."

---

[59] Castiglioni, 8; Asakura, 95., See also Kurata, 35 for details on an 1888 Tokyo *misemono* of a mummified ogre arm and head with prominent fangs and horns, advertised in the daily *Jiji shinpō* 時事新報 (Current Events) newspaper with an illustration.

[60] See Markus for details.

[61] Foster, 48-49.

[62] On this, see Faure and Doniger.

[63] Mikles and Laycock, 3–4.

Bibliography

Primary Sources

Fujisawa Morihiko 藤沢衛彦, ed. *Nihon densetsu sōsho* 日本伝説叢書. Awa no maki 阿波の巻. Tokyo: Nihon Densetsu Sōsho Kankōkai, 1917.

Honda Rōshō 本田了祥. *Gankai ama no teasobi: hōgi sōzoku no kōhanryo* 願海あまの手遊：法義相続の好伴侶. Kyoto: Hōzōkan 1903.

Honda Ishirō 本多猪四郎, dir. *Gojira*. Toho, 1956; Classic Media, 2013. 1 hr., 38 min. Blu-ray Disc, 1080p HD.

Kōyo 厚誉, Tsujimoto Motosada 辻本基定, Shimada Masataka 島田雅喬. *Saigoku sanjūsansho Kannon reijō ki zue* 西国三十三所観音霊場記図会. 1804. Digital MS. Waseda University Library Kotenseki Sōgō Database: Japanese and Chinese Classics. August 20, 2022. https://www.wul.waseda.ac.jp/kotenseki/html/ha04/ha04_01807/index.html

Museum of Fine Arts, Boston. "Kannon-ji in Ōmi Province, No. 32 of the Saikoku Pilgrimage Route Saikoku junrei sanjûniban Kanonji Ōmi), from the series Miracles of Kannon (Kannon reigenki)" August 22, 2022. https://collections.mfa.org/objects/175728/kannonji-in-omi-province-no-32-of-the-saikoku-pilgrimage

Noguchi Toshinaga 野口年長. *Awa no ochibo* 粟の落穂. 1856.

Tanaka Makoto 田中允 ed. *Mikan yōkyoku shū zoku* 未刊謡曲集続 *6. Tokyo: Koten Bunko, 1990.*

Terajima Ryōan 寺島良安. *Wakan sansai zue* 和漢三才図会. 1712. Volume 1. Tokyo: Nihon Zuihitsu Taisei Kankōkai, 1928. National Diet Library Digital Collections. August 20, 2022. https://dl.ndl.go.jp/info:ndljp/pid/1772984.

Toriyama Sekien 鳥山石燕. *Toriyama Sekien Gazu hyakki yakō zen gashū* 鳥山石燕画図百鬼夜行全画集. Tokyo: Kadokawa, 2005.

Sakamoto Juntaku 坂本純沢 and Sakamoto Kōsetsu 坂本浩雪. *Suiko jūnihin no zu* 水虎十二品之図. Late Edo period. National Diet Library Digital Collections. August 20, 2022. https://dl.ndl.go.jp/info:ndljp/pid/2543033

Shōyo Chōdō 聲響超道. *Hōnen shōnin gyōjō ryakuden* 法然上人行状略傳 (*Enkō daishi ryakuden* 圓光大師略傳). 1818. Bukkyō University Library Digital Collections. August 20, 2022. https://bird.bukkyo-u.ac.jp/collections/titles/honenshoningyojoryakuden/

Secondary Sources

Abé, Ryūichi. "Revisiting the Dragon Princess: Her Role in Medieval Engi Stories and Their Implications in Reading the Lotus Sutra." *Japanese Journal of Religious Studies* 42, no. 1 (2015): 27–70.

Asakura Musei 朝倉無声. *Misemono kenkyū. Shimai hen* 見世物研究. 姉妹篇. Tokyo: Heibonsha, 1992.

Castiglioni, Andrea. "The Human-Fish: Animality, Teratology, and Religion in Premodern Japan." *Japanese Journal of Religious Studies* 48/1 (2021): 1–44.

Cohen, Jeffrey Jerome. "Monster Culture (Seven Theses)." In *Monster Theory: Reading Culture*, edited by Jeffrey Jerome Cohen, 3-25. Minneapolis: University of Minnesota Press, 1996.

Doniger O'Flaherty, Wendy. *The Origins of Evil in Hindu Mythology.* Berkeley: University of California Press, 1976.

Faure, Bernard. *Rage and Ravage: Gods of Medieval Japan, Volume 3.* University of Hawai'i Press, 2022.

Figal, Gerald. "Civilization and Monsters: Spirits of Modernity in Meiji Japan. Durham, NC: Duke University Press, 1999.

Foster, Michael Dylan. "The Metamorphosis of the Kappa: Transformation from Folklore to Folklorism in Japan." *Asian Folklore Studies* 57, 1-24, 1998.

———. *The Book of Yōkai: Mysterious Creatures of Japanese Folklore.* Oakland: University of California Press, 2015.

Foster, Michael Dylan. *Pandemonium and Parade: Japanese Monsters and the Culture of Yōkai.* Berkeley: University of California Press, 2009.

Hirano, Katsuya. *The Politics of Dialogic Imagination: Power and Popular Culture in Early Modern Japan.* Chicago: University of Chicago Press, 2014.

Hur, Nam-lin. *Death and Social Order in Tokugawa Japan: Buddhism, Anti-Christianity, and the Danka System. (Harvard East Asian Monographs, number 282.)* Cambridge, Mass.: Harvard University Press. 2007.

Itō Ryōhei 伊藤龍平. *Edo genjū hakubutsushi: yōkai to mikakunin dōbutsu no hazama de* 江戸幻獣博物誌 : 妖怪と未確認動物のはざまで. Tokyo: Seikyūsha, 2010.

Klein, Susan Blakeley. "When the Moon Strikes the Bell: Desire and Enlightenment in the Noh Play Dojoji." *Journal of Japanese Studies* 17, no. 2 (1991): 291–322.

Knowledge Capital. "'Yōkai genjū hyakumonogatari' kaisai: Nihon hatsukōkai no yōkai genjū no miira ga tōjō" 「妖怪幻獣百物語」開催: 日本初公 開の妖怪幻獣 のミイラが登場! August 20, 2022. https://kc-i.jp/Content/263.

Komatsu Kazuhiko 小松和彦. *Yōkaigaku shinkō: Yōkai kara miru Nihonjin no kokoro* 妖怪学新考: 妖怪からみる日本人の心. Tokyo: Kodansha Gakujutsu Bunko, 2015. Kindle.

———. *An Introduction to Yōkai Culture: Monsters, Ghosts, and Outsiders in Japanese History.* Tokyo: Japan Publishing Industry Foundation for Culture, 2017.

Kurata Yoshihiro 倉田喜弘, ed. *Bakumatsu Meiji misemono jiten* 幕末明治見世物事典. Tokyo: Yoshikawa Kobunkan, 2012.

Marcon, Federico. *The Knowledge of Nature and the Nature of Knowledge in Early Modern Japan.* Chicago: University of Chicago Press, 2015.

Markus, Andrew L. "The Carnival of Edo: *Misemono* Spectacles From Contemporary Accounts." *Harvard Journal of Asiatic Studies* 45/2 (1985), 499-541.

Matsuyamashi 松山市. "Shi shitei bunkazai: sekken ichiguchi" 市指定文化財: 石剣1口. August 23, 2022. https://www.city.matsuyama.ehime.jp/kanko/kankoguide/rekishibunka/bunkazai/shi/isiteji_sekken.html

Mikles L. Natasha and Joseph P. Laycock. *Religion, Culture, and the Monstrous: of Gods and Monsters.* Lanham: Lexington Books, 2021.

Murakami Kenji 村上健司. *Yōkai jiten* 妖怪事典. Tokyo: Mainichi Shinbunsha, 2013. Kindle.

Nakamura Teiri 中村禎里. *Kappa no Nihonshi* 河童の日本史. Nihon Editā Sukūru Shuppanbu, 1996.

Ōmi Kyōdo Gangu Kenkyūkai 近江郷土玩具研究会, ed. "Kannonshōji no ningyo: kaisaku densetsu ni chinami sōsaku" 観音正寺の人魚: 開創説にちなみ創作. *Ōmi no gangu* 近江の玩具. Bessatsu Ōmi bunko 別冊淡海文庫 13. Hikone: Sanraizu Shuppan, 2004. 158-160.

Papp, Zília. *Traditional Monster Imagery in Manga, Anime and Japanese Cinema.* Leiden: Brill, 2010.

Pitelka, Morgan. *Spectacular Accumulation: Material Culture, Tokugawa Ieyasu, and Samurai Sociability.* Honolulu: University of Hawai'i Press, 2016.

Smits, Gregory. "Conduits of Power: What the Origins of Japan's Earthquake Catfish Reveal about Religious Geography." *Japan Review* 2012. 24: 41–65.

Takahashi Ayako 高橋綾子 and Fujii Shuhei 藤井修平. "Shingata korona uirusu wazawai no Amabie ni miru yōkai no shakaiteki kinō 新型コロ ナウイルス禍のアマビエにみる妖怪の社会的機能 (Social functions of Yokai, considering Amabie as an example, during the COVID-19 calamity). *Shinrigaku kenkyū* 心理学研究 (*The Japanese Journal of Psychology*), 2022, Vol.93(1), 58-64.

Teeuwen, Mark, and Fabio Rambelli, ed. *Buddhas and Kami in Japan: Honji Suijaku as a Combinatory Paradigm.* London and New York: Routledge Curzon, 2003.

Yamaguchi Naoki 山口直樹. 山口直樹. *Yōkai miira kanzen file: ketteiban*妖怪ミイラ完全 file: 決定版. Tokyo: Gakken, 2010

―――. *Nihon yōkai miira taizen: yami ni ugomeku igyō no monotachi ni matsuwaru ayashi no hakubutsushi* 日本妖怪ミイラ大全: 闇に蠢く異形のものたちにまつわる妖しの博物誌. Tokyo: Gakken, 2014.

Yanagita Kunio 柳田國男. *Hitotsume kozō: sono hoka* 一目小僧: その他. Tokyo: Oyama Shoten, 1934.

―――. *Shintei Yōkai dangi: Yanagita Kunio korekushon* 新訂妖怪談義: 柳田国男コレクション. Tokyo: Kadokawa, 2014. Kindle.

Yoda, Hiroku and Matt Alt. *Japandemonium Illustrated: The Yokai Encyclopedias of Toriyama Sekien.* Mineola, New York: Dover Publications, 2016.

Yumoto Kōichi 湯本豪一. *Konjaku yōkai taikan: Yumoto Kōichi korekushon* 今昔妖怪大鑑: 湯本豪一コレクション = *Yokai Museum: The Art of Japanese Supernatural Beings from the YUMOTO Koichi Collection.* Tokyo: PIE International, 2013.

―――. *Konjaku yōkai ruirui: Yumoto Kōichi korekushon* 古今妖怪纍纍: 湯本豪一コレクション = *Yōkai Wonderland: More from the YUMOTO Koichi Collection: Supernatural Beings in Japanese Art.* Tokyo: PIE International, 2017.

―――. *Yōkai* ezōshi: Yumoto Kōichi korekushon 妖怪絵草紙: 湯本豪一コ レクション *Yōkai Storyland: Illustrated Books from the YUMOTO Koichi Collection.* Tokyo: PIE International, 2018.

Yumoto Kōichi Memorial Japan *Yōkai* Museum (Miyoshi Mononoke Museum). "Kōshin (Kaiki enchō) (Natsuyasumi kikakuten): genjū miira daihakurankai – oni kara ningyo made – kaisai ni tsuite" [更新（会期延長）]【夏休み企画展】幻獣ミイラ大博覧会-鬼から人魚まで-開催について. August 20, 2022. https://miyoshi-mononoke.jp/2021/07/1423.

Contributors

Allan E.C. Wright

Allan E.C. Wright earned his PhD at the University of Alberta and is an Assistant Lecturer in the History, Classics, & Religion Department. His previous monograph is titled "Better to Reign in Hell, than Serve in Heaven:" Satan's Metamorphasis from a Heavenly Council Member to the Ruler of Pandaemonium.

Heather Macumber

Heather Macumber is Associate Professor of Biblical Studies at Providence University College in Manitoba, Canada. The use of monster theory as a critical lens is the subject of her recent publications that focus on Daniel, John's Apocalypse, and the Dead Sea Scrolls. Her book *Recovering the Monstrous in Revelation* is published with Lexington Books/Fortress Academic.

Gregory E. Lamb

Gregory E. Lamb earned his Ph.D. in Biblical Studies (with New Testament emphasis) at Southeastern Baptist Theological Seminary (Wake Forest, NC), where he serves as an Adjunct Professor of NT Greek. Gregory also serves as Lead/Solo Researcher for the Docent Group. His dissertation on human flourishing in Philippians is forthcoming in Mohr Siebeck's WUNT II monograph series and is titled, *Living and Dying Well in Philippians: A Comparative Analysis of Ancient Sources.* Gregory's research interests are wide-ranging with contracted, forthcoming books titled, *The Rich Man and Poor Lazarus* (Luke 16:19–31; Fortress Academic), *Literary Survey of the Second Temple Period for Biblical Studies* (Pickwick/Wipf & Stock), and *A Father's Tears: A Biblical Theology of Fatherhood, Fatherlessness, and Single Parenting* (Wipf & Stock). Additionally, Gregory is a regular presenter at academic conferences worldwide such as SBL/ISBL, AAR, IBR, Tyndale, and DFG, and has published numerous articles and book chapters in the field of biblical studies.

Helena L. Martin

Helena L. Martin is a doctoral student in Religious Studies at Yale University dedicated to disability-informed historical criticism. Her master's thesis at Yale Divinity School, "Sin and Sign: Disability in the Gospels," used philology, literary and historical criticism, and critical theory to reread popular healing stories in the New Testament. The connections between monster theory and disability theory animate her work as she investigates societies' constructs of the deviant outsider.

Dunja Jelesijevic

Dunja Jelesijevic is an Assistant Professor in Comparative Religion and Asian Studies within the Department of Comparative Cultural Studies at Northern Arizona University.

Laura Nuffer

Laura Nuffer earned her PhD in East Asia Languages and Civilizations from the University of Pennsylvania. She is currently an assistant professor at Colby College and works primarily on medieval and early modern Japanese literature, with a particular focus on folklore and animal studies.

Kevin Bond

Kevin Bond holds a doctorate in Buddhism and East Asian Religions from McMaster University, Canada. He is currently an Associate Professor in Religious Studies at the University of Regina where he teaches courses on Asian religions and the supernatural in Japanese culture. His research focuses on the social history of medieval and early modern Japanese Buddhism and Daoism, and has published on such topics as Buddhist material culture, war, theatre, and deity cults. His most recent research examines military divination and spellcraft among medieval *samurai* battlefield rituals.

Index